AF251399

The Carpet and the Connoisseur

THE CARPET AND THE CONNOISSEUR

The James F. Ballard Collection of Oriental Rugs

Walter B. Denny with Thomas J. Farnham

SAINT LOUIS ART MUSEUM

The Carpet and the Connoisseur: The James F. Ballard Collection of Oriental Rugs
is published in conjunction with an exhibition presented at the Saint Louis Art
Museum from March 6 to May 8, 2016.

© 2016 Saint Louis Art Museum.
All rights reserved. No part of this publication may be reproduced, stored in a
retrieval system, or transmitted in any form or by any means, electronic or
mechanical, photocopying, recording, or otherwise, without prior permission in
writing from the Saint Louis Art Museum.

SAINT LOUIS ART MUSEUM

One Fine Arts Drive, St. Louis, MO 63110
www.slam.org

Edited, designed, and produced by HALI Publications Limited, London

Printed in Italy by EBS – Editoriale Bortolazzi, Verona, Italy
This book is typeset in Baskerville Monotype 10/13 and Fruitiger 8/11.5
The paper is 150gsm GardaMatt art

Library of Congress Cataloging-in-Publication Data

Names: St. Louis Art Museum, author. | Denny, Walter B., author. | Farnham,
    Thomas J., author.
Title: The carpet and the connoisseur : the James F. Ballard collection of oriental
    rugs / Walter B. Denny ; With Thomas J. Farnham.
Description: St. Louis, MO : Saint Louis Art Museum, 2016. | Includes
    bibliographical references and index. | Issued in connection with an exhibition
held at the Saint Louis Art Museum from March 6 to May 8, 2016.
Identifiers: LCCN 2015047463 | ISBN 9780891780724 (alk. paper)
Subjects: LCSH: Rugs, Oriental--Exhibitions. | Ballard, James Franklin,
    1851-1931--Art collections--Exhibitions. | Rugs--Private
    collections--Missouri--Saint Louis--Exhibitions. | St. Louis Art
    Museum--Exhibitions.
Classification: LCC NK2808 .S77 2016 | DDC 746.7/509507477866--dc23 LC record
available at http://lccn.loc.gov/2015047463

Cover: Pl. 12, Large Fragmentary Ushak Quatrefoil Carpet
West-central Anatolia, 16th century

ISBN 978-0-89178-072-4

Image Credits
figs. 7–10, 12, 14, 17–19
© Metropolitan Museum of Art/Art
Resource, NY
fig. 13
© Gemäldegalerie der Staatlichen
Museen zu Berlin, Preußischer
Kulturbesitz. Photo: Jörg P. Anders
fig. 15
San Giovanni e Paolo, Venice, Italy.
Cameraphoto Arte Venezia /
Bridgeman Art Library
fig. 16
Photo: Walter B. Denny
fig. 20
Fundação Calouste Gulbenkian, Lisbon
fig. 21
Harvard Art Museums/Arthur M.
Sackler Museum, Photo: Imaging
Department © President and Fellows of
Harvard College

Contents

Director's Foreword

St. Louisan James F. Ballard (1851–1931) was one of the most important American collectors of Oriental carpets at the turn of the twentieth century. Celebrated for his singular approach to collecting at a time when most other rug connoisseurs were acquiring classical Persian and Indian carpets, Ballard traveled the world, purchasing Anatolian carpets from provincial centers in Turkey. His willingness to acquire many works that in his day were virtual orphans, without firm provenance or art-historical pedigree, was unique. Today those rugs are among the most highly esteemed of his acquisitions. Ballard's scholarly approach to collecting included an understanding of carpet history as a continuum both broad and deep, and it served as an inspiration to subsequent generations of collectors.

Ballard ultimately divided his collection between The Metropolitan Museum of Art in New York and the Saint Louis Art Museum. Some of the greatest masterpieces came to Saint Louis as gifts from Ballard in 1929 and 1930. Another group of 45 rugs was donated by his daughter, Nellie Ballard White, in 1972. Her gift includes her father's most splendid Persian carpet and some of his most beautiful and important village and nomadic carpets, and it further illuminates his provocative and prescient outlook on collecting.

The Carpet and the Connoisseur: The James F. Ballard Collection of Oriental Rugs brings together for the first time a comprehensive selection of masterpieces that reaffirm the importance of the Ballard legacy not only for St. Louis but also for the world of carpet study in general. While the selection demonstrates strength in Anatolian material, it begins chronologically with three Cairene rugs, a Spanish rug, and examples of Lotto and Holbein carpets, all important survivors in a long tradition. We also include two nineteenth-century Persian pleasure tents, which until recently were the only examples of such works in an American museum.

We are grateful to guest curator Dr. Walter B. Denny for his extensive contributions to this project. His essay and entries offer unique technical and art-historical perspectives that illuminate the diversity and beauty of the works in the collection. Independent scholar Thomas Farnham's essay presents an insightful view of Ballard as a complex and colorful individual whose tastes and instincts as a collector were ahead of his time.

Philip Hu, associate curator-in-charge of Asian art, and Zoe Perkins, textile conservator, thoughtfully supervised the project's development to ensure that the Ballard collection is beautifully presented in the exhibition and in the catalogue pages that follow. *The Carpet and the Connoisseur: The James F. Ballard Collection of Oriental Rugs* exemplifies the Saint Louis Art Museum's ongoing commitment to preserving the diverse collections entrusted to us by generous donors such as James F. Ballard and Nellie Ballard White.

Brent R. Benjamin
Director

Chronology

1851 • James Franklin Ballard is born to James and Eliza Heath Ballard in Ashtabula, Ohio, on July 16, 1851. By the time James is ten years old, the family, which by then includes two sisters, has moved to Almont, Michigan, where James attends Almont public schools.

1874 • After working for several years as a druggist's assistant in Michigan and Tennessee, James moves to St. Louis. Now familiar with the retail drug trade, Ballard is employed as a traveling salesman for the wholesale drug firm Richardson and Company of St. Louis.

1878 • On June 24, James marries Emma Hill Hadley of Vincennes, Indiana. Emma, daughter of William Swain Hadley and Anna Hill, was born in Norwalk, Ohio, in 1856. She lives in St. Louis throughout her adult life, and is married to James for forty-seven years.

1878 • The couple's son, William Jay Ballard, is born.

1882–83 • James establishes Ballard-Snow Liniment Co., a successful drug manufacturing and merchandising company. He amasses a significant fortune before the age of fifty. One of his products, Campho-Phenique, a topical medication for cold sores, insect bites, and blisters, is still sold today. [FIG. A]

1885 • The couple's daughter, Berenice C. Ballard, is born. Berenice later marries and has a daughter, Emile B. Clark, who dies in infancy.

1890 • Another daughter, Nellie Ballard, is born to James and Emma. Nellie later marries David B. White and develops a keen interest in and appreciation for Oriental carpets. Like her sister Berenice, Nellie inherits carpets from her father and continues to build her collection after his death.

1892 • The couple has another daughter, Elizabeth S. Ballard, who dies in infancy. Elizabeth is buried in Bellefontaine Cemetery in St. Louis, with Emma's mother, Anna Hill Hadley.

fig. A
Campho-Phenique brochure and Liniment glass bottle

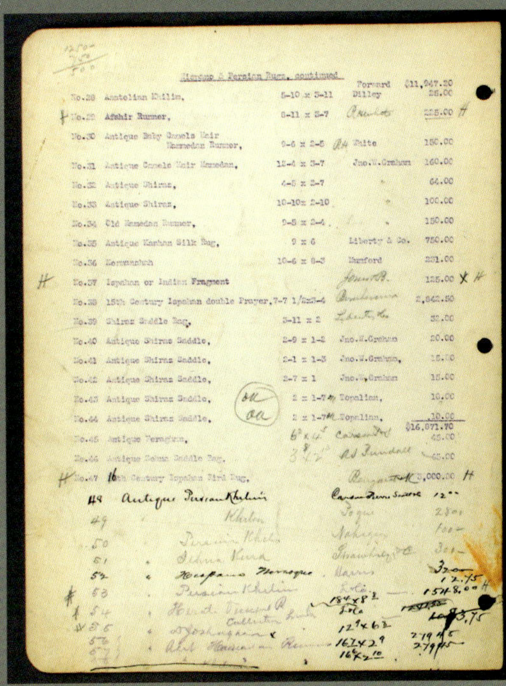

fig. B
Dealers' lists detailing rugs and prices

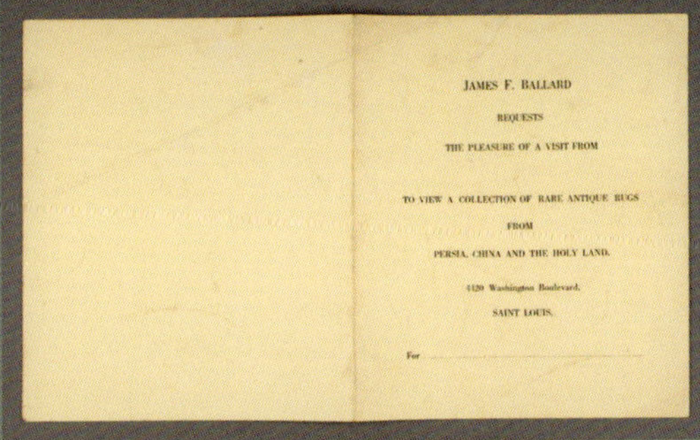

fig. C
Formal invitation to view rugs in the gallery at Ballard's home

1905   •   Ballard begins collecting carpets with an initial purchase in New York City.

1906   •   Ballard devotes more time to his new hobby, rug collecting. As well as buying carpets from East Coast dealers, he begins looking for examples internationally, including in London, Berlin, and Constantinople. He later travels to Asia Minor, Persia, India, and China in the search for Oriental rugs. [**FIG.B**]

1912   •   Ballard adds a brick, stone, and steel gallery measuring 22 x 44 feet to his home at 4420 Washington Boulevard in St. Louis. The fire- and burglar-proof gallery features one door and high windows. The decision is prescient, as four years later a devastating blaze at another St. Louis home will destroy a major art collection. For added protection, Ballard posts a twenty-four-hour security guard on the premises. He constantly exhibits different selections of carpets to friends and colleagues, often issuing printed invitations. [**FIG.C**] (Unfortunately, soon after he moves to New York in 1927, the house and gallery on Washington are demolished.)

1916   •   Ballard, likely with the assistance of his friend Arthur Dilley, compiles a catalogue of his entire collection. It contains descriptions of nearly 300 rugs. Ballard also begins publishing his collection with a limited edition catalogue of his Gördes carpets, and continues to fund future publications of his carpet exhibitions.

1919   •   Ballard begins loaning his carpets to exhibitions at museums that include the Metropolitan Museum of Art in New York, the Museum of Fine Arts Boston, the Carnegie Institute in Pittsburgh, the Cleveland Museum of Art, the Art Institute of Chicago, the Minneapolis Institute of Arts, and the Palace of Fine Arts, San Francisco. He continues to do so for at least the next ten years.

1920-21	•	Ballard travels to England, France, and Italy to purchase carpets.
1921	•	William Jay dies at age forty-three. He is buried in Bellefontaine Cemetery, St. Louis. During his lifetime, he had married and had two sons.
1922	•	Ballard presents a gift of 129 carpets to the Metropolitan Museum of Art after graciously inviting the Met's curator to select carpets from the collection that fill the gaps in the museum's holdings. In selecting the Met, Ballard wants to ensure that his rugs are shared with the greatest number of visitors.
1922-25	•	Ballard continues to travel all over the world, including a journey to Adrianople, in search of rugs for his collection. [**FIG.D**]
1923	•	The Ballard-Snow Liniment Co., having absorbed other enterprises, is incorporated in St. Louis as James F. Ballard, Inc.
1924	•	Although Ballard typically travels without his family in search of rugs, his wife and daughters accompany him on a buying trip to China, India, and Egypt.
1925	•	On June 10, Emma dies at age sixty-nine after physical frailty throughout her life. She is buried in Bellefontaine Cemetery, St. Louis.
1926-27	•	Ballard leaves St. Louis and relocates permanently to New York City. The move brings him closer to not only Berenice, who is also in the city, but also other prominent carpet collectors.
1926-29	•	Ballard buys two tents, perhaps in London from Liberty & Co. One is exhibited in April 1926 at the Albany Institute and Historical and Art Society. [**FIG.E**] In 1929 both tents are displayed with the Ballard collection of carpets at the City Art Museum (now Saint Louis Art Museum).
1927	•	Berenice travels with her father to Rangoon in search of carpets. By the fall Ballard's travels and acquisitions have allowed him to replenish his collection, which was diminished following his gift to the Met. He exhibits his carpets at the City Art Museum in St. Louis. In St. Louis Ballard actively

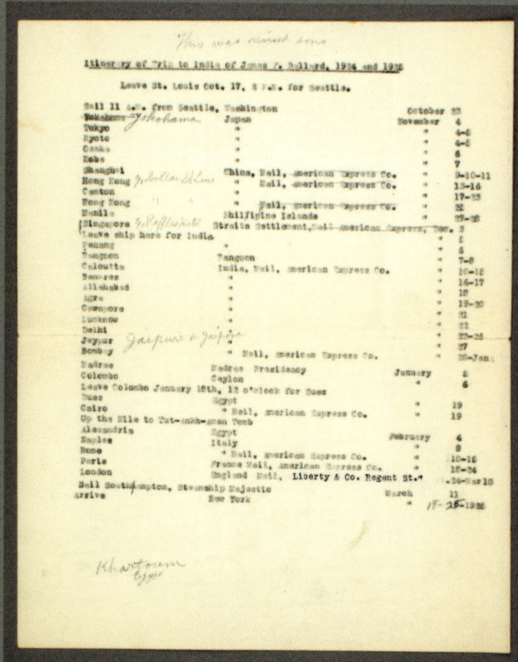

fig. D
A Ballard travel itinerary

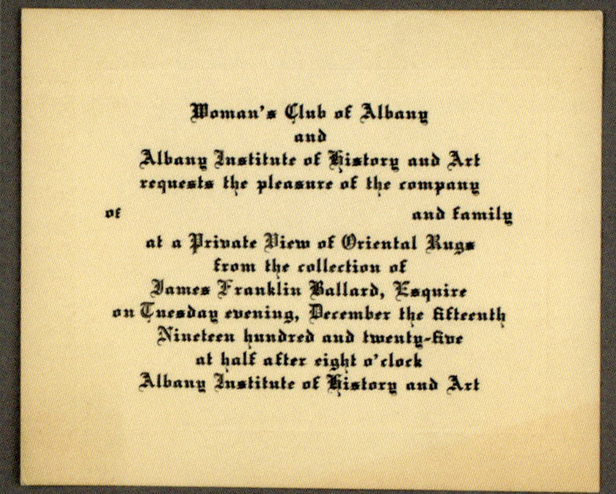

fig. E
Invitation to a private view of Ballard rugs at
The Albany Institute of History and Art, 1925

participates in the exhibition installation, which he did not do at the Met exhibition. According to a reporter at *The St. Louis Times*: "A keen-eyed little man with white hair and an agile step, Mr. Ballard, dressed in formal morning attire, was in the museum today, helping arrange his beloved carpets."[1]

1929 • Ballard gives more than seventy carpets from his collection to the City Art Museum in St. Louis. The gift is described as "The most important gift ever received by the Museum."[2] The Ballard carpets go on view in November, but unfortunately Ballard cannot attend as a blood disorder curtails his travels. He also gives sixty-four carpets to Nellie.

1930 • For the last year of his life, Ballard is ill. By this time, both Ballard daughters have developed an interest in carpets. Nellie spends extensive time with her father in New York City discussing rugs. Ballard gives seven more carpets to the City Art Museum in St. Louis.

1931 • James Ballard dies in New York City on April 23 of a rare blood disease, less than three months before his eightieth birthday. He is buried at Bellefontaine Cemetery, St. Louis.

1935 • Islamic scholar Maurice S. Dimand authors a final publication on the Ballard collection with Berenice and Nellie providing a dedication in memory of their father. The foreword was written by Ballard himself before his death.

1947 • Berenice dies and the seventy-four carpets in her collection are sold at Parke-Bernet Galleries on October 27. She is buried at Bellefontaine Cemetery, St. Louis.

1972 • After her father's death, Nellie continues his efforts to exhibit, lecture about, and publish his beloved carpets. Nellie also continues buying carpets and gives a group of forty-nine to the Saint Louis Art Museum.

1982 • Nellie Ballard White dies. The carpets remaining in the collection are inherited by her daughters Grace White Walker and Susan White Brooks Humphries. Nellie is buried at Bellefontaine Cemetery, St. Louis.

Ballard The Collector

Thomas J. Farnham

James F. Ballard is a familiar name to fanciers of Oriental carpets [**FIG.1**]. He donated major portions of two important carpet collections, one at the Metropolitan Museum of Art and another at the Saint Louis Art Museum. But if Ballard's name is memorable, his story as a collector is hazy. The lack of clarity results from two factors: Ballard's determination to control his own narrative, and the spotty record he left behind. He went to great lengths to present himself to the public as he hoped to be seen; in the process, the truth was often a victim. The documents he left behind are riddled with holes, and are missing crucial facts. As a consequence, understanding Ballard as a collector requires two things. First one must remove the narrative from his control and tell his story with less panache but greater verity; second, one has to salvage the few facts that do exist in his papers while giving due consideration to the probabilities (remembering they are no more than probabilities). The effort is certainly justified, for Ballard stands today, not alone but in extremely select company, at the apex of American carpet collectors.

No one, certainly on the day James F. Ballard acquired his first rug, would have predicted he would become one of the country's foremost carpet collectors. He was simply not the type. He was a mid-westerner. When he began to collect, at the beginning of the twentieth century, carpet collecting was an activity confined to that part of the United States from Washington, D.C., to Boston and was concentrated in and around New York City. To find a carpet collector in St. Louis, where Ballard spent his adult life, was about as likely as locating a Manhattanite who would acknowledge that St. Louis's Union Station was the equal of Grand Central Terminal.

Furthermore Ballard, before becoming fascinated with carpets, demonstrated no interest in collecting generally. Typically carpet collectors also surrounded themselves with other *objets d'art*. Henry Gurdon Marquand, former president of the Metropolitan Museum of Art, owned Old Master paintings as well as important sculptures; Benjamin Altman, the department store magnate, collected both Old Master paintings and Chinese porcelain; the collecting habits of Henry Walters of Baltimore, Charles T. Yerkes of New York, William A. Clark of New York, and George Walter Vincent Smith of Springfield, Massachusetts, knew no bounds; John D. Rockefeller, Jr. took more pride in his Chinese porcelain and tapestries than in his rugs; and Charles F. Williams, whose carpets now reside in the Philadelphia Museum of Art, also collected American furniture. Of the major carpet collectors of Ballard's era, only George Hewitt Myers, the founder of The Textile Museum, began collecting carpets without having shown any earlier interest in other media, but his zest for carpets was very quickly overtaken by his enthusiasm for textiles, a passion Ballard never came to share.

Unlike other contemporary collectors, Ballard was a prosperous businessman but not an individual of great personal wealth. Rockefeller, Yerkes, and others spent, on occasion,

more for a single carpet than Ballard spent on the first 300 rugs he acquired.[3] His home was commodious and pleasant but stood in the midst of other upper middle-class houses, some distance from the most prestigious neighborhoods in St Louis [**FIG.2**]. He did build an impressive art room onto his home, but it hardly compared with the galleries in the Altman and Yerkes mansions—much less the complete museums that Smith built in Springfield or Walters endowed in Baltimore or Myers created in Washington, or the wing of the Corcoran Museum the Clark family members provided to house their father's treasures.

The assets Ballard did accumulate were derived not from investments, as was the case with his fellow collectors, but rather from his indomitable will, his

fig. 2
Exterior of the Ballard Home, Washington Boulevard; Saint Louis Art Museum Archives

fig. 3
The Ballard Liniment Co. building; Saint Louis Art Museum Archives

fig. 3

seemingly endless capacity for work, and his tolerance of mendacity. All of these were apparently essential qualities for anyone engaged in the pharmaceutical business as it was practiced in the United States at the beginning of the twentieth century.

In 1865, at age fourteen, he went to work in a drug store. When he was twenty he became a traveling salesman for a wholesale drug company. His work completely consumed him as he proceeded from small town to small town to offer his products to local merchants. By his thirty-second birthday, he owned his own company, James F. Ballard Proprietary Medicines, a circumstance that meant not shorter but longer workdays. Other firms manufactured some of the products he sold, but most were items concocted at his facility at 500–502 North 2nd Street in St. Louis [**FIG.3**].

All the medications he offered had, according to Ballard, the ability to perform miracles, to cure nearly any illness. His claims for Swaim's Panacea were typical [**FIG.4**]. Originally manufactured in Philadelphia but purchased by Ballard in 1900, Swaim's professed to be a fool-proof remedy for "positively, surely, absolutely, All Diseases of the Blood, Eczema, Rheumatism, Scrofula, Syphilis (inherited or acquired), Cancer,

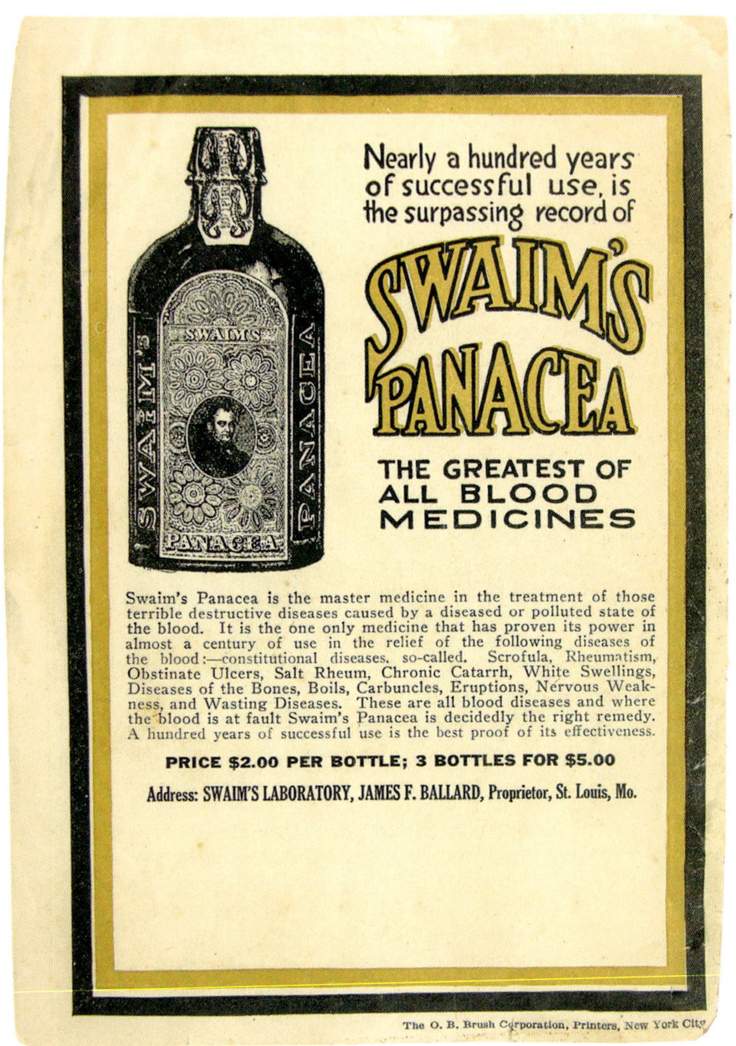

fig. 4
Advertisement for Swaim's Panacea; Saint Louis Art Museum Archives

Chronic Ulcers and all forms of Blood Poison." Like Swaim's, each of his other nostrums could, or so his advertisements proclaimed, heal a variety of illnesses. As a group, no problem known to medical science was beyond their curative powers—anything from "cholera morbus" to "diphtheria" to "frostbite."[4]

Again unlike his fellow collectors, Ballard refused to become what he called "a check-book collector," to depend on an elite dealer, perhaps Dikran Kelekian or Joseph Duveen, to select pieces for his collection. Marquand, because of his connection with the Metropolitan and his years of buying pictures, knew every important dealer in the United States and Europe and made good use of them. Clark, who maintained a residence in Paris, depended on many of the same sources. Benjamin Altman bought almost exclusively from Henry Duveen, and Rockefeller from Henry's nephew, Joseph Duveen. Henry Walters relied on Kelekian as well as Seligmann and Company, while Charles Williams asked for and received advice from the two foremost carpet scholars in the world, Wilhelm von Bode, the director of the Kaiser Wilhelm Museum in Berlin, and his colleague, Friedrich Sarre, the head of the Islamic Department at that same museum.

As different as Ballard was from the other individuals collecting carpets, he would, in time, aspire to join their ranks. He understood, as he stated, the advantages of pursuing a hobby, "something sufficiently interesting to make it possible to forget, for a time, the every-day cares and worries and get the mind into a new environment."[5] But his intent would go well beyond finding a way to while away his leisure hours. "As far back as there is any record of human activity," he declared, "it has been a custom of all nations, as greater wealth was accumulated, for people of the finer artistic perceptions to love, revere, and desire to acquire the best and most authentic productions of the art of earlier civilizations, to gather them into collections."[6] Collecting, he hoped, might one day allow him to stand with those "people of the finer artistic perceptions," with Altman and Clark and Myers.

The story of how Ballard bought his first rug has been much repeated, primarily by the collector himself. As he explained, in 1905 he was in New York on business when, quite by chance, he found himself with a few free moments and decided to stroll down South Park Avenue to where it becomes 4th Avenue. At the corner of 4th and 32nd Street, he happened to glance into the window of an Oriental rug store and saw a rug that intrigued him. Entering the shop, he asked to examine the piece and inquired about its cost. He considered the proprietor's price, $500, to be outrageous and he left empty handed. But that night he found himself haunted by thoughts of the rug and so returned to the shop the next day and, after some haggling, bought the rug for $375. He was fifty-five at the time and had for the past forty years devoted his energies exclusively to his work. That was about to change. His life was to take a new direction.

One might wonder if Ballard's first purchase was as spontaneous as he described. St. Louis had hosted the Louisiana Purchase Exposition during 1904. The fair included pavilions from sixty-two foreign countries and forty-three of the then forty-five states. Also featured were fifty educational and scientific displays, one of which was installed by Ephraim Benguiat, a recent arrival in the United States from Smyrna, Turkey, and a purveyor of Middle Eastern textiles and carpets. The "Benguiat Palace of Ancient Art" offered fairgoers a unique opportunity, the chance to examine carpets, embroideries, curtains, and velvets of a quality not previously seen in St. Louis. One item Ephraim offered was an early Persian animal carpet for which his brother, Vitall, had recently paid $38,000, an object so spectacular it could not be overlooked.[7] Whether Ballard even visited Benguiat's Palace will never be known but, had he done so, his appetite for carpets might well have been initially whetted by what he happened upon there.

Perhaps because an unidentified dealer to whom Ballard showed his first rug supposedly offered him $1,500 for it, he—beginner that he was—decided he intuitively knew an outstanding rug from a good one. He then proceeded to buy fifteen more rugs in 1905, all in quick succession, all of them at a small New York auction house, and all of them without the benefit of any second-party advice. A subsequent and more leisurely review of his new acquisitions convinced him that most of them were far less charming than he had first believed. Perhaps, he decided, a dose of professional guidance could be helpful. His budget meant he should avoid the top dealers, but there were others who could help, individuals with reputations for experience and competence and for selling rugs of the kind that fit within his means. He began by turning to John W. Graham in Philadelphia, Quill Jones in New York, A.H. Revel and Company in Chicago, Liberty & Company in London—a city he visited regularly on business—and especially Arthur Dilley in Boston.

Much of the advice dealers could provide was less than reliable. Other than that, locating information about Oriental rugs when Ballard started collecting demanded a major commitment of time and energy, especially as compared with the situation today. In 1905 only two public American museums, the Metropolitan Museum of Art and the Boston Museum of Fine Arts, could claim carpet collections of any importance; today significant carpet collections can be found at dozens of institutions. Virtually all of them, as well as museums in other parts of the world, permit their collections to be viewed on the Internet, thus providing access to hundreds of high-resolution carpet images. Finding first-rate photographs of carpets in 1905 meant finding a copy of the catalogue of the 1891 Vienna carpet exhibition, a volume that might have been tracked down in Chicago but probably nowhere else west of the Appalachians.

Scholarly publications about carpets were equally elusive. Certainly no periodical covered the subject then as HALI, *The International Magazine of Carpets, Textiles and Islamic Art* does today. At least one writer has erroneously suggested that Ballard was a member of the Hajji Baba Club, the first rug society in the United States, a group committed to expanding the knowledge of carpets. Unfortunately Ballard died two years before the club came into existence. Because of the dearth of available resources, he had to travel in uncharted territory, in a veritable wilderness.

He did take advantage of the few rug books he could find. John Kimberly Mumford's *Oriental Rugs*, first published in 1901, was the obvious starting point. The author—a newspaper reporter who had spent most of his career writing about the coal industry—traveled throughout the Middle East gathering as much information as he could about the carpet industry as it then existed. Unfortunately the details he provided on early rugs were sketchy.

Determined to examine all the limited material he could find, Ballard apparently studied with equal care the dealer pamphlets or brochures that were easily found in rug stores. These pamphlets, broadcast by the thousands, sought to introduce consumers to Oriental carpets, products as unfamiliar to Ballard's fellow Americans as horseless carriages or radio sets. These brochures, while presenting bizarre theories about the meanings of carpet designs and embellishing dealer lore with the appearance of scholarship, offered a consistent theme: owning an Oriental rug and studying its design can transport one "from the prosaic Occident to the mysterious Orient, from the bustling West to the dreamy East," can cause a person to wonder if his or her rug might have been "the most valued possession of some swarthy fanatic" or if it graced "the tent of some desert conqueror" or if it was "the Hearth rug of some dusky bandit."[8]

This genre theme was one that resonated with Ballard. When he explained his own fascination with Oriental carpets, he provided essentially the same interpretation the dealer pamphlets offered. Of all the objects one might collect, he contended, early Oriental rugs head the list: "first, because of the extreme beauty of the colors and designs; second, because of their symbolic importance; and third, on account of their historical and religious significance, all of which makes a most fascinating and interesting story. These symbols and designs carry us back to past ages," he maintained. "They are full of love, passion, sentiment, religion, mysticism, tragedy, and tribal tradition… Some of these rugs have passed through war, riot, bloodshed—mute witnesses of robbery, pillage, and murder. They have made pilgrimages over the hot sands of deserts, on the backs of camels…"[9] Levon Babayan, the author of one of the most popular of the pamphlets, *The Romance of the Oriental Rug*, or any of the other pamphleteers, could not have made the point more vividly.

Ballard explained the allure rugs held for him for the first time in 1916. It would remain the explanation he continued to provide for the rest of his life. Nearly a decade after he first expounded on the subject, he again discussed his fascination: "A rug seemed to satisfy the love of colour in me, and once I got started found that rugs were not only charming from the colour point of view, but that they were alluring for other reasons. Each rug was, in a sense, a romance of the Orient."[10] The aesthetic pleasure he derived from his rugs was obviously only part of their appeal; the mystery and romance they brought to his life—qualities he believed no other media possessed—were what ultimately made rugs so compelling.

Ballard and the authors of the brochures shared more in common than their appreciation for the romance of Oriental rugs. They also shared the conviction that Gördes (Ghiordes) prayer rugs represented as fine an example of carpet art as existed, a conviction held by many who admired Oriental carpets during the early twentieth century.[11] Ballard was explicit: "Antique Ghiordes Prayer Rugs constitute the most artistic expression of Turkish weaving."[12] During his first ten years of collecting, he bought forty-one of them. London's Liberty & Company, the famous Regent Street shop, provided more Gördes rugs to Ballard than any other dealer, nearly all of them recommended by A.E. King, who headed Liberty's carpet department and who eventually became Ballard's close friend and traveling companion. The Boston dealer Arthur Dilley endorsed Gördes prayer rugs even more wholeheartedly than did King and forged an even closer bond with Ballard.[13] While Ballard rarely paid more than $1,000 for any of his Gördes rugs and often spent far less than $400, he did pay $3,500 for a piece Tiffany and Company offered and $3,000 for one acquired from Quill Jones.[14]

In October 1914 Ballard published an article about Gördes rugs in *International Studio*.[15] The following year, he invited—by printed invitation—selected St. Louisans to visit his home to view "A Masterful Piece of Ghiordes Weaving of the 16th Century." The culmination of his concentration on these rugs came in 1916 with the appearance of the first of what would become his many catalogues, *Illustrated Catalogue and Descriptions of Ghiordes Rugs of the Seventeenth and Eighteenth Centuries from the Collection of James F. Ballard*.

Ballard's friend Arthur Dilley contributed, perhaps in a major way, to the writing of both his *International Studio* article and his Gördes catalogue. In 1914 Ballard convinced Dilley, whose Boston carpet business was struggling, to move to New York and to shift his attention from merely trading in carpets to writing and lecturing about them as well. When Ballard, still deeply involved in the day-to-day operations of his business, offered to employ him to help with his publications, Dilley, a former prep school English instructor who fancied himself a master of English prose, leapt at the opportunity; he had long aspired to support himself with his pen.[16] In 1916 Ballard compiled, for his own use, a catalogue of his entire collection. It contained descriptions of nearly 300 rugs. The likelihood that Dilley, not Ballard, wrote many and probably most of those descriptions, which were interwoven with the literary flourishes Dilley venerated, cannot be proven, but it is highly likely.[17]

After 1916 Ballard continued to enjoy Gördes rugs, but added few more examples to his collection. He also paid less attention to two other early favorites, Ladik and Kula prayer rugs, of which he owned fifty-five in 1916. These three Turkish groups—all more Persian

than Turkish in appearance—basked in the reflected popularity Persian carpets then enjoyed. Fortunately for the sake of his collection, Ballard's interests became too broad to allow any of the three, or in fact any single classification of rugs, to remain the focal point of his attention.

The 1915 private show at his Washington Boulevard home was possible because he had, in 1912, added a gallery or art room to his residence, a space where his carpets could be conveniently displayed. Fire-proof and burglar-proof and constantly under the watchful eye of a guard, the art room made possible not only private showings but also allowed Ballard better to enjoy his rugs, the number of which had become, by the time the room was added, sufficiently large to overwhelm his living quarters.

A photograph of his art room, probably taken about 1916, discloses a bit about his early taste in rugs [**FIG.6**]. On the floor in the foreground are two late nineteenth-century,

Serab camel-hair runners that now reside in the Saint Louis Art Museum; despite their elegance, they never appeared in a Ballard exhibition.[18] Neither did the large northwest Persian carpet located between the two runners. It eventually became the property of Ballard's daughter, Berenice, and was sold along with other items from her estate in 1950. Its current whereabouts are unknown.[19] The rug at the end of the room is an eighteenth-century Gördes cemetery rug now in the Metropolitan Museum of Art.[20] Another Gördes rug, also in the Metropolitan,[21] is on the right next to a small southwest Persian piece decorated with a Shah Abbas motif. That rug appeared in only one Ballard exhibition, and its current location is a mystery.

Although Ballard began his study of Oriental carpets by reading Mumford's book and studying dealer brochures, he quickly graduated to works of real substance. He studied Wilhelm von Bode's and Ernst Kühnel's *Vorderasiatische Knüpfteppiche aus älterer Zeit*, published in 1914, a work of monumental importance both then and now. He must have been especially proud of his copy of F. R. Martin's magnum opus, *A History of Oriental Rugs before 1800*. Published by the Swedish dealer in 1908, this folio edition included a volume of text and three of plates and remains even today essential reading for anyone investigating carpets. Because depictions of important rugs were nearly impossible to find in 1908, Martin's volume, with its numerous meticulous plates, was a godsend for carpet scholars.

fig. 7
Cairene Medallion Carpet, 17th century; Metropolitan Museum of Art, New York, Gift of James F. Ballard, 22.100.54

Wilhelm R. Valentiner's *Catalogue of a Loan Exhibition of Early Oriental Rugs*, the catalogue of a 1910 carpet exhibition at the Metropolitan Museum of Art, probably served Ballard nearly as well as did Martin's work. Valentiner had assembled, described, and illustrated —although not with the high-quality plates Martin provided—fifty elegant classical carpets. Ballard's library also included several other essential volumes. A. A. Bogolyubov's *Tapisseries de l'Asie Centrale,* published in St. Petersburg in 1908, demanded the attention of the few people then interested in Turkmen rugs. Vincent Robinson, a London dealer, published two editions of *Eastern Carpets, Twelve Early Examples,* one in 1882 and another in 1893 and each with plates depicting outstanding carpets. Ballard owned both. His library would have been the envy of any early student of carpets and stood as a measure of his commitment to carpet scholarship.[23]

Ballard knew better than to limit his research to what he could find in books; he insisted on seeing actual carpets, not merely depictions of them. He visited museums in London, Paris, and especially Berlin often enough to know their collections nearly by heart. He probably spent as much time at and derived as much benefit from the 1910 Metropolitan Museum of Art exhibition as any other visitor.

The extent and diversity of his own collection became clear when Ballard in 1916 exhibited sixty-two of his rugs. The event took place at Marshall Field and Company in Chicago. While Turkish rugs dominated the show, only a single Gördes prayer rug was included. Various classical rugs were well represented, among them an early sixteenth-century Isfahan; an Isfahan double prayer rug that had been exhibited at the "Meisterwerke muhammedanischer Kunst" exhibition in 1910 in Munich; two sixteenth-century Cairene rugs; a Mamluk carpet; a very early Spanish rug; and a diminutive Polonaise rug Ballard found in 1915. Eighteenth- and nineteenth-century Persian rugs were a small but much-appreciated presence at the show.

Underappreciated in 1916, when most Turkish rugs—other than Gördes, Kula, and Ladik pieces—were considered infra dig, but absolutely spectacular when seen from the perspective of the twenty-first century, were his Ushak rugs. Later critics have accused Ballard of valuing only those Turkish rugs that were "not too Turkish," his Gördes, Kula, and Ladik rugs being obvious examples. Those criticisms are exaggerated. At a time when the Altmans and the Rockefellers and the Yerkeses of the collecting world sought only Persian carpets, when Joseph Duveen would have recommended a machine-made carpet before a Turkish rug, when even Bode and Sarre considered Turkish rugs to be poor cousins of Persian carpets, Ballard recognized the magnificence of a Lotto rug or a Variant Star Ushak or a Variant Medallion Ushak, all of which he included in the show. Furthermore anyone who would doubt his fondness for bold Turkish rugs should be reminded of the spectacular Karapinar rug he also

displayed. His appreciation of them was not a perception
he learned from the dealers with whom he traded. His
ability to see in Turkish rugs what others did not might
have been encouraged by their prices—they were easily
afforded—but it was also intuitive, part of his growth as a
collector. Similarly, his looking beyond Gördes rugs and
the other Persian lookalikes revealed another aspect of
that maturation.[24]

The more Ballard studied rugs and finely honed his
collection, the more he came to believe the Marshall
Fields exhibition had fallen short, had let him down.
He disliked the store's decision to title his show a
"Home Furnishing Exhibit." Labeling his masterpieces
"Home Furnishings" deprecated both them and him.
Henceforth, he promised himself, he would exhibit his
rugs only at museums or academic institutions, locations
where they would be understood and admired.

His first opportunity to do so came in early
1919, three years after the Marshall Field show. The
Pennsylvania Museum and School of Industrial Art
organized a loan exhibition of carpets and textiles from
Asia Minor. Invited to participate were Ballard and
several collectors from the Philadelphia area: Charles
F. Williams, whose collection included exceptional
classical Turkish carpets; John D. McIlhenny, who, like
Ballard and Williams, had learned to value Turkish
rugs; and Philip M. Sharpless, the owner of only a
handful of rugs, among them a remarkable Lotto rug

fig. 8
Fragment of a Northwest Persian
medallion carpet, early 16th century;
Metropolitan Museum of Art, New
York, Gift of James F. Ballard,
22.100.67

and a Dragon rug that many believe to be the finest example in existence.[25] The Philadelphia collectors provided thirty-nine Turkish rugs while Ballard lent a total of eighty-eight, most of them pieces he had included in his Marshall Field show. In addition, New York dealers Dikran Kelekian, Hagop Kevorkian, and P. W. French and Company lent 120 velvets, brocades, and embroideries, nearly all of them world-class objects. Ballard, who hated to be outshone, initially believed his pieces would dominate the show. But, by the time it closed, he realized they had not. Never again, he decided, would he be surpassed.[26]

The opportunity to make his point came quickly. The Cleveland Art Museum was planning an exhibition to be held later that same year. It would include rugs as impressive as those displayed in 1910 at the Metropolitan Museum of Art. The museum requested loans from major dealers and collectors. Joseph Duveen, probably the most important art dealer in the world at the time, agreed to lend the second Ardabil carpet, the mate to the one in the Victoria and Albert Museum.[27] Dikran Kelekian agreed to participate, as did the New York collector Harry Payne Bingham. John D. McIlhenny lent three rugs, including a Lotto rug that any museum would have been proud to own and a Mamluk carpet of equal quality.[28] Also represented were carpets from P. W. French and Company and the estate of J.P. Morgan.

Ballard supplied more rugs, sixty-six, than any of the other lenders. Those he did lend illustrated both his determination to stand with the nation's premier collectors and his increasing sophistication as a connoisseur. For example, he was now willing to purchase both fragments and heavily restored pieces, confident in his ability to appreciate the original artistry of those artifacts from the elements that survive. He included three fragments in the Cleveland show, two Mughal fragments and one Persian [**FIG.8**]. He sent an early, large medallion carpet, one he thought had been made in Persia but is now considered a seventeenth-century Caucasian weaving, probably woven in Kuba [**FIG.9**]. Included as Plate I in the exhibition catalogue, it proved to be one of the show's stars. Another Ballard Caucasian piece was a large Dragon rug, one he had shown before. He also contributed six early Persian pieces, two of them Polonaise rugs, one a seventeenth-century Isfahan tree carpet, and another a floral carpet from eastern Persia.[29]

His Ushaks, still in 1919 the victims of arbiters' distaste, would be regarded as showstoppers today. These and his other pieces, even when compared with those owned by world-class dealers and better-known collectors, offset the disappointment of the earlier Philadelphia exhibition. They demonstrated to him and others his ascendance as a collector, as an individual who—despite his more limited financial resources, his insistence on following his own instincts, and his having to function on the outskirts of the carpet collecting coterie—knew and understood carpets as well as anyone.[30]

As Ballard added more important rugs to his collection, he also identified inferior pieces he no longer wanted; these he sometimes gave away, sometimes sold. He certainly did sell rugs, despite his frequent assertions to the contrary. In 1925, in an interview with a reporter from *The New York Herald*, he repeated what he had stated many times before: "I have never sold a single rug that I have ever purchased and I never intend to... [because] real rugs are like real paintings and must be loved and cared for."[31] In fact he had been selling unwanted rugs for years and, just two years before he spoke with the *Herald* reporter, he sold a group of nineteen rugs for $4,417.50 to Garfield D. Merner of 7001 Washington Boulevard in St. Louis.[32] Why Ballard insisted on maintaining his fiction is unclear. Perhaps he hoped to create the illusion that he could, from the day be bought his first rug, distinguish between a mediocre piece and a good one. Whatever the reason, he persisted in this deception throughout his life.

Maintaining his plan to buy only important rugs, Ballard purchased several between the close of the Cleveland exhibition and the flurry of exhibitions that followed. From October 8 until December 31, 1921, his rugs decorated the Metropolitan Museum of Art. Although he included many of his previously seen Gördes, Ladik, and Kula rugs, he also lent an ancient Persian carpet, a product of the fifteenth century, the work of the White Sheep Turkmen, rulers of Tabriz until 1502. Also from the fifteenth century was a Spanish carpet that won the heart of *The New York Times* reporter who covered the show.[33] Not so early but equally beautiful was the splendid Isfahan Tree carpet from the seventeenth century he had shown in Cleveland. Once again Ballard demonstrated his appreciation of fragments; he sent a large Vase carpet fragment to the show [**FIG. 10**]. He had displayed a seventeenth-century Dragon rug on several earlier occasions but, at the Metropolitan, he exhibited a second Dragon rug, this one showing significantly more age than his first. The rugs that attracted as much attention as any others were seven Ottoman medallion carpets probably made in Cairo in the sixteenth and seventeenth centuries [**FIG. 7**].[34] The Ottoman carpets, all but one of them displayed for the first time and all of them reverberating with Persian influence, delighted those people reluctant to accept the bolder Turkish products.[35]

During November, while his rugs were on display at the Metropolitan, Ballard began an exchange of letters with Edward Robinson, the museum's director; the subject was the possibility of giving part of his collection to the Met. The excitement his rugs generated among New Yorkers apparently convinced him that donating them there would generate more enthusiasm for rugs than his relentless series of exhibitions ever could. Never one to ignore his own reputation, he certainly understood a donation like the one he contemplated would carry him beyond what he had already accomplished, acceptance by carpet

fig. 11
Some of Ballard's rugs at
Liberty & Co., London, in 1923

enthusiasts. It would mean joining company with the likes of Henry G. Marquand and J. P. Morgan and other patrons of the Metropolitan, "people of the finer artistic perceptions." Determined that his generosity not be overlooked, he insisted on being proclaimed the rug's donor "with due notice to the press."[36]

On Thursday, May 18, 1922, Ballard formally offered the museum the opportunity to accession any of his rugs that would enhance its existing collection. The Metropolitan's board wasted no time in replying. On Monday, May 22, it responded: "your generous offer accepted with thanks." At the same time, it formally designated Ballard a "Benefactor of the Museum," its highest honor.[37]

Joseph Breck, the Metropolitan's Curator of Decorative Arts, selected 125 of Ballard's rugs. Many had been among the sixty-nine exhibited at the museum during 1921. The others were rugs Breck culled from Ballard's complete catalogue of approximately 300 rugs. The 125 chosen would, Breck believed, fill voids in the museum's existing collection. More than half, sixty-five, were Turkish or Ottoman products, including fifteen Gördes prayer rugs. Among the remaining sixty rugs, fourteen were Persian, nineteen Caucasian, fifteen Turkmen [FIG.12], nine Chinese, and three Spanish.

When asked why he had chosen the Metropolitan to receive his gift, Ballard's reply was invariably the same: "It is here because I think it belongs here. Here in New York 5,000 people will see the rugs to one in other places. I want people to see and understand the great beauty to be found in rugs."[38] And then, hinting his largesse had only begun, he concluded: "Of course, I shall not neglect my home city."[39]

Ballard added four rugs to his original New York gift. The first was a spectacular Ottoman court prayer rug from the sixteenth century, one he had originally seen in the Bode and Kühnel book, at the time never imagining the rug would someday be his. Probably the acquisition of no other rug in his collection brought more joy to Ballard than his purchase of the Bird rug he found in Istanbul. Made in Ushak in the sixteenth century, the rug is decorated with palmette motifs that resemble bird heads, hence its name. It went to the Metropolitan, as did a Garden carpet he bought in 1923, one he had first encountered in F. R. Martin's great tome. That carpet had belonged to Carl Robert Lamm whose home in Sweden, Näsby Castle, had once been among Europe's most-visited private museums. Ballard paid $5,600 for it at the American Art Galleries, New York's premier auction house. These three objects—along with yet another Gördes prayer rug—brought the total number of rugs he gave the Metropolitan to 129.[40] Because he had previously agreed to lend his rugs for exhibitions in Minneapolis, Chicago, and San Francisco, the entire group of 129 rugs reached the museum only in the autumn of 1923. A special exhibition of the new acquisitions proved to be a high point on the museum's calendar that year.[41]

The rugs Ballard added to his gift are typical of the kinds of acquisition he sought during the remainder of his life. Convinced since the time of the Philadelphia Museum exhibition that only exceptional rugs deserved his attention, he concentrated exclusively on objects he thought met that criterion. Evidence of the extent of his success can be seen in a photograph taken at Liberty & Company in London, probably in early 1923 [FIG.11]. The photograph shows five rugs Ballard had just purchased and one he had owned for several years but had apparently sent to Liberty for restoration. At the far left is a so-called small-pattern Holbein rug, one of the earliest of this type known. Next to it is an even older Lotto rug, arguably a product of the late fifteenth century. The large medallion Ushak carpet above the mantle remained in the Ballard family until it was sold in 1950, part of Berenice Ballard's estate. Located below the mantle are an important sixteenth-century

small-medallion Ushak rug, a seventeenth-century
Indo-Persian rug—the weakest member of the group—
and the rug he had apparently had repaired, an Ushak
prayer rug that went to the Metropolitan.[42]

As much as Ballard sought only important rugs for
his collection, he, like any collector, made mistakes. He
purchased a seventeenth-century Çintemani Ushak at
the same time he discovered his Bird rug. He planned
to give both to the Metropolitan but either changed
his mind or the museum rejected the Çintemani rug;
in either case, it never found a home in New York.
He, of course, did not know what modern scholars
would subsequently learn about the rug. Only a small
portion of it is original, nearly its entire border being
the work of a restorer, one who employed aniline dyes,
clear evidence the restorations were completed only
a few years before Ballard bought it. He also chose
badly when he bought the Indo-Persian rug seen in
the Liberty & Company photo. Rugs of this type were
readily available, and few connoisseurs would consider
this one distinguished.[43]

Overall Ballard chose wisely more often than not; he
knew carpets as well as anyone then collecting. This was
acknowledged in 1926 by the London firm of Cardinal
and Harford. It was, at the time, attempting to sell the
so-called Emperor's Carpet, one of the pair of animal
carpets supposedly given by Czar Peter the Great to
Emperor Leopold I of Austria when Peter visited Vienna

fig. 12
Yomut Turkmen main carpet,
Turkmenistan, late 18th–early
19th century. Metropolitan
Museum of Art, New York, Gift of
James F. Ballard, 22.100.44

in 1698.[44] Cardinal and Harford invited several experts to comment on the carpet, including A.F. Kendrick of the Victoria and Albert Museum, Arthur U. Pope, then the leading authority on Persian art, and Ballard. Clearly the St. Louis pharmaceutical salesman had attained a notable plateau, had joined an exclusive fraternity of carpet experts.[45]

Several of Ballard's final additions to his collection offer further testimony to his knowledge of rugs, the most important of them being a Vase carpet he acquired from Friedrich Sarre. During the 1920s, Turkmen pieces, like bold Turkish rugs, remained underappreciated, and had yet to attract the attention they would later enjoy. Ballard, again demonstrating his prescience, bought several, in particular a splendid Tekke main carpet. Vastly older is the Mudéjar large-pattern Holbein fragment he discovered. Although the fifteenth-century weavers who made this carpet resided in Spain, they derived their design from Anatolian models.[46]

Turkish rugs remained Ballard's specialty. Those he obtained during the 1920s include several of genuine merit. Among them were a unique Variant Star Ushak rug from the sixteenth century, once the property of Vitall Benguiat; a Konya medallion rug of similar age; the best Gördes, Kula and Ladik prayer rugs he ever owned; and a Karapinar rug that generated little excitement among his contemporaries but is today considered among the most desirable pieces he owned.[47]

If Ballard, after 1922, set himself apart through the quality of his collection, he also attracted attention thanks to the frequency with which his name appeared in newspapers from around the world. Journalists from St. Louis to Boston, from London to Cairo, and from Bombay to Singapore, wrote about his pursuit of rugs [FIG.5]. Attracting so much notice from so many reporters must have required the efforts of an industrious publicist. While no evidence exists to prove Ballard employed such an individual, there can be little doubt that he did, given the number of column inches devoted to his exploits and given the sameness of the accounts. On the other hand, abundant evidence does verify that he hired French's Press Cutting Agency, a London firm, to maintain a complete file of his clippings.[48]

The articles, based on Ballard's own inventive narratives, chronicled his astonishing adventures: accounts of how he dashed to Peking to buy an imperial Chinese carpet after learning the deposed emperor badly needed cash;[49] of how he spent seventeen years searching for a Bird rug only to find one in Istanbul after being held prisoner of war by Greek troops;[50] surviving a bombardment by Turkish soldiers, and witnessing "the horrors of Smyrna," the city ablaze and its harbor "filled with the dead bodies of men, women and children."[51] In October 1922 he told *The New York Times* that building his collection required him to travel 275,000 miles—not a surprising number given his claim that finding his imperial Chinese carpet dictated a trip of 30,000 miles,[52] and locating his Indo-Persian rug[53] meant a journey of 40,000 miles.[54] Rarely did he, according to his own accounts, acquire a rug with ease. Fifteen years were spent locating one of his Ottoman rugs, and obtaining an Ushak that came "from the harem of the tenth Sultan of Turkey" could not have been an easy task.[55]

Ballard also continued to expound on the benefits of collecting rugs, as he did to a *New York Herald* reporter in 1925: "To the rug connoisseur a genuine antique opens up a world of mystery and romance."[56] More than one journalist managed to decipher a shrouded meaning in his remarks, to understand that carpet collecting had, after 1922, taken on an added significance for him. One of these journalists, writing in *The Furniture Trader Advisor,* a London publication, hinted at this new emphasis: "A large part of the attraction of rug collecting has to do with the romance of the whole subject, and in his travels Mr. Ballard seems to reflect the spirit of the ages in which Oriental art reached its zenith."[57] A hometown newsman was even more perceptive: "More precious to Mr. Ballard, however, than the rugs that he collected, were the adventure and romance of assembly, the delights of pursuit."[58] After his gift to the Metropolitan and his recognition as a connoisseur, after he had attained a degree of celebrity, he began to prize his travels even more than his collecting. Rugs, in a word, became both an excuse for constant travel and the means of enveloping himself with the same exoticism he had long attached to rugs. Like them, he, himself, could now claim to have passed "through war, riot, bloodshed," to have witnessed "robbery, pillage, and murder."[59]

Much to his disappointment, his travels came to an abrupt end in April 1929 when he fell seriously ill with a blood disorder eventually diagnosed as filariasis, a parasitic disease transmitted by blood-feeding insects. Two years earlier he had visited Egypt, where, it is assumed, an infected mosquito transmitted the disease to him. After his wife, Emma, died in 1925, he had moved with his elder daughter, Berenice, from St. Louis to New York. It was there, at his home at 171 West 57th Street, that he convalesced.

At the time of his move he went to considerable lengths to explain that settling in New York was "not a case of loving St. Louis any less." Instead, he said, it made sense "for the convenience of my European trips" and because New York is where "a large number of my friends, among them the art and rug collectors, reside." In 1927, he reaffirmed his devotion to St. Louis by reminding its residents of his promise to donate part of his collection to its City Art Museum. On October 27 he was explicit: "St. Louis not only has a favorable chance, it has the only chance [of receiving my rugs.] It will be the only city considered." Both the *St. Louis Post Dispatch* and the *St. Louis Daily Globe-Democra*t had, the previous day, stolen his thunder by unequivocally stating that his rugs were coming to their city.[60]

The first sixty-six arrived in the spring of 1929. Because he remained seriously ill, his younger daughter, Nellie Ballard White, arranged for their transfer. The Administrative

Board of Control of the City Art Museum, acknowledging the gift of "some seventy rugs," sent him a letter of thanks on June 5, 1929.[61] On November 21 the rugs went on display in the museum.[62] The exhibition's opening, which he was too ill to attend, was a grand, by-invitation-only affair that featured a "Promenade Concert" performed by the St. Louis Symphony Orchestra.

Although the Metropolitan had seven years earlier selected 129 Ballard rugs for its collection, those that came to St. Louis were by no means an inferior lot. Ballard had made many of his most advantageous purchases after 1922. As a consequence, his inventory of rugs at the time of the City Art Museum bequest included both a spectacular array and wide variety of pieces. Nearly every rug-producing region from Spain to China was represented. Both his large-pattern Holbein from Spain and his "hundred antiques" carpet from China were included. Two Indian fragments that Breck inexplicably failed to select for the Metropolitan came to St. Louis. Ballard's gift even included two tents, probably Persian, which are as difficult to display as they are spectacular when erected. As usual, his long suit was his Turkish contingent. Those carrying artists' names—Holbein, Lotto, Tintoretto, and Ghirlandaio—would cause any curator's heart to race. Along with them came certain Gördes, Ladik, and Kula prayer rugs that justify Ballard's devotion to them. Even more spectacular were the southwest Anatolian, Yürük, Mudéjar, Ushak, "Transylvanian," and Karapinar rugs that found homes in the City Art Museum. The following year, 1930, seven more Ballard pieces, including his much-acclaimed Tekke Turkmen main carpet, joined the collection. Also that year, Maurice Dimand, soon to become the Curator of Near Eastern Art at the Metropolitan, was commissioned to prepare a catalogue of seventy of the St. Louis rugs.[63]

Besides those he presented to the museum, Ballard in 1929 gave another sixty-four rugs to his daughter Nellie. She had moved to New York to be with him as he struggled to regain his health, and she appreciated rugs nearly as much as he did. Her interest seemed to validate his own quarter-century commitment to them, and her descriptions of the auctions and exhibitions she attended allowed him, if only vicariously, to experience them with her. His other daughter, Berenice, owned seventy-four rugs when she died in 1947; at least seventeen of them had been her father's. Whether they came to her at the same time Nellie received hers is uncertain. In fact, with only two or three exceptions, when and how she acquired any of them remains a puzzle.

Despite his physicians' best efforts and Nellie's care, Ballard's health continued to deteriorate. His preoccupation with rugs, on the other hand, remained vigorous. As late as March 1931 he added a new rug to his collection, again a Gördes prayer rug, a reminder of his early favorites and a fitting choice to be his final purchase.[64] He would enjoy it only briefly, however, because a month later, on April 23, 1931, now nearly eighty, with both Nellie and Berenice at his bedside, he died at Madison Avenue Hospital.

His daughters, each in their own way, succeeded in keeping the Ballard name synonymous with carpets. Together they financed the publication of Maurice Dimand's catalogue, a project their father had initiated but had not lived long enough to complete. Nellie followed her father's example by exhibiting her collection, which now included the glorious Vase carpet Ballard had acquired from Friedrich Sarre [CAT.1] as well as four animal rugs she had bought from a French family, owners of the rugs for a century and a half.[65] In 1972, she gave forty rugs to the City Art Museum, by then known more precisely as the Saint Louis Art Museum; later she donated five additional pieces. Aside from the four animal rugs, nearly all those she gave had been her father's.[66]

Berenice's rugs remained with her until her death. On October 27, 1950, on order of her heirs, Parke-Bernet offered them at auction in New York. Because of the quality of her rugs, the sale attracted both serious carpet collectors and important dealers. George Hewitt Myers attended the auction and bought an Ushak opposed-arch rug and a Spanish medallion rug for the Textile Museum. Joseph V. McMullan found two "Transylvanian" rugs he later gave to the Metropolitan, while Henry Francis du Pont selected three pieces—a Kula runner, a Feraghan carpet, and an Ushak medallion carpet—for Winterthur. The New York dealer Karekin Beshir came away with a Kula prayer rug that had once been Ballard's.[67] As notable as any of those was a carpet Berenice Ballard herself bought in 1941 at the Mrs. Henry Walters sale. This seventeenth-century Persian rug, woven in silk with gold and silver thread, contains an unusual scene inspired by a Flemish tapestry. It now resides in the Metropolitan thanks to C. Ruxton Love, who bought it at the sale.[68]

Today James F. Ballard occupies a prominent place in the pantheon of carpet collectors. When he began assembling his collection, few people would have predicted such a conclusion. He seemed to lack the qualifications a collector should have. He was prosperous but could claim no great fortune; a mid-westerner, not—like most collectors—an East Coast resident; a person with no collecting experience; and certainly not an individual who, with checkbook in hand, would depend on a major dealer to assemble a collection for him. Surprisingly these seeming handicaps account in large measure for his achievements. Because he lacked the funds to compete with the Rockefellers and the Clarks or to open his checkbook to dealers like Kelekian or Duveen, he avoided the widely accepted fallacy that only Persian carpets were worthy of a collector's attention. He bought what he could afford, frequently the underappreciated, and in doing so broke new ground.

Unlike his contemporaries who collected other objects besides rugs, he remained single-focused and so became a connoisseur, an acknowledged carpet expert, a distinction few collectors of his generation could claim. Only after his collection had taken on a character of its own did he move to New York and begin hobnobbing with the East-Coast crowd, a clique whose members would have discouraged his acquiring the sorts of pieces he had learned to prize. After his early fascination with Gördes, Ladik, and Kula prayer rugs, a thralldom cultivated by Arthur Dilley and A. E. King, he developed the courage to rely on his own eye, to avoid received opinions. In the process, although he made mistakes and acquired some inelegant pieces, he created a collection of monumental significance.

But James F. Ballard should be remembered as much for the influence he exerted as for the objects he bought. Through his exhibitions and bequests—and, yes, even because of his incessant quest for attention—he compelled future collectors to acknowledge the glories of "Transylvanian," Karapinar, Turkmen and bold Ushak rugs. Also, and of utmost importance, he convinced countless other people, individuals whose first encounter with an early Oriental rug was an encounter with one of his, that carpets could be more than floor coverings; that they could indeed, as he so loudly proclaimed, be art.

The Ballard Collection in Context

Walter B. Denny

CARPET STUDY AND ISLAMIC ART

On initial consideration by an informed layperson, the position occupied by carpets within the broad spectrum of Islamic arts would appear to be both unique and perhaps even pre-eminent. Architecture apart, knotted-pile carpets of the Islamic world are certainly as a group the largest works of Islamic art in size; they are also large in number. They are beyond any argument the works of Islamic art best known and most completely documented outside of the Islamic world. This is especially true in Europe from the early modern period onward. And from the realms of folklore—the flying carpets of Arab legend—to commerce, the knotted-pile carpet is perhaps more emblematic of Islam and its cultural traditions than any other artistic medium save architecture.

To the scholar of carpets, this initial impression is underlined by a series of still more important factors. Within the world of Islamic art, the carpet is the only medium that finds expression in all levels of Islamic society, from the small agricultural village and pastoral nomadic encampment, through the urban commercial workshop, to the rarified level of the court manufactory, where carpets were produced for the use of royalty and to serve as royal gifts. No other Islamic artistic medium—for that matter no other artistic medium in the Western tradition—can make claim to such a wide range of social and cultural embeddedness in both manufacture and use. Viewed in the broad historical context, only textiles made for domestic furnishings and for clothing can claim to equal carpets in economic importance in the Islamic world.

The same pre-eminence applies if we look at the central iconic images of Islamic art. Two of the most important of these are the arcade (symbolizing the mosque) and the single arch, often with a lamp (alternately symbolizing the gateway to paradise or by implication the mihrab, the niche in a mosque that indicates the *qibla* wall facing Mecca). While architectural in origin and reflected in many different media, they achieve their most numerous and most important artistic representations in knotted-pile carpets of the *saff* (a carpet woven with a design of a row or rows of arched compartment forms) and *sajjadah* (a so-called prayer carpet, woven with a design of a single arch, niche, or gateway representation) types [**FIG.13**].[69] The major forms of Islamic art are calligraphy, floral, vegetal and geometric ornament, and the figural art of humans and animals. All find some of their most numerous, largest-scale, most opulent, and most iconic manifestations in the art of the Islamic carpet.

If we look to museums of Islamic art, the art of the carpet likewise predominates. The new installation of Islamic art at the Victoria and Albert Museum in London is arrayed around the dramatic presentation of the Ardabil carpet, sheltered beneath reflective glass, and illuminated for only a few minutes in each hour. In New York, Paris, Berlin, and Vienna, as in Qatar, Kuwait, Cairo and Istanbul, current or prospective installations of Islamic art present

Distichon in imaginem Georgij Gysenij
Ista refert vultus, quam cernis Imago Georgij
Sic oculos vivos, sic habet ille genas
Anno aetatis suae XXXIIII
Anno Dom. 1532
Nulla sine merore voluptas
.G. Gisze.

carpets as centerpieces of great collections that attempt both to explain and to epitomize the achievements of the cultures of the Islamic world. Considering the carpets' great size, brilliant color, and impressive workmanship and materials, such display is almost as a matter of necessity. Given these simple, indisputable facts, we might then ask why it is that, in the world of Islamic art scholarship, carpets are by far the least studied and least discussed of major artistic media. We might ask why a large proportion of the major published work on Islamic carpets is the product of collectors, dealers and popularizers; much of it does not therefore meet the prevailing standards for scholarly work. We might ask why carpets, while indubitably popular with museum-goers, are so rarely accorded serious exhibitions in major institutions. Above all, we might ask why Islamic carpets have for most of the past hundred years been the subject of almost as much indifference on the part of historians of European material culture as they have been by scholars of the art of the Islamic world. They have, after all, been an integral part of Western material culture since the late Middle Ages, and are depicted countless times in European and American painting as symbols of wealth, sanctity, or social status.

There are of course several quite simple answers to these questions. Carpets are designed for daily use of a very low status, under one's feet and under one's furniture. The "Oriental" carpet on one's living room floor is dying a slow death from dirt, spills, and the abuses of shod and sometimes muddy feet. Yet it is a work of the same technique and often stems from the same lineage, if rarely the same artistic level, as works of art in museums. It is perhaps no surprise that the low status of the floor covering in effect "rubs off" on the museum object to a greater extent than the high status of the museum object "rubs off" on the floor covering. Carpets are not only status symbols but also conspicuous consumption in the literal sense. Like rare and expensive food and wines, haute couture clothing, high-status automobiles, or luxurious hotels and travel, carpets are regarded as expensive items to be used up—consumed or destroyed—as a demonstration of status and wealth. Mr. Getty used one of the Ardabil carpets on the floor of his London living room, and the Rockefellers did the same with other classical masterpieces in their New York mansion; and they did so without second thoughts. Thus it is no surprise that the stories of Jesus entering Jerusalem on Palm Sunday, where his followers spread their cloaks in the dusty road to make a royal pathway, or of Sir Walter Raleigh's precious cape placed in the mud to make a clean passage for Queen Elizabeth, are not concerned with moralizing over a sacrifice of precious and beautiful works of textile art. Rather they focus on the exaltation of the personages for whom the precious possessions are sacrificed.

A second answer has to do with the fact that, virtually alone among works of Islamic artistic production, carpets can be bought everywhere today in a worldwide marketplace— one that, by repute, deservedly or not, is a place where a buyer needs to beware. Carpet dealers have a somewhat dubious reputation; a term such as "rug merchant" or *marchand de tapis* has pejorative connotations in many languages besides English and French. Many of the myths of the marketplace have been augmented by popular publications on carpets written by dealers and collectors anxious to bolster the market value of their holdings. Hand-crafted objects are readily available as a common form of floor covering and are reasonably inexpensive by comparison with paintings, furniture, or sculpture. In combination, these factors have not helped the art of the carpet to attain either a popular or a scholarly status in our times. Furthermore the forging of older and more valuable types of carpet experienced a first golden (or better, gold-tone) age around the turn of the twentieth century, and a second one around the turn of the twenty-first. Such fakery has had a negative effect on collectors and on museums; concern over being taken in by forgeries has even led to imputations being leveled against objects that more careful study has revealed to be blamelessly genuine.[70]

Another problem bedeviling rug scholarship is the notion, notably held in certain American museum quarters today, that the only carpets worthy of exhibition in an art museum are "high-art" carpets belonging to the court manufactory category, or their close commercial imitators. During the past half-century, carpet scholarship has come to regard carpet art and production over the past seven centuries as an integrated and highly interrelated series of traditions and artistic practices. This point of view expresses a high regard for carpets in which the impact of court arts, such as manuscript illumination and miniature painting, can be clearly seen. Yet it finds itself at odds with the concept of artistry in the commercial, nomadic and village traditions that both nurtured and were nurtured by the court tradition. Such a view expresses even more doubt about the "other" major category of Islamic carpet weaving, slit-tapestry weaving or the kilim technique, which recent scholarship has shown to be related with the history of the knotted-pile carpet in an intimate and highly complex way.[71]

The practice that has emerged over the past half-century of studying and classifying carpets with the aid of structural analysis is generally a rather simple, straightforward and scientific process of describing the basic materials and simple techniques by which all carpets are created. However it has been quite unjustly viewed by some scholars of Islamic art as deeply arcane and difficult to learn—and a somewhat unworthy occupation for a dignified scholar, involving as it frequently does the elevation of the posterior above the head while kneeling on the floor to look closely at carpet structure through a magnifier. This is today often further tainted with the accusatory term connoisseurship which, when combined with the mundane activity of counting knots—or anything—has contributed to the relative neglect of carpet studies by academic specialists in today's universities. This neglect has, however, a bright side. In the broad context of the study of Islamic art, there is no area of greater excitement, potential for important discovery, and room for innovative thinking, than the area of carpet study. And one might imagine, therefore, that some of those involved in this area of study, the present writer included, are in a perverse way grateful for the excitement, the opportunities, the discoveries and the freedom accorded them in their work through the neglect of others.

JAMES BALLARD, COLLECTOR

James Ballard is discussed in detail elsewhere in this volume, but before looking at the works of art he gave to St. Louis, it is useful briefly to consider his relationship to those works of art. Ballard was by all accounts an archetypal American entrepreneur. A recent paper on collecting in the United States actually used the term "snake oil salesman" to describe the origins of Ballard's fortune. In a world anxious to cast its heroes and its politicians as pristine champions of virtue, we have to remember that, despite the alleged civilizing properties of great art, many of the world's greatest collectors certainly had their feet of clay. But despite his talent for self-promotion, it can be argued that James Ballard's historical role in the world of carpets transcends that of any other scholar or collector of his or any other time.

Like many collectors of his era, whether of painting, *objets de vertu*, or carpets, Ballard relied to a great extent on the advice of dealers, a few of whom may have been scallywags and tellers of dubious tales. This notwithstanding, Ballard was able to break out of the conventional mold of collecting in his time to an extent that would eventually fundamentally alter the way we all look at carpets. If we look at the text of Ballard's early catalogues— whether that inspired directly by his own comments, by the information given to him by dealers, or at a later date written by scholars he retained to publish his work—we find by today's standards fairly little of value.[73] The attributions are often out of date, the technical understanding of carpets is sometimes flawed, and the historical and geographical context poorly understood. These are all predictable and quite unremarkable characteristics of any academic discipline in its infancy. What is remarkable about the Ballard collection, in its three parts—the gift to the Metropolitan Museum of Art of 1922, the gift to the Saint Louis Art Museum of 1928, and the residual bequests and gifts to Saint Louis by members of the Ballard family in 1971 and later—is the vision behind the totality of the collection.

Here, for the first time, we encounter a collector who saw the entire artistic spectrum of the Islamic carpet as an artistically integrated whole, in which the internal boundaries of time and genre were essentially of minor importance. In this he differs from the Rockefellers, Clarks, Fricks, and their ilk. And he did not hesitate to juxtapose what were then regarded as museum masterpieces (so expensive that he often could not afford them) alongside examples often regarded by his contemporaries merely as high-class (if that) floor covering (which he could amply afford to buy). Ballard was almost certainly looking beyond the temporary prestige of having great works of art on his floor, toward a legacy for his name that would be established by gifts to major museums. (By contrast, most of the Rockefeller carpets were eventually sold and not donated.) Whatever his motivations, James Ballard's collection was essentially more than three-quarters of a century ahead of its time. And there can be no doubt that, if Ballard hoped his donating of art to major museums would result in a kind of immortality beyond the realm of patent medicines, his hopes have to a great extent been realized.

THE BALLARD COLLECTION

When beginning research on the Ballard collections of carpets in St. Louis—both the original and residual bequests— I had no idea that I would shortly thereafter begin an appointment at the Metropolitan Museum of Art that would permit me an equally detailed examination of the Ballard Collection items there. The enriched perspective thus gained perhaps allows for a fuller understanding and appreciation of the Ballard collection, and certainly for a clearer view of its historical legacy. The collection, or rather the three collections, is of interest on a number of fronts.

First, of course, they contain many masterpieces of carpet weaving that are of immense importance for the historian of art; carpets such as the St. Louis four-lobed medallion Ushak [CAT.12],[74] or the Metropolitan's coupled-column Ottoman prayer rug [FIG.14],[75] occupy permanent niches in the pantheon of masterworks in carpet history. Second, as we have mentioned, the Ballard collections in certain ways embody what at the time of collecting was an uncommon approach to the history of carpets, which turns out to have been historically ahead of its time. This is the concept that carpet weaving across time, space, and social and economic strata constitutes in many ways a unified artistic phenomenon with cross-fertilizing components and a common ancestry. Third, in contrast, James Ballard's collections also inevitably reflect certain areas of interest, and certain art historical and aesthetic judgments, that today are regarded less favorably than at the time Ballard was collecting. Among these is Ballard's attention to collecting west Anatolian seccade or "prayer rug" production from Gördes and Kula, which today are not highly esteemed by scholars and collectors. Another example is his early twentieth-century taste for extensive "restoration" of carpets—by which I mean reknotting, reweaving, and even replacing or reinterpreting substantial parts of old carpets in order to give them the appearance of aesthetic wholeness that was desired at the time.

This practice contrasts remarkably with present taste and practice, which favor the conservation and stabilization, rather than the restoration, of old pieces, and do not shrink from the museum display of carpet fragments or fragmentary examples. By today's standards, some Ballard carpets have extensive areas of restoration that over time have drastically faded and changed in color; these are no longer considered worthy of exhibition except in the context of the history of restoration. It is somewhat ironic that, had they been left unrestored, they would be far more acceptable for exhibition as works of art today.[76]

In terms of its scope, the Ballard collection in St. Louis is vast. In addition to the four major geographic carpet-weaving areas of Central Asia, Iran, Transcaucasia and Anatolia (the latter represented with enormous richness), it includes significant representation of carpets from Spain, Egypt and Syria, while India's Mughal tradition is represented by two brilliant fragments. When we look at the very great differences in aesthetic among these carpet groups, it becomes again obvious that Ballard's collection is not so much the creation of a single individual's taste, as it is a single individual's concept of the unity and diversity present in the world of carpet art. In short, it is a collection made to inform the mind and to influence public and scholarly taste, as well as to delight the beholder.

Masterpieces in Saint Louis

Walter B. Denny

A PAIR OF PERSIAN CARPETS

In James Ballard's day, the prices paid for the most important Persian carpets in the world art marketplace were already sky-high; in fact, once inflation is taken into account, their prices were often at levels not attained again until early in the twenty-first century.

The Ballard collection contains a few superb examples of seventeenth-century Kerman carpets in the so-called "Vase" technique, and of these cat. 1, given to St. Louis by Nellie Ballard White in 1972, is both a very fine and a very typical example. The carpet's wide range of intense colors apparently appealed to Ballard. Although, quite typical for Vase carpets, this example has been cut down from its original size, the overall artistic quality of the carpet and its design, including three of the small eponymous vases, is excellent. The complex and overlapping floral lattices are fluid and clear, and the carpet has survived in quite good condition with good colors.

The carpet far surpasses in condition and quality the fragmentary example Ballard gave to the Metropolitan Museum in 1922 [FIG.10]; it is a mystery why it remained in the family's collection until 1972. One suspects that the St. Louis Vase carpet was a family favorite that was simply too hard to part with until the later date. It is also quite significant that in his collecting Ballard avoided buying the most popular classical Persian rugs of his own day: the seventeenth-century "Indo-Isfahan" carpets that survived in rather large numbers and were highly popular with collectors such as the New Yorkers Henry Clay Frick and Senator William A. Clark. In retrospect this was probably also prescient, as these carpets, many of which have survived in very poor condition, are generally not held in the highest esteem among Persian carpets today.

The other end of the spectrum of Persian carpet history, until recently neglected by scholars, is exemplified in St. Louis by an early nineteenth-century northwest Persian carpet [CAT.2] that also arrived at the Saint Louis Art Museum in 1972. From a period that until recently was thought to be largely devoid of significant carpet weaving, this masterpiece of the dyer's and weaver's art, probably created by ethnic Kurds, is one of the outstanding masterpieces of the Ballard collection. The design, an overall lattice of large palmettes, traces its lineage back to the seventeenth century and before. But Ballard's example is above all a symphony of spectacular colors and spectacular wool, only matched among large carpets in St. Louis by the famous four-lobed medallion Ushak carpet. Again, this carpet did not form part of the original donation of 1929, but rather entered the Museum in 1972. This is perhaps opportune, because it is not until recently that the artistic merits of carpets such as these have been accorded the attention that they have always richly deserved.

The present catalogue of items selected for exhibition from the Ballard collection in St.

the City Art Mueum. However, these two examples are both of significantly high artistic quality. The two works, both incorporating designs of complex floral palmettes in a network of vines, stand in effect as pillars at opposite ends of the chronology of classical Persian weaving. If considered together with the entire Ballard collection in its three parts—New York 1922, St. Louis 1929, and St. Louis 1972—these two Persian carpets may be regarded as a paradigm of Ballard's taste, economic circumstances and collecting philosophy. He avoided the priciest and most fashionable Persian carpets; but the examples he acquired expressed an interest, unusual for his time, in the Persian carpet tradition as a continuously evolving artistic continuum that was subject to continual artistic self-renewal over a period of several centuries.

THE ANATOLIAN TRADITION

The Ballard collection is deservedly most famous for its important examples of the carpet-weaving tradition of Anatolia, the Asian part of today's Republic of Turkey. Early Anatolian carpets named after the European painters of the Renaissance who depicted them, including examples of "Holbein," "Bellini," and "Lotto" design types, are well represented, in a way that again gives rise to many questions. For example: Ballard donated one Lotto and three Bellini carpets to the Metropolitan Museum in 1922;[77] why, seven years later, did he donate to St. Louis three Lotto carpets (later to be joined in 1972 by a fourth), one Bellini [FIG.17] and one small-pattern Holbein (a very important type until recently represented in New York only by a small fragment donated in the late twentieth century)?

From the weaving tradition of Ushak, the most prolific carpet-producing area in Anatolia from the fifteenth through the eighteenth centuries, Ballard donated four examples to Saint Louis in 1929, later joined by two others in 1972. These include the only reasonably complete early quatrefoil Ushak rug in North America [CAT.15]. It served as the model for the much later Ballard quatrefoil rug in New York (22.100.115)[78] and countless other Anatolian carpets through the centuries. The other examples are: a very beautiful early example of the so-called double-ended Ushak prayer rug type [CAT.13] that served as a model for the later Ballard "Transylvanian" rugs in St. Louis and New York;[79] an unusually small, almost tiny early Star Ushak carpet [CAT.11], again with a rich lineage of later weaving; and a carpet that many consider to be the greatest masterpiece of the Ballard collection in St. Louis, [CAT.12]. This last, although today comprising only about two-thirds of its original size, must be ranked among the finest examples of Ushak weaving to survive into our time, unsurpassed in the brilliance of its colors, and unique in its design.

Of the four Ushak examples in the 1929 donation, the first three are all excellent examples of well-known types, each of which has a distinct lineage of descendants in the Ballard collection and in the surviving corpus of early Turkish carpets. But the four-lobed medallion Ushak carpet points out another aspect of Ballard's collecting: it shows that Ballard did not shrink from acquiring unique and otherwise unknown design types. If one thinks of the major "stars" of Ballard's collection, many of them fall into this category of rare types that in James Ballard's day were relatively unknown: the coupled-column Ottoman prayer rug in James Ballard's day were relatively unknown: the coupled-column Ottoman prayer rug in the Metropolitan [**FIG.15**];[80] the St. Louis four-lobed Ushak under discussion; the overall-patterned small Ushak rug in the Metropolitan (22.100.116);[81] the unique fine-patterned Ushak in St. Louis [**CAT.14**]; the beautiful small Konya medallion rug in St. Louis [**CAT.36**]; and certainly the breathtaking medallion rug with off-set knotting in St. Louis [**CAT.33**], a masterpiece of early weaving from southeast Anatolia.

Finally, although numerous examples of the very common ogival-medallion Ushak carpets have survived and many were available for purchase in Ballard's time, he seems to have avoided them in the same way he avoided the so-called Indo-Isfahan Persian carpets of the seventeenth century. St. Louis received in 1972 a very small and relatively late example of the type [**CAT.16**], which presents twin advantages for the Museum of very good colors, and atypically very small (and hence easy-to-exhibit) size.

Any discussion of outstanding masterpieces in the Ballard Collection cannot neglect two unusual carpets from Anatolia. They reflect the village weaving tradition of the seventeenth century and later, one inextricably linked both culturally and artistically to the earlier classical examples. The first of these, the above-mentioned medallion carpet with offset knotting [**CAT.33**], belongs to a tradition of weaving that frequently employs a knotting scheme where the horizontal rows of colored wool knots, instead of stacking up vertically on pairs of warps directly above the knots in the row below, are often offset one row from the next by a single warp. This technique allows for much steeper verticals in the design, and thus greater artistic freedom for the weaver; it is thought by scholars to indicate the carpet's origin in the weaving tradition of Kurdish peoples from south-central and southeastern Anatolia.

The central field of this Ballard carpet incorporates a layout that is classical in the extreme: a medallion, pointed at the vertical ends, connected vertically to two oblong rectangular cartouches and two triangular pendants, on an indigo ground whose wool, freely dyed in small lots, betrays an intense "vibrato" of lighter and darker values known as abrash. But it is the white-ground border that elevates it from the ranks of the unusual into the pantheon of carpet masterpieces: an artistically exciting alternation of split-leaf vegetal forms and oblongs based on an eight-pointed star cartouche from classical Persian carpets, brilliantly colored, and executed with a bold disregard for fussy details that produces an indelible visual impression. Only one other carpet, a much larger example with multiple medallions that came to light more recently, can be firmly placed in the same place, time and weaving milieu.[82]

What a contrast then to compare this village weaving from the wild southeast of Anatolia to the incredibly elegant red-ground medallion carpet from central Anatolia [**CAT.36**]. Also a village product, this carpet impresses by its impeccable symmetry, the elegance of its white outlining of medallions, pendants, and corner-pieces, the smooth corner articulation, and the brilliantly colored crenellated *elem* "skirts" or "flaps" at each end, with their stylized tulips in a wide range of color variations. In Ballard's day only one major museum, the Museum of Islamic Art in Berlin, had the prescience actively to pursue the collecting of Anatolian carpets of this period and type, which today are recognized as among the supreme accomplishments

SMALL WONDERS

In finishing this brief look at the Ballard Collection in the context of time and space, we turn finally to two of the smallest items in St. Louis, woven at around the same time but very far apart in space.

The first of these is an unusually small carpet [CAT.5] with a central, highly geometric design of three square compartments each containing a hexagonal red field with an eight-pointed star surrounded by various floating motifs. Rugs such as these were once dubbed by scholars, perhaps inappropriately, "chessboard" carpets. A significant number have survived.

They are documented in European painting around the year 1600, and have long been recognized as having some technical and color relationships with the so-called Mamluk carpets of Egypt. Such carpets have a tendency to vertical "stretching" of the design, an unusual combination of hexagon and octagon, and design relationships to a number of groups of extremely rare and very early carpets from the Near East.

They are generally thought to have been woven in what we today call Syria. They have unusual, very shiny but somewhat intractable wool that resists being spun, a highly distinctive color range, and an unusual structure. The group was apparently produced in a commercial manufactory, in one of Syria's main commercial centers—whether Damascus, Aleppo, or possibly Homs or Hama we do not know. The vast majority of the production employs designs identical to that of the St. Louis carpet, but almost always with at least two rows of compartments horizontally and many more vertically. More recently, scholars have identified other carpets in museums that, although they have very different designs mainly based on Anatolian and Persian curvilinear prototypes, are identical in coloration and technique to the chessboard carpets.[84]

A particular design characteristic of the entire group is the careful planning of the corner articulation of the borders. The Ballard example in St. Louis is unique in its small size, and unusual in its relatively good state of repair, despite the loss of both ends. The Metropolitan Museum had to wait until 1969 to acquire its own rather badly worn chessboard carpet from Joseph V. McMullan,[85] who may rightly be regarded as Ballard's true heir in collecting philosophy and aesthetic taste.

The other Ballard "small wonder" to be discussed here is one of two tiny fragments of large Mughal carpets woven in India in the early seventeenth century [CAT.49]. From the small fragment the overall design of the field can be deduced: a diagonal lattice of white leaf-like forms, on top of another lattice of green and blue vines, bearing leaves, floral buds, and large complex floral palmettes. The design is fluid and three-dimensional; forms overlap, and the subtle shading of the two halves of each green leaf suggests varying reactivity to light.

Is there anything about this fragment, at first glance so artistically different from the bulk of the Ballard collection, which might suggest some personal relationship between object and collector? The answer to this question would appear to lie in the realm of color, for the seventeenth-century Mughal fragment of a carpet of truly royal quality from north India has one outstanding characteristic that even trumps its typically elegant and precise

India has one outstanding characteristic that even trumps its typically elegant and precise Mughal design: brilliant, intense, vibrant and compelling color dyed into pashm, yarn crafted from the soft undercoat of the Kashmir goat that we sometimes call cashmere.

It is easy to imagine the man who acquired the brilliantly colored, four-lobed Ushak carpet immediately falling under the spell of this small, almost miraculously intact scrap of imperial splendor from the era of the Taj Mahal because of the extraordinary impact of its colors. And so it is that this small wonder also found its way into the Ballard Collection.

THE BALLARD COLLECTION IN HISTORY

As James Ballard would have liked, the St. Louis collection of Ballard carpets has had a long history of attention and exhibition. First Ballard's own catalogues of early loan exhibitions, then Maurice Dimand's handsome hardbound volume setting out the collection, eventually Daniel Walker's writing on the collection, and now this present volume, have each highlighted various aspects of the collection and the collector. These writings serve collectively as a chronicle of changing tastes and emphases in scholarship and museum practice.

Because Ballard was, as we have characterized him, a carpet collector ahead of his time, it has taken, and will take, a good deal of time for scholarship on the collection to catch up with the scope and complexity of the collection itself. By the standards of the Gilded Age, the Ballard collection is unusual: in its interest in wild cards and unique items, its incorporation of fragments and fragmentary examples, and its concentration on the village weaving of Anatolia. An individual who collected the beautiful red carpets of Turkmen weavers from Central Asia with the same fervor that he acquired masterpieces from imperial Ottoman looms must have seemed to many to be eccentric, if not actually quite daft. Today we are of course the grateful beneficiaries of Ballard's peculiar madness (which may far better be characterized as gifted foresight). His gift to St. Louis will keep on giving, as his collection continues to yield up new secrets to new generations in the time to come.

A Short Note on Carpet Technique

Why do we include technical and structural data on carpets in this catalogue? First and foremost, as the entries themselves make clear, the basic technical characteristics of a carpet are a primary indication of the carpet's place and time of weaving, as well as a major determinant of the carpet's visual and hence artistic impact. A pile carpet consists of two major parts: the pile itself, which is the napped surface that we see when we look at the front of a carpet, and is composed of many thousands of individual knots; and the foundation, which consists of lengthwise warp yarns and widthwise weft yarns, that serve as the basic structure on which the knotted pile is constructed in the weaving process. In this catalogue we have taken the innovative step of showing a close-up detail of both the front and the back of an identical 10 cm square section of each carpet. This should illuminate the technical data for the reader, and make the catalogue entry easier to understand.

Analyzing a carpet is itself normally a very simple process that anyone can learn how to do in basic fashion in a few minutes. The following protocol is observed:

Warp: First, we have to determine that we are looking at original warps in the carpet, and not, as so frequently is the case in the Ballard collection, with restorations. The upper and lower ends of the carpet are where warps normally protrude as a fringe and therefore are easy to see; they are also those areas typically most likely to have been completely restored, often with materials that differ from those of the original work in significant ways.

Once we have an original warp in view, we look carefully to determine its material (usually either wool or cotton, sometimes silk or goat-hair, more rarely a mixture of materials), its color (undyed or dyed; undyed wool comes in a wide range of colors), and then its spin and ply. The direction of spinning of the original yarn can be clockwise—what we call S-spun—or counter-clockwise—what we term Z-spun. The overwhelming majority of carpets utilize Z-spun yarns, so the appearance of S-spun yarns is usually a cause for particular interest.

Normally, to make the warps of a carpet thicker and stronger, a number of Z-spun yarns (two or three wool yarns, or up to a dozen or more cotton yarns) are S-plied together to make a stronger and thicker warp yarn. As a rule of thumb, the direction of the ply of individual yarns together (S or Z) is always the opposite of the direction of the original spinning of single yarns. Warps in a carpet, when observed from the back, may either be on one single level, or may be arranged during the weaving process into two different levels, where one warp in each pair is higher or lower than the other.

Weft: After determining that the weft we want to look at is original and not a restoration, we examine it carefully, usually from the back of the carpet, where it is easier to see between the rows of knots. In carpets with complicated structures, it always helps to find a damaged area, such as a hole or seriously worn area, or a fraying end or edge, where the weft can be more easily seen. We then look at the material (cotton, wool, and silk are the most common ones); the color (wefts are far more likely to be dyed different colors than warps, which are usually undyed); the direction of spin (unless the rug was woven in Egypt in early times, this will almost always be counter-clockwise or Z-spun); and the number of times and the pattern in which the weft has been passed horizontally across the rug between each row of knots.

In the simplest case, a weft is passed (shot) once in one direction and once in the opposite direction between each row of knots. Between shots, devices on the loom called a heddle and a shed stick can be manipulated so that the shed (the space between alternate warps) can be made wide enough to pass the weft yarn (usually wound on a wooden device called a shuttle) from side to side, first going over ever other warp, and then under every other warp. This fundamental process of weaving with warp and weft yarns results in a woven fabric.

Sometimes the pattern of passing the weft from side to side becomes more complex. Between each row of pile knots there may be four or more alternating wefts. Or there may be a single weft going in one direction only. Often there are parallel pairs of wefts in a single pass or shot, and sometimes three or more wefts parallel in a single shot. Sometimes the first pass of the weft will be pulled tightly, forcing the warps into two levels; the next pass, through a shed space reversing the upper and lower warps, may be made very loosely. The result is first a straight weft, and then a sinuous weft—and the warp will be on two levels.

Straight and sinuous passes may be made with different numbers or materials of weft. Generally, therefore, the analyzed wefts in a carpet may prove to be more complicated than the warps, and thus may often tell us more about where and when, and even (rarely) for whom, a carpet was made.

Pile: Once again, we have been very careful to ensure that our pile data is based on original pile in the Ballard carpets, and not on restored areas. Most pile carpets consist of horizontal row after row of small tufts of colored wool (silk and cotton are far more rare) that are tied as knots on a pair of warps; these tufts or knots altogether form the pile surface of the carpet, with its pattern, texture, and reactivity to light. The pile gives the carpet its visual impact; pile yarns are usually dyed in a variety of colors, and pile yarn normally consists of at least two Z-spun yarns plied S. The most common red dye is made from the root of the madder plant; indigo is the most common source of blue; and yellow comes from many different sources, including a weed termed "weld" in English. In Persian and Egyptian rugs especially, a purplish-red dye made from the dried bodies of insects is frequently used.

We may rarely encounter pile knots tied on a single warp, or on as many as four warps. In most areas of the Islamic world that practice rug weaving, however, the normal practice is to tie each knot on two warps. The knot may be tied so that the two ends come up to the front of the rug between the two warps (the so-called symmetrical knot) or it may be tied in such a fashion that each of the two ends of the knot is separated from the other by a single warp (the co-called asymmetrical knot). Such asymmetrical knots are open either to the left or the right, and the practices of knotting are normally very specific to certain areas and traditions, and thus can tell us a great deal about the origins of a rug.

Depending on the fineness and the crowding of warps and wefts, the pile on a rug may either be very fine (6,400 knots per square decimeter or higher, about 20 x 20 = 400 knots per square inch) or very coarse (600 knots per square decimeter or less, about 6 x 6 = 36 knots per square inch). The pile may be very short, in order for the outlines and detail on a finely knotted rug to be crisp and clear, or it may be fairly long, in order for the lush texture and color of a coarsely knotted rug to be emphasized.

Edges and ends: Looking at the edges and ends of a carpet, we can sometimes see distinctive features employed by certain weaving groups or that are particular to certain geographical areas. However, edges and ends are generally the first parts of a carpet to succumb to wear and mistreatment, and are often replaced and restored. So it is relatively unusual to find a very old carpet with completely intact original edges and ends.

General questions: In looking at a carpet, we ask other questions that are perhaps a little more subjective. Is the carpet thick and stiff, or is it thin and supple? Are the colors bright and clear, or do they show evidence of chemical alteration or darkening due to grime? If the rug is worn, is the wear in irregular patches, or uniform over the entire rug? Looking at the back, do we see evidence of re-napping, patches, or entire areas of reweaving? Looking from the front, do we see evidence that worn spots have been painted with dyes, or evidence of replacement of corroded dark-brown knots? With each carpet examined, we gain new insights, new experience, and new knowledge.

Definitions and approximation: Finally, textiles of all kinds incorporate a certain degree of "stretchiness" which means that, practically speaking, any measurements given for a carpet, especially for a carpet of large size, must necessarily be approximate rather than "exact" in any scientific sense. The fibers and yarns in carpets are highly reactive to temperature, humidity, and weight stress; depending on whether the carpet is laid flat or hung, whether the humidity environment is low or high, and whether the temperature is low or high, the dimensions of a carpet may change rather significantly. For this reason, all dimensions of carpets listed here are accompanied by the qualification "approximately."

Compared to many areas of art-historical study, carpet studies and carpet nomenclature are still, relatively speaking, in a formative stage. For the present publication, for reasons of both practicality and art-historical humility, we have often utilized the term "probably" when speaking of matters that are still not completely settled, especially those of provenance.

Persian Carpets

The two Ballard Persian (Iranian) carpets selected for this volume serve in essence as bookends to the great Iranian tradition of commercial weaving. In the seventeenth century, when the Safavid Empire was ruled from its capital in Isfahan, carpets were produced for the royal court in Isfahan itself, and in other traditional centers of very high-quality carpet weaving, such as Herat and Kashan. Many of these carpets produced to royal order, such as the famous "Polonaise" carpet with silk pile and metallic-thread brocading, were intended as royal gifts, but in fact represent a kind of sideshow to the major weaving traditions of Iran.

With the benefit of historical hindsight we are able to see that, for seventeenth-century Iran, it was the commercial carpet production of Kerman in central Persia that proved the most important, both for the volume and fame of its production at the time, and for its artistic impact on subsequent weaving in Iran and Transcaucasia. The so-called "Vase" carpets of Kerman, represented by an iconic example in the Ballard Collection, utilized a vast range of colors; a very robust construction in which the multi-ply cotton warps were crowded onto two levels; a complex and peculiar system of wefting that apparently was invented to try to keep the vertical/horizontal knot ratio as close to 1/1 as possible; and a dazzling repertoire of beautiful designs, many of them utilizing the overall lattice layout with stylized blossoms and tiny flower-vases that we see in the St. Louis example.

However, the design range of carpets produced in Kerman during these years (and well through the eighteenth century) also encompassed a wide variety of patterns and motifs beyond the traditional "Vase" carpets. For this reason, when scholars today use the term "Vase" carpet or "Vase-technique" carpet they are usually referring to all carpets woven in Kerman with this unusual technique, and not simply the best-known design type.

The commercial tradition of weaving large carpets with floral designs was well established in Iran by the end of the seventeenth century. It had long been assumed that important large-scale carpet production in Iran all but ceased following the Afghan invasion in the early eighteenth century, which brought the Safavid dynasty to a close in 1722. This widespread assumption has more recently been convincingly challenged in a doctoral thesis based on a wide range of Iranian and foreign documents, travel accounts, and dated carpets, from which it emerges that Iranian carpet production continued at a high level from the fall of the Safavids until the purported date of the carpet revival in Iran around 1870.

James Ballard's spectacular single-wefted long carpet from west Iran supports this conclusion. It is probably from an area with a large population of Kurdish weavers. In its brilliant colors, beautiful wool, richly complex design and phenomenal state of preservation it makes a memorable artistic impression. This carpet not only demonstrates the continuity of the Iranian weaving tradition, but in its well-preserved state it provides us with a glimpse back in time. It also offers an insight into the original appearance of many equally beautiful but much older and consequently more worn examples of Iranian carpet-weaving that have survived.

Further reading: On the "Vase" carpets and their history, see Beattie 1976; on the more recent Iranian weaving of the eighteenth and nineteenth centuries, see Maktabi 2007

1

"Vase-Technique" Carpet

Kerman, South-central Iran, 17th century
Gift of Nellie Ballard White, 285:1972

Although reduced in both width and length, with some parts of the border extensively rewoven, this very handsome, probably fairly early, Vase carpet is in quite good condition, with a typically wide range of colors and a tightly designed floral lattice. An example of the eponymous motif of a vase of small flowers, which gave the entire group of Kerman carpets woven in this technique its name, may be seen in the center at the very bottom of the field; two others, like the first depicted above a sway-backed "sconce" motif, are slightly above the midline of the carpet. This important carpet was not a part of the original 1929 James Ballard gift to St. Louis, but entered the Museum in 1972.

This carpet, in common with most Vase carpets that use this layout, shows bilateral symmetry side to side, and the lattice of white vines forming the major sectors of the layout is echoed by a smaller-scale lattice of blue vines designed to appear underneath the major lattice. The blossoms on these vines are typical for all Vase carpets of this layout: many show a stylized lotus blossom with eight petals, resembling a butterfly; other composite flowers show petals of alternating colors. Some large leaf-palmettes have deeply serrated edges, while others are smooth. Yet others contain sprays of small flowers, and still others have a trident-like appearance. The vast bulk of the floral forms are depicted at a roughly 45-degree angle—only those in the center lines of the lattices are shown upright. If we look at rosette forms, designed to be the same height and width, such as the two at the top corners of the carpet, we note a vertical stretching of the design away from a 1/1 knot ratio. The design is in theory infinite—it is simply cut by the four borders—but there is no vertical repetition of the design in the entire length of the carpet. The apparent regularity of the vine lattice, is contradicted by the variety of the floral forms. The border has been designed to work out smoothly at the corners, and at each end it was conceived from the outside in, resulting in a very small lotus in the middle of the bottom border, and two large ones in the middle of the top one. Border improvisations apart, the entire carpet was probably woven following a knot plan or *talim*—a set of instructions for weaving—that assumed the finished product would have a vertical-to-horizontal knot ratio close to 1/1. The finished carpet was destined for the marketplace; many examples were sold locally in Iran, while others were exported to the Ottoman Empire, Transcaucasia, and into Europe. The large number of colors, high knot count, fine materials, complex designs, and extremely robust construction probably meant that these were high-end products, far more expensive than the Ushak carpets woven in Anatolia to the west [CAT.14, 15, 18].

The design repertoire of carpets produced from the later sixteenth century through the end of the seventeenth in Kerman (and well into the eighteenth century as well) encompassed a wide variety of patterns and motifs beyond the traditional lattice layout with flower-vases. For this reason, when scholars use the term "Vase carpet" or "Vase-technique carpet" they are usually referring to all carpets woven in Kerman with this unusual technique, and not simply the best-known design type. Many carpets in other museums echo the general design and layout of the Ballard carpet in St. Louis. Among these are a red-ground example in the Thyssen Collection in Madrid, carpets in the Berlin Museums, Metropolitan Museum of Art, and the Victoria and Albert Museum. Among those bearing other designs, perhaps the most famous is the carpet recently de-accessioned by the Corcoran Gallery in Washington, D.C., notable for its design incorporating huge sickle-shaped serrated leaves. Other, slightly earlier examples assigned to Kerman, such as the "Sanguszko" carpet formerly on long-term loan in the Metropolitan Museum of Art, utilize a medallion format. They often include animals and humans in their iconographically complex designs, which are full of arcane symbolism and hidden meanings. Vase-technique carpets incorporating a design of stylized Chinese dragons and other animals, only surviving in a few fragments, appear to have served as the inspiration for both design and layout of the famous Dragon carpets of Transcaucasia [CAT.45].

In terms of its condition, its colors, its artistry, and its size, this carpet may fairly be singled out as the greatest Persian carpet collected by James Ballard; left out of the original 1922 and 1929 gifts to New York and St. Louis, its entrance into the St. Louis collection in 1972 marked a major addition to the Museum's holdings.

Further reading: Beattie 1976

Length: Approximately 346 cm

Width: Approximately 147 cm

Warp: Undyed white cotton, two Z-spun yarns plied S; alternate warps very strongly depressed

Weft 1: Sinuous, undyed white cotton, one Z-spun yarn; shot two parallel between every row of knots (2//)

Weft 2: Straight: light-brown (apparently undyed) wool, one Z-spun yarn, shot once between every row of knots

Pile: Wool dyed dark maroon-red, pinkish red, very dark blue, medium blue, light blue, dark blue-green, light green, olive green abrashed to very dark olive-green at bottom of carpet, grey-green, tan, orange-tan, dark yellow, corrosive medium brown, black, and undyed white; all pile consists of two Z-spun yarns plied S

Knot: Asymmetrical open to the left; approximately 50V x 64H per decimeter

Edges: Rewrapped, not original

Ends: Fragments of original ends were found; warps are folded back and tightly bound with blue-dyed cotton wefts

Detail

Reverse view

2

Long Rug with Blossom Lattice Design

Northwest Iran, early 19th century
Gift of Nellie Ballard White, 292:1972

A miracle of brilliantly dyed wool pile in superb condition, this large carpet, with its almost 1/1 knot ratio and robust construction, was probably woven by ethnic Kurdish weavers in northwestern Iran. It is a testament to the continued vitality of Iranian weaving in the post-Safavid period.

It has long been thought that important large-scale carpet production in Iran all but ceased following the Afghan invasion of Iran in the early eighteenth century, which brought the Safavid dynasty to a close in 1722. This widespread assumption has recently been challenged by Hadi Maktabi. As a doctoral scholar at Oxford University, Maktabi surveyed a wide range of Iranian and foreign documents, travel accounts, and dated carpets. He concluded that in many areas of Iran, carpet production continued at a high level from the fall of the Safavid dynasty in 1722 well into the second half of the nineteenth century.

A fine example of support for Maktabi's conclusions is this spectacular single-wefted long carpet from northwest Iran. It is from an area with a large population of Kurdish weavers, and was probably woven, as many large Iranian carpets were, on a vertical roller-beam loom. The finished carpet was gradually wound up around the lower roller beam as the remaining warp was unrolled from the top one. The central field, with a dark indigo ground color, is ornamented by a tightly packed arrangement of diverse floral forms, without the defining lattice of vines seen in the Ballard Vase-technique carpet [CAT.1]. The weaver employs both lateral symmetry and vertical repetition; but the lateral symmetry is one of form only, and not of color, which means that those major floral elements with predominately yellow coloration set up an impression of lower-right to upper-left diagonals in the field. A close examination of the major border quickly tells us that the corners are skillfully articulated, with a slight crowding in the upper right-hand corner. Pronounced abrash or vertical color variation, seen especially in the medium blue and medium red, adds variety and warmth to the design, whose highly saturated colors and soft wool appeal to the sense of touch as well as that of sight.

Ballard's taste prized a later product of a Persian market town, such as this carpet, on an equal level with an earlier "classical" example such as his Vase-technique carpet [CAT.1]. His approach was an inspiration to later generations of collectors, and especially to Joseph V. McMullan, who included, along with several earlier classical Persian carpets, a carpet similar to this one in the first portion of his collection given to the Metropolitan Museum of Art, New York in 1968 (68.219).

Further reading: Maktabi 2007

Length: Approximately 561 cm

Width: Approximately 206 cm

Warp: Mixed undyed brown and white wool; two Z-spun yarns plied S (ends restored with multi-ply white cotton warp), one level

Weft: Mixed undyed brown and white wool, one Z-spun yarn; with rare exceptions (one visible in the back detail) the wefts are shot one direction only between every row of knots, usually with a single weft, and more rarely with two parallel (2//), or three parallel (3//) wefts between each row of knots

Pile: Wool dyed dark red, medium red, yellow, dark blue, medium blue, bright green with great abrash variation, tan, dark brown, black-brown, and undyed white wool; all two Z-spun yarns plied S

Knot: Symmetrical, approximately 38V x 36H per decimeter

Edges: Two bundles of two warps wrapped in red pile yarn

Ends: Stripped, machine-made edging sewn on

Detail

Reverse view

Mamluk Carpets

The term "Mamluk carpets," like so many carpet terms, persists despite outliving its original descriptive usefulness, and the term "Cairene carpets" that was originally proposed as a substitute is also flawed. The two Ballard carpets in this category were probably made in Egypt, although the later one in particular may have been woven elsewhere in the eastern Mediterranean, possibly in Syria. Both were almost certainly made after 1517, when the Mamluk dynasty was deposed by the Ottoman Turks, and Egypt and Syria had become Ottoman provinces. Furthermore, the term "Mamluk carpets" actually applies to two distinct groups. One, made with five or more colors of wool pile and complex designs related to other early carpets in Iran and Anatolia, was largely woven during the fifteenth and early sixteenth centuries when the Mamluks actually ruled in Egypt, although a few later examples probably dating from Ottoman times can be identified as well. The other group, woven in three colors, with a more limited repertoire of motifs, was mostly made after the Ottoman conquest in 1517. As happens so frequently with carpet typology, we have to rely on the matter of technique to make our definition, as time and place are lacking a reasonable quantity of definitive documentation.

Both these carpets are distinguished from all others in the Ballard Collection by one major technical characteristic: the yarns were spun clockwise (S-spun) and thus multi-ply yarns were plied counter-clockwise (Z-plied). They are woven in only three colors, without use of black-dyed wool for outlining or of undyed white wool for design accents. And as the detail photographs of the back indicate, they were woven with the warps on two levels. Unlike contemporaneous Turkish carpets from Anatolia, Mamluk carpets are woven with the asymmetrical knot.

Even odder than the technical peculiarities is the combination of limited colors, very soft wool, and a highly individual but limited design repertoire. Both carpets have a central octagonal medallion, a similar border, and a similar array of secondary motifs in the field. They both feature tiny fan-shaped motifs in red that are representations of papyrus leaves, a motif known in Egyptian art for millennia. The tightly arranged warps and more loosely packed wefts of the later example result in a vertical stretching of the design, and it also incorporates at each end depictions of date-palm trees and pointed, arrowhead-like cypress trees.

From the structural analyses, we might expect these carpets to look very much alike. But they create very different impressions, because the same basic colors and materials vary significantly from object to object. Why should that be? Some suggest that there were different centers of production, and that some carpets in this category were produced away from Cairo. Others say it merely means that there were different workshops in Cairo using different standards for dyeing, design, and weaving in different decades or centuries.

Side by side the Ballard Mamluk carpets, pose this question of differences in an eloquent manner, but are considerably less forthcoming in providing answers. To me, the structural differences, especially the stretching of the design, suggest a difference in dating, with the more distorted design reflecting a later production. Color is a different matter, since the outcome of the dyeing process depends on: the dyestuffs and mordants used; the temperature and origin of the water used in the dyeing process, which will contain various dissolved salts that will affect the final colors; the amount of time the wool is left in the dye-pot; and the particular wool used, which varies according to the breed and the age of sheep, the time of year it was clipped, and the minerals present in the forage eaten by the sheep themselves.

The color differences strongly suggest a difference in wool and water (analysis of the dyestuffs shows that they are basically identical), and thus may indicate that one of these carpets—most likely the one we have dated later—may have been woven outside Cairo and perhaps even outside of Egypt. As intelligent as I believe these surmises to be, they remain hypotheses for the present, not to be confused with widely accepted art-historical fact.

Further reading: See Thompson 2006, 164–65, for a discussion of Mamluk carpets remarkable in its thoughtfulness and good sense

3

Mamluk Three-color One-medallion Carpet

Egypt, late 16th century

Gift of James F. Ballard, 121:1929

Published: Dimand 1935, pl. LIX

Normal substantial texture and handle; faded repairs up the middle and patches of very heavy wear, but some areas of thick intensely colored pile remain.

What is presented here as the earlier of the two Ballard Mamluk carpets is one of the smallest of its type to have survived. Worn, with faded reknotting along its vertical and horizontal fold lines, it exhibits a border of elongated cartouches and small roundels, and a central field composed of a central octagon with triangular projections turning it into an eight-pointed star. The extra length of the carpet is created by horizontal bands of three small medallions both above and below the central octagon/star. The two outermost medallions in each band consist of eight radiating rectangular "tabs" around a central circle, while the middle medallion in each band shows sixteen star-points around each central circle, half of them 90-degree points, and half 45-degree points. These basic motifs may be considered to be elements of vocabulary; they can be related to motifs in early Anatolian carpets (the medallions) or arts of the book (the borders).

On the other hand, the combinations of motifs (what we might term the vocabulary and syntax) and the coloration (which we can compare in language to rhetoric and spoken nuance) are completely original to Egyptian weaving of this time and place.

With no white, no black, and three hues of the same value and intensity, carpets such as this represent a considerable challenge to photograph and to print in color. Confronted "in the wool," however, they provide an almost mesmerizing effect, aided by the shimmering impression produced by the subtle vertical variations in horizontal stripes of color known as abrash.

There are numerous examples of small three-color Mamluk carpets known. A number of comparative examples with motifs and layouts similar to the Ballard example in St. Louis are listed in Okumura 2007. The largest single collection of Mamluk carpets is in The Textile Museum, Washington, D.C.

Length: Approximately 190 cm

Width: Approximately 135 cm

Warp: Greenish-yellow wool, three S-spun yarns plied Z, alternate warps heavily depressed

Weft: Golden yellow wool, one S-spun yarn, one sinuous and one straight weft between each row of knots

Pile: Wool dyed dark-red, blue, and green; two S-spun yarns plied Z

Knot: Asymmetrical open left, approximately 55–56V x 52–53H per decimeter

Edges: Both stripped and reselvedged

Ends: Both stripped, a tricolor silk fringe added probably in the 19th century

Detail

Reverse view

4

Mamluk Three-color Centralized-design Carpet

Egypt or possibly Syria, 17th century
Gift of Nellie Ballard White, 299:1972

Unusual Mamluk rug, atypical colors, strange knot-ratio asymmetry, very unusual vertically stretched design. May have been woven well into the seventeenth century or even later. Cypress and palm trees in panels at each end.

The printed numbers and words of the structural and technical information of this carpet are much like those used in the analysis of its sister carpet [CAT.3], but the overall visual impression is much different. Within the category of three-color Mamluk carpets the variation to be found is in fact enormous. Here we see the traditional cartouche and roundel borders found in the previous example, but the difference in width between the side and end borders, as well as the elongation of the central octagon, immediately inform us that there is a significant disparity in the number of knots per decimeter between horizontal and vertical coordinates. While we give the same names to the colors—red, blue, green—the visual effects of these colors, both in published photographs and in the objects themselves, is dramatically different.

Certain design motifs in this carpet also suggest a later date. One of these, repeated four times in the carpet, is the small date-palm tree serving as a divider in the top and bottom bands of three small medallions across the rug. To either side of each of these motifs are others, vaguely appearing like highly elongated hexagons. These are in fact stylized cypress trees, a motif with a long lineage in Syrian and Egyptian weaving from the fifteenth century onward.

A published example with similar vertical stretching of the design is found in the Philadelphia Museum of Art (1943-40-63); see Ellis 1988, 121–23.

Length: Approximately 193 cm

Width: Approximately 132 cm

Warp: White undyed wool, three S-spun yarns plied Z, alternate warps moderately depressed

Weft: Undyed white wool, one S-spun yarn, shot irregularly: five shoots (2// + 3//), six shoots (3// + 3//), eight shoots (4// + 4//)

Pile: Wool dyed light-blue, red, green, all consisting of three S-spun yarns plied Z

Knot: Asymmetrical, open left, approximately 36 V x 46–48 H per decimeter, resulting in a design that is stretched vertically

Edges: Both overcast, not original

Ends: Both stripped

Detail

Reverse view

A Syrian Carpet

In Maurice Dimand's 1935 catalogue this small carpet was labeled "Turkish, Asia Minor, XVII Century." The attribution was based on the mistaken assumption that the carpet had a symmetrical knot, and on the use of a row of repetitive motifs based on a geometric strapwork interlace, a design it shares with the "Holbein" carpets known to have been woven in Anatolia. A considerable number of carpets in this design, coloration, and technique are known. Our best information is that they were woven in Syria; their depiction in a few European paintings confirms a seventeenth-century date. They are probably the carpets mentioned in Italian Renaissance inventories as "*tappeti Damaschini*", that is "Damascus carpets."

The conventional name for this group was the "chessboard" group, but while the eight-pointed stars in hexagonal surrounds are contained within rectangular compartments, there is little resemblance to the alternating colors on a chessboard. The group's cohesion is determined not by design but by technique. It is distinguished by: an asymmetrical knot; a design that is almost always stretched vertically, sometimes to a very high degree, due to loose weft packing, with warps crowded together on two levels; a very peculiar kind of coarse, hard, shiny wool or animal hair that does not hold its spin well; and a small range of colors—red, light blue, green, yellow, and white, with corrosive black outlining.

Once their peculiar wool and structure had been recognised, art historians began to notice carpets with radically different designs, mostly curvilinear and probably Iranian in origin, woven in the same technique and with the same wool, texture and appearance front and back, as the "chessboard" group. It was also noticed that there was always a carefully worked-out adjustment on all four corners of the border, no matter what border design was used (the range is enormous), even if it required that the field design was left with an "awkward moment," such as a row of incomplete field motifs at the top of the carpet. The Ballard carpet is a sterling example. This workshop practice was followed irrespective of the design and size of the carpet (the Ballard rug is one of the smallest of the entire group).

The carpets were obviously not Anatolian (colors, knot structure, wool, and stretched design are unlike any known group of Anatolian carpets); and the colors, asymmetrical knot, corner articulations, and small arrowhead-shaped motifs were reminiscent of the so-called "Mamluk" rugs of Egypt, especially the earlier or "five-color" Mamluk rugs we have alluded to. For these reasons an intermediate geographical origin between Anatolia and Egypt—Syria—was proposed for these carpets. Although this has now gained general acceptance, the actual place of manufacture remains in doubt.

The "chessboard" subgroup, which has survived in the largest numbers, includes the typical repeating rows, either stacked or staggered, of strapwork stars seen in the Ballard example. Other carpets in the same technique but radically different designs include a spectacular red-ground example with elongated cloudbands in the Berlin Museums (86, 601), and two examples in the Vakıflar Carpet Museum, Istanbul, one with small blue cloud bands on a dark-brown ground (A-216) and the other with an overall diapered design on a red ground (A-172).

The remains of two gigantic medallion carpets, each once over 10 meters in length, were discovered in the depot of the Museum of Turkish and Islamic Art in Istanbul (845–47, 848–49 and 868). They may indicate that the Syrian manufactory was attempting to compete with the Ushak medallion carpets of western Anatolia, a staple of the Middle East carpet trade from the second half of the fifteenth century until well into the eighteenth. Two more large border fragments in the same technique, but with one-of-a-kind designs, are in museum collections. One, in the Metropolitan Museum of Art, a gift of Marshall and Marilyn R. Wolf (1990.169), is covered with the traditional *Çintemani* motif of three pearls and wavy flames; the other, in the Museum of Islamic Art, Doha, has a layout of repeating cartouches and eight-lobed medallions, ubiquitous in sixteenth- and seventeenth-century Islamic art.

Further reading: Some of the most up-to-date thoughts on this group of carpets are articulated by Jon Thompson; see Thompson 2006, 123–65. See also Spuhler 1986, 261–69, Ellis 1988, 128–31; Denny 1999, 6–7. Also Denny, Walter, "Islamic Carpets in European Paintings", Metropolitan Museum's online resource, the Heilbrunn Timeline of Art History

5

Small "Chessboard" Carpet

Syria or Damascus, early 17th century
Gift of James F. Ballard, 110:1929
Published: Dimand 1935, pl. XV (as "Turkish Asia Minor, XVII century"); Walker 1988, No. 4

Unusually for rugs of this type, the knot count at the bottom of the rug is more or less the same horizontally and vertically, and the star motif is therefore radially symmetrical; at the top of the rug, owing to much looser packing of the rows of knots and wefts, the design is considerably more vertically stretched.

James Ballard's little carpet, with its field consisting of a vertical row of three-plus strapwork eight-pointed stars, steep diagonals, and hexagonal compartments around octagonal motifs, is typical of the "chessboard" subgroup of Syrian carpets. Although it is missing knots from each end (allowing us to see the very straight protruding warps that have lost their spin and twist), we can easily see how the weaver took great pains to provide a graceful articulation at all corners of the carpet, even at the expense of having to insert only a tiny part of a repeat at the top of the field. It is also instructive to see how the density of the knotting decreased markedly as the weaving process continued, with the result that the design on the upper half of the carpet is considerably more stretched than that of the bottom, and its diagonals are as a consequence considerably steeper.

"Chessboard" carpets are rarely depicted by European painters. Most dateable representations are found in paintings created after 1600. An especially attractive depiction is that in the Metropolitan Museum of Art (91.26.11) painted in 1659 by Gabriël Metsu (Dutch, 1629–1667); it shows a musical party, with the thick-piled carpet draped over a table.

Other carpets in the "chessboard" design of this Ballard example include a small McMullan carpet in the Metropolitan Museum of Art (69.267), a carpet collected by George Hewitt Myers in The Textile Museum (R34.34.1), two examples in the Berlin Museums (I.14, and 76, 1557), and a carpet from the Joseph Lees Williams Memorial Collection in the Philadelphia Museum of Art (1955-65-6).

Length: Approximately 167 cm

Width: Approximately 91 cm

Warp: Undyed white stiff coarse wool, two Z-spun yarns plied S, alternate warps strongly depressed, not uniformly wrapped on loom

Weft: Wool dyed pinkish-brown, one Z-spun yarn, one straight plus one sinuous shoot between each row of knots, very irregular weft packing

Pile: Coarse stiff wool, light-blue, dark-blue, grey-blue, light blue-green, medium blue-green, red, yellow-cream, corrosive dark brown, undyed white; all two Z-spun yarns plied S

Knot: Asymmetrical open left, approximately 32–35V x 35–41H per decimeter

Edges: Original selvedges both replaced

Ends: Both stripped

Detail

Reverse view

A Spanish Carpet

In many respects Spanish carpets are the oddest subgroup of Islamic weaving. Unlike carpets woven in the Middle East and North Africa, Spanish carpets utilize a unique and peculiar structural technique called the Spanish knot, which immediately distinguishes them when one looks closely at the back or the front of the carpet. The tying of knots in staggered horizontal rows on single warps, together with the use of multiple parallel wefts shot in one direction only between each row of knots, means that small bits of the warp are clearly visible on the back of a Spanish carpet, and on the front of a worn example. On the front of a Spanish carpet, vertical lines in the design prove on close observation to be zigzag lines, as the knots in each succeeding row are offset by one warp.

The origins of this technique are shrouded in mystery. However, it is apparent that in the "pre-historic" period of carpet study (the period of knotted-carpet weaving before ca. 1300) there were a number of ways of producing a knotted-pile fabric that fall outside of the conventional system of stacked horizontal rows of either symmetrical or asymmetrical knots tied on two warps—the method that characterizes most carpets surviving into our time.

Coupled with this unusual technique is the peculiar fact that almost all early Spanish carpets—those thought to have been woven in the later fourteenth and the fifteenth centuries—have designs that are largely copied from those of Anatolian carpets. For this reason, James Ballard's handsome if somewhat worn Spanish carpet in St. Louis is sometimes known as a Spanish "large-pattern Holbein" carpet. The design was borrowed from an Anatolian carpet of that name, a carpet design immortalized in Hans Holbein's famous double portrait of *The Ambassadors* in the National Gallery in London. In this painting, a carpet with a design of large octagons is clearly depicted on a table laden with a curious collection of objects.[87]

To sum up the peculiar situation of the St. Louis Spanish carpet: a design type probably originating in central or eastern Turkey in the thirteenth century is woven in significant numbers in western Turkey by the late fourteenth and early fifteenth century, and widely exported around the Mediterranean basin; it is almost immediately copied by Spanish weavers at the other end of the Mediterranean in a completely different technique; around 1535 a German painter depicts an example of the original Turkish carpet type in a portrait of two Frenchmen; and in the late nineteenth century a German art historian gives all carpets with this design, Turkish and Spanish, the name "large-pattern Holbein" carpets.[88]

In addition to carpets in the Spanish knot with the large-pattern Holbein design, Iberian weavers also wove carpets in other Anatolian-inspired designs and layouts. Among them is the well-known "small-pattern Holbein" design [CAT.18], the most important surviving example of which is in the Museum of Fine Arts, Boston. An even more complex artistic lineage can be found in Spanish carpets produced in imitation of Anatolian carpet adaptations of Chinese silk designs.

In this case, a fourteenth-century Chinese silk damask fabric of the Yuan dynasty depicting row upon row of lotus blossoms with trailing aquatic roots was adapted in fourteenth-century Anatolia to carpets. An example survives in the Museum of Turkish and Islamic Art in Istanbul.[89] Other carpets with the same design were evidently exported to Spain, where they were copied (in different colors and with the Spanish knot) in local products; one has survived today in the collection of the Textile Museum in Washington, D.C.[90] Yet other Spanish carpets appear to be direct and original adaptations of designs found in Islamic silks; an example given by Ballard to the Metropolitan Museum of Art is typical of the genre.[91]

Spanish carpets continued to be produced in Iberia after the Reconquista by Muslim artists—Mudéjars—working for Christian patrons. The so-called "Admiral Carpets", the finest surviving example of which is found in the Philadelphia Museum of Art,[92] again use the typical Spanish knot, and their designs are complex conflations of Islamic and non-Islamic iconography and motifs. Recent scholarship has also suggested intriguing Jewish connections for some carpets in the group, part of the complex and troubled history of "conversos", Jewish converts to Christianity in post-Reconquista Spain.[93]

6

Spanish Carpet in "Large-pattern Holbein" Design

Spain, 15th century

Gift of James F. Ballard, 122:1929

Published: Dimand 1935, pl. XII

As it is missing both ends and both sides, it is possible that this carpet may have originally been larger; the wear pattern in two vertical bands suggests there may have been a third vertical row of octagonal medallions, and a wide border on each side. Despite the ravages of time this is a powerful and colorful work: one of the most interesting and probably one of the earliest of the type to have come down to us. The foundation wool is coarse and hard.

Typically for Spanish versions of the "large-pattern Holbein" design, the octagonal motifs of this central field fragment are set in almost square compartments. This lends credence to the theory that the complex technique of the Spanish knot, with multiple parallel wefts in one direction only, was devised in order to achieve a 1/1 vertical to horizontal knot ratio.

Each octagon in a square compartment is defined by a narrow border with a red motif on a white ground that may derive from a squared-off form of Kufic style Arabic script. The octagonal frame of each major motif is decorated with a common Anatolian design of S-shaped motifs within elongated hexagonal cartouches; the octagons, sometimes referred to as "wheels" in early European inventories, are based on an interlaced ribbon or strap that creates small geometric forms as it defines a larger octagonal medallion. The Anatolian prototype was probably woven well into the fifteenth century. Over time the original geometric strapwork still observable in the earliest examples, such as the famous large-pattern Holbein carpet in Berlin, has more or less dissolved, leaving only a white strapwork star at the very center of each octagon. The result: in a process called "motif-ground confusion," the original geometric strapwork arabesque that created a background of octagonal stars and elongated hexagonal "bars" has disappeared. Over time the design has evolved into the background, and the background has evolved into the design.

The rich coloration of Ballard's carpet, especially the extensive use of a bright yellow as well as the dark green ground of alternate horizontal rows of octagons, is typical of Spanish carpets with Anatolian designs. It shows a complete mastery in Spain of the art of dyeing wool. In its original state, the entire carpet field that has survived was almost certainly surrounded with a wide border also exhibiting a design based on a geometric interlace, echoing the so-called "kufesque" borders found on the known complete carpets in this group, originating in a squared-off and decoratively interlaced form of Arabic script.

Although only a large fragment, the Ballard carpet is a worthy representative of its type, and a testament to the existence of a common Mediterranean visual culture in the late medieval and early modern periods. In carpets, as in silk textiles, the late medieval period demonstrates the importance of the far-flung commercial routes of the time, including the so-called Silk Road from the eastern Mediterranean into Central and East Asia. Together with established European and Mediterranean trade routes, these Eurasian commercial networks linking the great Mediterranean trading centers of Spain, France, Italy, the Balkans, Syria, and Egypt, brought an astonishing variety of luxury goods to world markets, and provided artists with an almost inexhaustible source of challenges and inspiration.

Similar carpets in this layout are found in, among others, the Cleveland Museum of Art (1952.511), Metropolitan Museum of Art (53.79), Victoria and Albert Museum (784-1905), The Textile Museum (R44.2.7), and the Philadelphia Museum of Art (1955-65-3).

Length: Approximately 274 cm

Width: Approximately 155 cm

Warp: Undyed white wool, uniform, two Z-spun yarns plied S, one level

Weft: Undyed white wool, uniform, one Z-spun yarn shot four warps parallel (4//, more frequently) or three parallel (3//, less frequently) between each row of knots)

Pile: Wool, red, green, dark-blue, yellow, corrosive dark brown and undyed white, all two Z-spun yarns plied S

Knot: Spanish (tied around one warp in offset staggered rows), approximately 44V x 43H per decimeter

Edges: Both completely stripped

Ends: Both completely stripped

Detail

Reverse view

Lotto Carpets

Like the so-called "Holbein" and "Bellini" carpets, the "Lotto" carpets are named after a specific depiction by a European painter, in this case an altarpiece, *The Charity of Saint Anthony*, painted by the northern Italian painter Lorenzo Lotto in 1542, in the church of San Giovanni e Paolo in Venice [**FIG.15**].

All four Lotto carpets in the Ballard collection in St. Louis (and the single Ballard Lotto carpet in the Metropolitan Museum), show the same general design of a geometric pattern of stylized split leaves and blossoms in yellow on a red ground; the conceptual basis of the design comprises two different elements, one cruciform and the other more four-square, arranged vertically in staggered horizontal rows. Most of these carpets were woven in west Anatolia. Technical similarities with the commercial carpets of Ushak suggest that area as the possible source for many if not most carpets of this design type.

In a famous article on Lotto carpets, the American carpet scholar Charles Grant Ellis observed that there must have been a near mania for them in Europe over the centuries, because so many survived there, and so many were depicted over the centuries by painters in Italy, England, Hungary, Germany, and France. Like Holbein carpets, Lotto carpets were also copied in Spain, another indication of the popularity of the type in Europe.

Although they do not appear in paintings until the first half of the sixteenth century, the overall arabesque design that characterizes the group is firmly rooted in what some have termed an international Islamic style of the second half of the fifteenth century. In this, networks of vines and split-leaf forms known in Turkish art as *rumi* and in Iranian art as *islimi* were used in a wide spectrum of arts, in the realms of the Timurids, Turkmen, Ottomans, and Mamluks. The adaptation of a curvilinear prototype to the carpet medium produced a strongly geometric form of what had been an extremely curvilinear one. Over time, as the design was produced and then evolved in a wide variety of geographical locations in Anatolia, three distinct sub-groups emerged, which Ellis characterized as the classic, decorated, and kilim styles. The St. Louis collection contains four examples (two each from two of the three groups.)

The earliest and rarest examples of Lotto-pattern carpets that have come down to us use what is called an "open kufesque" border, found in **CAT.7**. It consists of a calligraphy-like interlaced band in white on a blue ground, in which the ligatures, the vertical elements of the letter-like forms, end in finials.

The term "kufesque" is used to describe artistic forms that, while strongly recalling the squared-off and geometric Arabic calligraphy known as kufic (after the city of Kufa in Iraq, where it supposedly originated) do not form real words, but only give the appearance of writing. Such ornament may first have arisen in carpets and textiles. There it could invoke the aura of sanctity of the written word, always revered in Islamic art, but at the same time avoid any disrespect that might result from actual words with religious meaning being trodden underfoot. The apotropaic or magical properties sometimes attributed to calligraphic

script in Islamic culture spilled over into European consciousness. Kufic inscriptions on the wooden doors of Le Puy Cathedral in France appear as early as the second half of the twelfth century, and a lengthy kufic inscription adorns the celebrated coronation mantle of the Norman King Roger II, embroidered in Palermo around 1133. A twelfth-century kufesque inscription cast in bronze is found on the tomb of Bohemund in Canosa, dated to at least as early as 1111; and in fourteenth-century Italian painting kufesque ornament appears on depictions of textiles with great frequency, making its presence felt in the garments and even the halos of the Virgin herself.

The next development chronologically of Lotto carpets appears to be the "closed kufesque" border seen in **CAT.8**. Here the white geometric arabesque on a blue-green ground has been simplified and changed to a more compact interwoven motif without extending ligatures. While it probably kept its protective connotations despite the distancing of the pattern from actual script, this border proved immensely popular. It appears in carpets of the small pattern Holbein group, many examples of which were probably produced in the same location as most of the early Lotto carpets.

By the seventeenth century, Lotto carpets were being produced in many locations. Most were in the popular small sizes in demand in Europe, and used a variety of border types common to many different kinds of Anatolian carpet. The so-called "ragged palmette" border of **CAT.9**, for example, was in wide use in the seventeenth century; it appears in the

shadows under a tablecloth in Caravaggio's *Supper at Emmaus* in the National Gallery, London, painted as early as 1601.

A splendid carpet with close affinities to sixteenth-century Lotto carpets, with Ushak-style lotus palmettes in field and border, was given by Ballard to the Metropolitan Museum of Art (22.100.113), along with a small seventeenth-century Lotto carpet (22.100.112) with a medallion border.

The popularity of the design both at home and abroad, together with the use of a repetitive pattern in the design, also led to the production of commercial carpets all using the same border and field designs. They have a widely varying range of sizes, a phenomenon we can also see in the "small-pattern Holbein" carpets. While the majority of depictions in European painting show relatively small carpets such as that in the eponymous painting by Lotto (which also shows a very large example of an extremely rare carpet of the so-called "para-Mamluk" group) arrayed on the steps of the dais in front of St. Anthony. A fairly large example (5 meters long) is preserved in the Museo Nazionale del Bargello in Florence. Later Lotto carpets were highly prized as votive gifts to churches in Central Europe, and many examples similar to **CAT.10** are found in the churches of Transylvania. Ballard's four Lottos in St. Louis provide an excellent vantage point to see the variety and unity of Lotto designs in superb examples in good condition.

Further reading: Ellis 1975, Ellis 1986, Ellis 1988, Denny 2002, Ionesco 2005

7

"Lotto" Carpet

Central Anatolia, late 15th–early 16th century
Gift of James F. Ballard, 104:1929
Published: Dimand 1935, pl. XXI; Carboni 2006,
text p. 124, illus. p. 125; Walker 1988, No. 2

Normal and typical supple handle; despite the patches of wear this carpet has glorious colors and must certainly be one of the oldest surviving rugs of its type, in an unusually small size.

This carpet, certainly the earliest of the Ballard Lottos, shows the yellow-on-red arabesque in its simplest form, but its place in the sequence is largely determined by the border. Like the borders of many early Turkish classical carpets from Anatolia, its design evokes a monumental inscription in kufic, a geometric form of the Arabic alphabet. Arabic letters are used in almost all Islamic countries, regardless of their language, in the same way the Roman alphabet has now found currency in many languages around the world. What appears to be an inscription in Arabic, with the decorated finials of the letters to the outside of the carpet and the bases of the letters near the field, is not in fact actual writing; instead it is a design that gives the appearance of writing (thus avoiding the question of potentially sacred writings being trodden underfoot). For this reason the rather endearing term kufesque has been proposed, and widely accepted, as an adjective for such borders.

By the end of the fifteenth century, this type of white-on-blue script-like border was gradually replaced in Anatolian rug weaving by a geometrical interlaced pattern of closed forms without ligatures and finials, as seen in the slightly later Ballard Lotto carpet [CAT.8]. By the seventeenth century, as indicated in the later examples discussed below, weavers used a wide variety of different border types along with the familiar yellow-on-red Lotto field design.

It is probable that smaller Lotto carpets such as this, as well as many if not most smaller early Anatolian carpets made for the marketplace, were generally produced as part of a cottage industry. In order to utilize the weaving talent of village women who could not work outside the home in urban workshops, entrepreneurs loaned out small looms that could be placed in the homes of talented women weavers in small towns and villages. The weaver of this particular carpet made great efforts to articulate the corners of the complex borders in the rug, including making the script ligatures on the top border face inward. As a result, the field of the carpet ended up being slightly asymmetrical both horizontally and vertically. These small design adjustments and compromises in carpet construction add immeasurably to the variety and interest of the artistic outcome in carpets such as this example.

A similar carpet (08.167.1), came into the Metropolitan Museum of Art by purchase in 1908, which may have influenced Ballard's giving the majority of his Lottos to St. Louis (see Denny 2014). A small fragment of a similar carpet was given to the Metropolitan by Joseph V. McMullan in 1972 (1972.80.6). Two comparable carpets are also in the Philadelphia Museum of Art, one in the Joseph Lees Williams Memorial Collection (1955-65-9) and the other in the John D. McIlhenny Collection (1943-40-68); see Ellis 1988. Another example, with more repairs and slightly more faded colors, entered the collection of the Philadelphia Museum of Art in 1967, in the White Collection (1967-30-308).

Length: Approximately 170 cm

Width: Approximately 109 cm

Warp: Undyed white wool, two Z-spun yarns plied S, alternate warps very slightly depressed

Weft: Dyed red wool, one Z-spun yarn, shot twice (1 + 1) between each row of knots. Typically for early Lotto carpets, there are several areas where the wefts are not continuous from side to side, but are doubled back, leaving diagonal "lazy lines" on the back of the rug

Pile: Wool dyed yellow, red, light blue, dark blue, blue-green, corrosive dark-brown and undyed white; all two Z-spun yarns plied S

Knot: Symmetrical, slightly pulled to the left, approximately 37 V x 30H per decimeter

Edges: Both overcast, not original

Ends: Both stripped, overcast

Detail

Reverse view

8

"Lotto" Carpet

Central Anatolia, first half of the 16th century
Gift of James F. Ballard, 101:1929
Published: Dimand 1935

Normal and typical supple handle; despite a few reweaves the carpet is in a very fine state of preservation, and the dark brown is less corroded than in many early examples.

This carpet represents the next stage in the evolution of the Lotto design. The "open" kufesque border ornamentation of the first carpet [**CAT.7**], with its finials strongly suggestive of Arabic kufic letters, has metamorphosed into a simpler "closed" plaited pattern of white ribbons on a blue ground, a development which had probably taken place by the early sixteenth century. This Ballard carpet, in good condition, is one of the most attractive Lottos to have come down to us. In common with its slightly earlier counterpart, it is of a relatively small size convenient for display in a museum, unlike other early examples of much larger size.

Carpets made in this size were suitable for floor covering in any context. However, their proportions and size may also have enhanced their appeal in European markets, where small carpets such as this were commonly displayed in the houses of prosperous merchants and nobility, placed on a table top (Mack 2001). On festive occasions, such small carpets were displayed draped over the balustrades of exterior balconied courtyards and arched loggias; Such carpets formed an important part of public ceremonies in Renaissance Venice, and numerous paintings from the fifteenth and sixteenth centuries show carpets displayed in this fashion. Paintings by Mansueti, Carpaccio, and above all by Gentile Bellini, show the balconies of Venetian palaces decorated with such carpets. Venetian sources inform us that many of these carpets were loaned by enterprising rug merchants, as a way of displaying their goods and adding to their cachet and price (Denny 2007). A well-known painting in the Hungarian National Museum in Budapest (Batári 1994), showing a group of Hungarian diplomats receiving an audience from the Russian tsar around 1600, demonstrates that, in the absence of large ceremonial carpets, dozens of smaller ones were commonly spread on floors for certain important state ceremonies.

An example of a Lotto-pattern carpet with the "closed" kufesque border was painted by Lorenzo Lotto himself in 1547 (*Portrait of Giovanni della Volta with his Wife and Children*, National Gallery, London). Surviving examples are rare; a heavily restored carpet from the John G. Johnson collection is in the Philadelphia Museum of Art.

Length: Approximately 202 cm

Width: Approximately 114 cm

Warp: Undyed white wool, uniform, two Z-spun yarns plied S, alternate warps very slightly depressed

Weft: Dyed red wool, one Z-spun yarn, shot twice (1 + 1) between each row of knots.Typically for early Lotto carpets, there are several areas where the wefts are not continuous from side to side, but are doubled back, leaving perceptible diagonal lines ("lazy lines") on the back of the rug

Pile: Wool dyed yellow, red, light blue, dark blue, blue-green, mildly corrosive dark-brown and undyed white; all two Z-spun yarns plied S

Knot: Symmetrical, slightly pulled to the left, approximately 40V x 36–37 H per decimeter

Edges: Both overcast, not original

Ends: Less than one cm remaining of red and blue-green tapestry weave at each end

Detail

Reverse view

9

"Lotto" Carpet

Probably west Anatolia, 17th century
Gift of James F. Ballard, 100:1929
Published: Dimand 1935, pl. XXII;
Walker 1988, No. 3

Normal and typical supple handle; in a fairly good state of preservation.

In a third stage in the developmental sequence of Lotto carpets in St. Louis, we can see the ultimate development of the Lotto pattern in western Anatolian weaving. In this particular carpet the delicate fringing on the edge of the split leaves and palmette blossoms observable in the two earlier examples has evolved into a bolder saw-toothed silhouette; the border now consists of a series of discrete floral elements separated by yellow and red dividers, which has replaced the complex interwoven geometry of the kufesque borders.

This example has splendid strong colors, and similar carpets, exported to Europe in significant numbers, have survived in Protestant churches in northern Romania and southern Hungary. In Calvinist churches in particular, the theological position that banned works of statuary and religious paintings depicting humans, deemed to reflect Roman Catholic "idolatry", seems to have softened with regard to carpets such as these. They apparently maintained a kind of religious neutrality in the eyes of their European owners, even when they carried demonstrably religious Islamic meaning (as in prayer carpets depicting the gateway to paradise) or even readable Arabic inscriptions, which were of course not readable by their European owners. The distinctive border, sometimes termed the "ragged palmette" border, was used on many different kinds of Anatolian carpets in addition to those with the "Lotto" pattern, from the seventeenth well into the nineteenth century.

Similar examples are found in the Brukenthal Museum, Sibiu, Romania, one from the evangelical Lutheran Church of Viscri (Weisskirch), and another from the evangelical Lutheran church of Muercurea (see Ionescu 2005).

Length: Approximately 198 cm

Width: Approximately 119 cm

Warp: Undyed white wool, two Z-spun yarns plied S, alternate warps very slightly depressed

Weft: Dyed brownish-red wool, one Z-spun yarn, shot twice (1 + 1) between each row of knots. Typically for early Lotto carpets, there are several areas where the wefts are not continuous from side to side, but are doubled back, leaving perceptible diagonal lines ("lazy lines") on the back of the rug

Pile: Wool, uniform thickness; yellow, red, red-brown, medium blue, dark blue, corrosive dark-brown and undyed white; all two Z-spun yarns plied S

Knot: Symmetrical, slightly pulled to the left, approximately 34V x 32H per decimeter

Edges: Both overcast, not original

Ends: Top: stripped; Bottom: less than one cm blue tapestry weave

Detail

Reverse view

10

"Lotto" Carpet

Central or west Anatolia, late 17th–early 18th century
Gift of Nellie Ballard White, 300:1972

Heavy corrosion of brown, much pile wear, repaired at two different times, extensive renapping; the handle is stiff and dry, typical of this group of later Lotto carpets.

In this final example we see a very characteristic late form of Lotto carpet that today also survives in large numbers as votive gifts found in churches in central Europe, and has sometimes been dubbed the "Transylvanian" type of Lotto carpet. It has a bold border of small cartouche medallions, and a very small central field. The smallest of the four Ballard Lotto carpets (**CAT.7** is missing both of its original ends), it shows the persistence of the Lotto design not only within the west Anatolian weaving tradition but also in European collecting taste.

The strict bilateral symmetry of the design demonstrates that the weaver, instead of tying successive rows of knots from one side of the carpet to another, at the outset worked from the middle outward to the edges. When the time came to finish off the carpet at the top, owing to the small size of the vertical loom used in the weaver's cottage, both the border design and the field design were interrupted; the weaver resumed her original practice of tying knots from the center of the rug toward the edges so that the top border would show the same bilateral symmetry as that of the bottom one.

Lotto-design carpets with similar field and border combinations are found in many collections, among them the Philadelphia Museum of Art (John G. Johnson Collection, catalogue 1160) discussed in Ellis 1988, and in various "Transylvanian" collections (Ionesco 2005). Ballard gave a similar carpet to the Metropolitan Museum of Art in 1922 (22.100.112); this was joined in the Metropolitan by a small McMullan carpet in 1972 (1972.80.7) and by a much larger (and possibly earlier) carpet with the same border, purchased with the support of the Seley Foundation in 1978 (1978.24).

Further reading: Ellis 1975, Ellis 1989, Denny 2002

Length: Approximately 175 cm

Width: Approximately 117 cm

Warp: Undyed white wool, two Z-spun yarns plied S, alternate warps very slightly depressed. While on the loom the bottom half of all of the warps were dyed orange, and the stripped rugs show orange on the bottom but white at the top

Weft: Dyed dull orange-brown wool, one Z-spun yarn, shot twice (1 + 1) between each row of knots As is typical for Lotto carpets, there are areas where the wefts are not continuous from side to side, but are doubled back, leaving perceptible diagonal "lazy lines" on the back of the rug

Pile: Wool dyed yellow, red, orange, light blue, medium blue, corrosive dark-brown and undyed white; all two Z-spun yarns plied S

Knot: Symmetrical, slightly pulled to the left, approximately 32V x 28 H per decimeter

Edges: Both heavily restored, not original

Ends: Top: stripped; Bottom: heavily rewoven

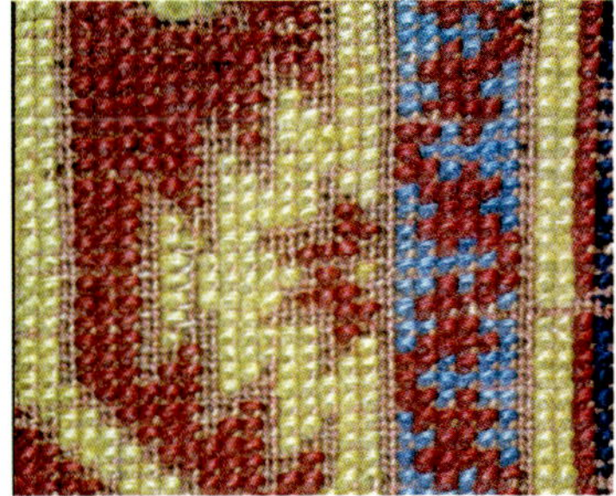

Detail

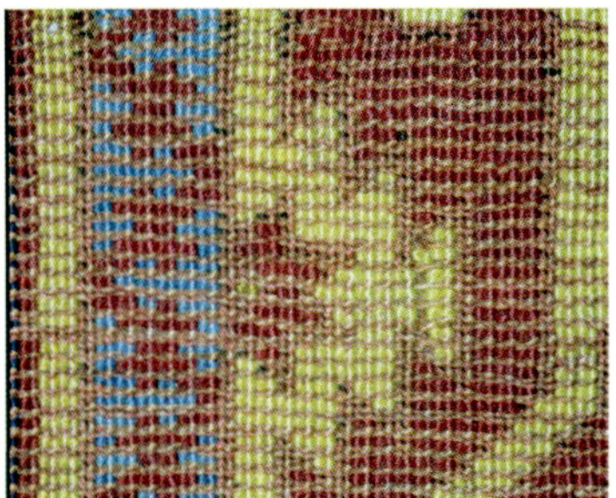

Reverse view

Ushak Carpets

In the later fifteenth, sixteenth, and seventeenth centuries, the commercial weaving ateliers in the district around the western Anatolian city of Ushak probably produced more square meters of carpets than the rest of the carpet-weaving world combined. Large numbers of Ushak carpets have survived into our own time, again probably more than any other group of early carpets, due to the large numbers originally woven, and their donation in large numbers to numerous mosques in what is today the Republic of Turkey.

As our technical entries make clear, the carpets grouped under the Ushak label share a basic weaving technique with other classical Turkish rugs from Anatolia. But they have two characteristics not found in other classical Turkish rugs we have examined: the designs are almost always curvilinear rather than geometric both in conception and in execution; and the coloration is overwhelmingly red and dark blue, with light blue, yellow, and some green, used as secondary colors, along with dark brown (for outlining) and small amounts of undyed white wool for design accents. The exceptions to this rule are the so-called "small medallion" Ushak carpets, whose actual place of origin in west Anatolia may be different from the rest of the group.

Another characteristic of almost all Ushak carpets is the infinite repeat nature of the design, which in concept continues in all four directions beyond the arbitrary confines of the border of the carpet. The eight-lobed "star" medallions are always treated as a part of an infinitely repeating design, a common Ushak design practice also evident in almost all of the earlier so-called "medallion Ushak" carpets and common in most lesser-employed Ushak design layouts as well.

Many Ushak design types are depicted in European painting from the sixteenth century onward. Using collateral dating— the comparison of undated carpets with dateable works in other media such as building decoration and bookbinding—the British scholar Julian Raby and the Italian scholar Alberto Boralevi posited a fifteenth-century dating for the earliest Ushak carpets. They placed them among the earliest exemplars of what the German scholar Kurt Erdmann called the "carpet design revolution": the weaving of carpets following curvilinear designs originating in the arts of the book or architectural tile decoration, rather than relying on the geometry of the loom as a basis for designs.

Carpets with the "star Ushak" design are probably the earliest to be woven in the Ushak manufactories. The origins of the design and layout are almost certainly to be found in architectural decoration; for example, there are very close parallels to both "star Ushak" and "medallion Ushak" major design motifs to be found in the tile decoration of fifteenth-century Islamic monuments from Bursa (tomb of Mehmed I, ca. 1421) to Tabriz (the so-called Masjid-i Kabud or Blue Mosque, ca. 1465).

A reconsideration of Kurt Erdmann's "carpet design revolution of the fifteenth century" has been prompted to a great extent by these resemblances, together with Julian Raby's dating of the "medallion Ushak" carpets to the later fifteenth century owing to the relations of their secondary ornamentation to the style of the Istanbul court under Sultans Mehmed II (r. 1451–1480) and Beyazid II (r. 1480–1512). Erdmann examined the depiction of certain textiles and carpets in the paintings of Behzad and other painters working for the Timurid court in Herat toward the end of the fifteenth century. He noted the transition from geometric patterns rooted in the foursquare knotted-pile medium into more fluid and curvilinear carpet designs based on the arts of manuscript illumination and bookbinding, concluding that it must have taken place in Herat in the late fifteenth century. More recently, however, others have taken notice of the emergence of curvilinear designs in Ushak around the same time, if not earlier. They have established the links between these Ushak designs (such as that of the Ballard star Ushak) and fifteenth-century architectural decoration in northwest Iran under the Turkmen dynasties, and in west Anatolia under the Ottomans.

As mentioned, probably the earliest Ushak design type, originating in the later fifteenth century, is the "Star Ushak" design. It is seen in the Ballard collection in CAT.11, a handsome example from the sixteenth century. Conceptually, the design consists of staggered horizontal rows of alternating eight-cusped "stars" and smaller cusped "diamonds" in blue on a red ground. The small-scale arrangement of small blossoms on vines against the red field displays the

typical butterfly-shaped lotus flowers that had, in the fourteenth century, become a standard element of Islamic design as a result of artistic contact with China during the Mongol domination of the Middle East. With extremely rare exceptions the curvilinear Ushak rugs do not use the geometric kufesque border, but instead show a wide variety of simple floral and vegetal border designs.

A second popular genre of Ushak carpet in the Ballard collection is the small medallion carpet [CAT.13]. Once dubbed "double-ended prayer carpets" by carpet scholars, small carpets such as these probably reflect bookbindings in their designs. The four corner-pieces of the central field, in yellow on red reminiscent of the Lotto carpets, are actually derived from curvilinear snake-like depictions of clouds in Chinese art. Ballard gave another carpet of this type to the Metropolitan Museum of Art (22.100.13)

The fragmentary carpet with its conceptually repeating staggered rows of large quatrefoil medallions [CAT.12], uses a design that is extremely rare in Ushak weaving. Even more unusual are the condition of its pile and the brilliant saturation of its colors, making it one of the most important among a small group of early Ushak carpets that have survived in such good condition, allowing us to imagine what all must have looked like at the time of the weaving. Thus they explain for us why these carpets were so very popular at home and abroad for such a long time.

The vast bulk of surviving Ushak carpets are in the oval medallion format depicted in the somewhat late example in the Ballard collection [CAT.16]. The central medallion, with its red and yellow split leaves on a blue ground forming a quatrefoil, is by the eighteenth century flattened on the sides, and the drawing of the border is irregular, but the colors are glorious. The blue arabesque on the red ground can be traced back from this carpet through three hundred years of Ushak weaving, to its origins in the court style of the Ottoman Sultan Mehmed the Conqueror (r. 1451–1480) in the fifteenth century. Carpets in the medallion format woven in Ushak can extend beyond ten meters in length, making them very difficult to exhibit; this Ballard example, although of late date, is not only in quite good condition but is of a very convenient size for display.

In considerably poorer condition, but again one of the few of its type to have survived relatively intact, is CAT.5, with its four-lobed medallions in repeat with diamond-shaped motifs. Like CAT.12 this carpet is essentially a variant on the early "star Ushak" design. Of all of the Ushak carpet designs in the Ballard collection, this "four leaf clover" medallion design was the most frequently paraphrased or copied by weavers of other Anatolian traditions. Its artistic offspring exist by the hundreds, especially in west Anatolian weaving of the eighteenth and nineteenth centuries. One of the finest examples is found in the Metropolitan Museum of Art, a gift from Ballard (22.100.15).

When Kurt Erdmann published his article on "Little-Known Ushak Designs" ("Weniger bekannte Uschak-muster") in 1963, this Ballard carpet was among the most interesting items of his discussion. Conceptually it fits in perfectly with the designs of the other Ballard Ushak rugs, although in this case the motifs—rather squat cartouche-like medallions—are in red, and the ground with its yellow arabesques is dark blue.

As well as the six Ballard Ushak rugs in St. Louis discussed here, there are several more in the larger collection. Together they are, like the Ballard Lotto carpets, a great vantage point for the study of Ushak carpets as a whole, and clearly show both the variety of Ushak designs and their remarkable lineage and influence.

Further reading: Erdmann 1963, Raby 1986b, Boralevi 1987, Denny 1999, Denny 2002

11

Small Star Ushak Carpet

West-central Anatolia, 16th century

Gift of James F. Ballard, 103:1929

Published: Indianapolis 1934, No. 74; Dimand 1935,
pl. XVIII; Walker 1988, No. 5

One of the favorite designs used by Ushak weavers, this pattern has its origins in the second half of the fifteenth century. This rug is distinguished by its unusually small size; largest examples approach five meters in length.

The first European depiction of a "star Ushak" carpet appears as late as the 1530s in a Venetian painting. Yet the earliest of these carpets may well have been the first group to have come from the Ushak manufactories in western Anatolia. The repetitive eight-lobed "star" medallions are always treated as part of an infinitely repeating design, a common Ushak design practice. The origin of the "star" design is probably to be found in architectural decoration.

Carpets of this type were woven in Ushak from at least as early as the last quarter of the fifteenth century until well into the seventeenth. They also spawned a host of later descendants in village weaving throughout Anatolia. The most splendid carpets in this design, probably dating from the first half of the sixteenth century, are exemplified by the first carpet given to the Metropolitan Museum of Art in 1958 by Joseph V. McMullan, the American collector most influenced by Ballard's approach to collecting, (58.63).

The bulk of McMullan's collection was to follow that carpet into the Metropolitan in two later gifts in the 1970s. In the first rotation of the newly reopened Metropolitan Museum Islamic galleries in 2007, the McMullan star Ushak was exhibited beside the Ballard star Ushak given to the Metropolitan in 1922 (22.100.110). Two splendid carpets in this design are found in Philadelphia, one from the Joseph Lees Williams Memorial Collection (1955-65-16) and one from the John D. McIlhenny Collection (1943-40-66).

Ballard's partiality toward carpets with this design is reflected in his gift of another to the Metropolitan Museum of Art (22.100.110) This particular example is one of the smallest early "Star" Ushak carpets to have come down to us.

Length: Approximately 167 cm

Width: Approximately 103 cm

Warp: Undyed white wool, two Z-spun yarns plied S; warps on one level

Weft: Dyed red wool, one Z-spun yarn, shot twice (1+1); discontinuous wefts that double back create diagonal "lazy lines" easily visible on the back of the carpet

Pile: Wool, dyed red, dark blue, light blue-green, yellow, corrosive brown, undyed white; all two Z-spun yarns plied S

Knot: Symmetrical, pulled slightly to left; approximately 47V x 27H per decimeter

Edges: Both extensively repaired; original flat selvedge evidently four separate warps wrapped in pale green wool

Ends: Both stripped and restored

Detail

Reverse view

12

Large Fragmentary Ushak Quatrefoil Carpet

West-central Anatolia, 16th century

Gift of James F. Ballard, 98:1929

Published: Dimand 1935, pl. XVI; Stokstad 2007, pl. 8–23;

Walker 1988, No. 6

Although both ends of this carpet have been extensively pieced together, and the carpet today is only about two-thirds of its original length, this brilliantly colored Ushak in a highly unusual design is one of the finest and earliest to have survived. Its soft wool and intense colors combining with an almost perfect 1/1 vertical/horizontal knot ratio to create an impression of great balance and nobility.

This fragmentary carpet, with its repeating staggered rows of large quatrefoil medallions, uses a design that is extremely rare in Ushak weaving. The wonderful condition of the pile and the brilliant saturation of its colors make it one of the most important among a small group of early Ushak carpets preserved in such good condition that they demonstrate what all surviving examples must have looked like when newly woven. This may explain why such carpets were so very popular at home and abroad for so long.

A very few other early Ushak carpets, including the Keshishian Carpet in the Textile Museum in Washington, D.C., have survived with anomalous and perhaps unique layouts such as this one, and in a similar state of pile preservation. Of special interest are the four radiating diagonal leaf palmettes in the middle of the quatrefoil medallions, each divided into a green and a yellow half, whose asymmetrical coloration gives a sense of rotation to the centers of the medallions, and imparts a subtle liveliness and a slightly off-balance character to the entire design. The background vine scroll on the red ground consists of small lotus blossoms, punctuated by pairs of wide light-green leaves with rounded contours that are a staple of late fifteenth- and early sixteenth-century Ottoman arts. The intact side borders show an alternation of two types of floral palmette framed by blue split-leaf form known in Turkish art as the *rumi* motif. Also of special interest, given the incredible saturation of the basic colors—red, navy, medium blue, green, and yellow, with a dark brown outlining—is the rare appearance of undyed white wool, almost always as tiny single-knot accents in the design.

The Ballard quatrefoil Ushak in St. Louis, despite its shortened state, is certainly among the most memorable and justly famed early Ushak pieces to have survived.

Length: Approximately 315 cm (originally probably at least 5 m long)

Width: Approximately 229 cm

Warp: Undyed white wool, two Z-spun yarns plied S, slight depression of alternate warps

Weft: Dyed red wool, one Z-spun yarn shot twice (1+1); discontinuous wefts that double back create diagonal "lazy lines" easily visible on the back of the carpet

Pile: Wool dyed red, light blue, dark blue, pale green, yellow, corrosive brown and undyed white; all two Z-spun yarns plied S

Knot: Symmetrical, pulled to the left; approximately 39V x 39H per decimeter

Edges: Machine-made wool selvedge attached on both sides

Ends: Machine-made wool selvedge attached both ends

Detail

Reverse view

13

Small "Double-ended" Ushak carpet

West-central Anatolia, late 16th century
Gift of James F. Ballard, 102:1929
Published: Dimand 1935, pl. XIX

This small medallion carpet is of a type traditionally ascribed to Ushak, although it does not exhibit many of the characteristics thought in general to define Ushak weaving. Despite its heavy wear and extensive restoration it is a good example of a type documented in European painting from the second half of the sixteenth century onward. The yellow arabesques in the corners of the field, derived from Chinese cloudbands, are especially attractive.

A second popular genre of Ushak carpet in the Ballard collection is the small medallion carpet. Because of their small size and proportions, together with the arch motif found at either end, these were once dubbed "double-ended prayer carpets" by carpet scholars. Small carpets such as these more likely reflect the layout of book-bindings and panels of architectural decoration in their designs. The four corner-pieces of the central field, arabesques of yellow on red strongly reminiscent of the designs of Lotto carpets, are actually derived from curvilinear snake-like depictions of clouds in Chinese art.

The actual function of small carpets such as these probably had little to do with Muslim prayer. The small size is often called *sajjadah* (Arabic: *sajjada*, modern Turkish: *seccade*), a word meaning "for prostration", referring to the touching of one's forehead to the carpet during prayer. They were convenient for use in Turkish interiors, and much sought after in Europe, where rugs of this type are well documented in European oil paintings. The medallion format with corner pieces is a common carpet layout from the Aegean to Central Asia. Carpets such as this, which from their color and construction were probably woven in the neighborhood of

Ushak, provide an interesting counterpoint to the larger and more typical Ushak carpets with their repeating patterns and heavy predominance of red and blue coloration.

Two similar carpets in the Metropolitan Museum of Art were given by Ballard's greatest admirer, Joseph V. McMullan, in 1974 (1974.149.10 and 1974.149.11), where they joined an example given by Ballard in 1922 (22.100.111) and another purchased in 1907 (07.116). Philadelphia has three examples, one from John D. McIlhenny (1943-40-59), and two from the Joseph Lees Williams Memorial Collection (1955-65-17 and 1955-65-18). The small Ballard carpet in the Metropolitan Museum with a field design reminiscent of Lotto carpets (22.100.113), discussed elsewhere, is most likely a member of this same group of small double-ended medallion carpets woven in the sixteenth century in the vicinity of Ushak.

Provenance: Dimand 1935 lists this carpet as "formerly in the Davanzatti (sic) collection", from which we can assume it was sold to Ballard by Vitall Benguiat, who at one time lived in the fifteenth-century Palazzo Davanzati in Florence, before pursuing his trade in North America

Detail

Reverse view

14

Ushak Carpet with Unusual Overall Pattern

West-central Anatolia, ca. 1600

Gift of Nellie Ballard White, 301:1972

Published: St. Louis 1932, No. 18; Indianapolis 1934, No. 64;

Walker 1988, No. 7

Despite extensive re-napping along vertical fold lines, this unusual carpet has survived in good condition, with intense colors. The highly unusual design is a testament to the remarkable inventiveness of the carpet-designers of Ushak, who produced a wide range of carpets in huge quantities over three centuries, many using innovative designs such as this one.

As well as the six Ballard Ushak rugs in St. Louis discussed here, there are several more in the larger collection. Together they are, like the Ballard Lotto carpets, a great vantage point for the study of Ushak carpets as a whole, and clearly show both the variety of Ushak designs and their remarkable lineage and influence. Ballard seems to have had a special interest in Ushak carpets with unusual patterns, a number of which ended up in both the Metropolitan and St. Louis donations; this example was part of the gift of Ballard's daughter to St. Louis in 1972.

The design consists of a series of rows of wide semi-oval red-ground medallions alternating with smaller almost diamond-shaped red-ground medallions against a dark-blue ground ornamented, like the large Ushak medallion carpets, with a leafy arabesque of plant forms ultimately derived from late fifteenth-century Ottoman court designs, and reflected in arts of the book and woodcarving of the period. The crowded and "squashed" design of the carpet, together with the flattening caused by the rather extreme knot ratio, makes a complex design appear even more complex, and also ensures that the end borders are a little more than half the width of the side borders. The impression of great richness is enhanced by the saturation of the colors, and the very limited use of undyed white wool in the pile. Kurt Erdmann was the first to discuss "lesser-known Ushak patterns" such as this before 1963. Today we recognize in Ushak weaving not only a huge volume of production but a very wide range of design types, all united by the familiar Ushak color palette and weaving technique.

Further reading: Erdmann 1963, Raby 1984, Boralevi 1987, Denny 1999, Denny 2002

Length: Approximately 386 cm

Width: Approximately 254 cm

Warp: Undyed white wool, two Z-spun yarns plied S, warps lie on one level

Weft: Dyed red wool, one Z-spun yarn, shot twice (1+1); discontinuous wefts that double back create diagonal "lazy lines" easily visible on the back of the carpet

Pile: Wool, dyed red, dark blue, light blue-green, yellow, corrosive brown and undyed white; all two-spun yarns plied S

Knot: Symmetrical, pulled slightly to left; approximately 47V x 27H per decimeter

Edges: Extensively repaired; fragments of original selvedge show four warps wrapped in pale green wool

Ends: Entirely restored

Detail

Reverse view

15

"Quatrefoil" Ushak Carpet

West-central Anatolia, late 16th–early 17th century
Gift of James F. Ballard, 99:1929
Published: Indianapolis 1934, No. 64;
St. Louis 1932, No. 18; Walker 1988, No. 7

The extensive faded renapping and reconstruction present in this carpet tend to distort and disfigure what is a remarkably handsome example of the type of Ushak carpet design most frequently copied by other Anatolian weaving centers.

Few examples of old Ushak carpets woven with this quatrefoil pattern have survived in good condition; the Metropolitan Museum has a small fragment of a similar carpet from the McMullan collection (1972.80.4).

In considerably poorer condition, but again one of the few carpets of its type to have survived relatively intact, is this carpet, with its four-lobed medallions in repeat with diamond-shaped motifs. Like **CAT.12**, this carpet is essentially a variant on the early "Star Ushak" design; here, the four lobes appear in the corners of the medallion on the diagonal axes, whereas in the much rarer design of **CAT.12** the four lobes appear on the vertical and horizontal axes.

Of all the Ushak carpet designs in the Ballard collection, this "four leaf clover" medallion design was the most frequently paraphrased or copied by weavers of other Anatolian traditions, and its artistic offspring exist by the hundreds, especially in west Anatolian weaving of the eighteenth and nineteenth centuries. Once again, the general inspiration for the layout probably lies in contemporary tilework building decoration, which in both Ottoman and Turkmen lands often favored repetitive patterns featuring large four-lobed medallions.

This carpet is probably fairly early in the sequence of surviving examples, as the knot ratio is reasonably close to 1/1, and consequently the pattern is spacious and has plenty of room to "breathe" visually. The knotted white straps connecting the corner lobes of the major X-shaped medallions are well executed and show a clear over-and-under knotting, a sophisticated detail that was lost in later examples. The spiky red-and-yellow lotus blossoms of the side borders were reduced to formulaic stars on the restored border of the bottom end.

Surviving early examples of this design type include the above-mentioned McMullan fragment in the Metropolitan, and a later complete carpet with this design, woven in central Anatolia, given by Ballard to the Metropolitan in 1922 (22.100.115). This was joined in the Metropolitan in 2009 by an even later carpet from the Dumas collection (2009.458.5) with the same design and layout.

Further Reading: McMullan 1966; Denny and Krody 2002

Length: Approximately 335 cm

Width: Approximately 206 cm

Warp: Undyed white wool, two Z-spun yarns plied S; very slight depression of alternate warps

Weft: Dyed red wool, one Z-spun yarn, shot twice (1+1) and three times (1+2//); discontinuous wefts that double back create diagonal "lazy lines" easily visible on the back of the carpet

Pile: Wool dyed red, pale-orange, medium blue, dark blue, blue-green, yellow, dark brown, undyed white; all two Z-spun yarns plied S

Knot: Symmetrical, approximately 37V x 33–36H per decimeter

Edges: Original edge mostly replaced, fragments of a flat selvedge with four bundles of two warps wrapped in blue yarn

Ends: Both stripped, extensively repaired and rewoven

Detail

Reverse view

16

Small Medallion Ushak Carpet

West-central Anatolia, 18th century
Gift of Nellie Ballard White, 302:1972

Despite major reconstruction in all four corners, the brilliant colors of this small Ushak carpet show that the Ushak tradition of weaving medallion carpets continued from the late fifteenth well into the late eighteenth century.

The popularity of the large medallion Ushak carpets over the centuries is quite remarkable. Although there is no surviving evidence of identical carpets in this format, the number of extant examples in the medallion layout, each one different from all the others, is truly amazing. The layout was best suited to the large, sometimes even gigantic, examples preserved in great numbers in the Museum of Turkish and Islamic Arts in Istanbul, there are occasionally carpets such as this one that, despite a very small size, attempt with some success to use the time-honored layout in their designs.

In this example the medallion has been crowded into the narrow width of the carpet, so much so that the sides are completely flat. The conventional leaf arabesques of the background, here in vivid blue against light red, recall the earlier prototypes, especially in the more spacious bottom half of the carpet. The corner pieces—actually quarters or near-quarters of eight-lobed brown-ground medallions with large vertical pendant elements—also valiantly evoke the classical carpets from Ushak of bygone centuries. A simple and somewhat formulaic border surrounds the field; the rich brown and the vibrant green, both additions to the earlier Ushak palette, give this small carpet with gigantic pretensions an additional element of attractiveness.

Length: Approximately 229 cm

Width: Approximately 132 cm

Warp: Undyed white wool, two Z-spun yarns plied S, warps lie on one level; extensive areas of reweaving and repair also include warps of white cotton, grey wool, and brown wool

Weft: Dyed red wool, one Z-spun yarn plied S; shot twice (1+1) and three times (1+2//); discontinuous wefts that double back create diagonal "lazy lines" easily visible on the back of the carpet

Pile: Wool, variable thickness, dyed red, orange, medium blue, light blue, green, yellow, corrosive brown, undyed white; mostly two Z-spun yarns plied S, except for some three-ply green, blue, yellow and red

Knot: Symmetrical, approximately 39–40V x 28–29H per decimeter

Edges: Reconstructed: fragments of original selvedge apparently three bundles of two warps wrapped in green wool

Ends: Top: fragments of apparently original elem show 4.5 cm of green tapestry weave; the same is found on the bottom, but the warps are dark brown, suggesting either that they were dyed on the loom or that they are reconstructions

Detail

Reverse view

Other Classical Anatolian Carpets

allard's preferences as a collector are powerfully evident in his collections, today divided between the Saint Louis Art Museum and the Metropolitan Museum in New York. He balked at the sometimes horrific prices being asked for early Persian carpets in the early twentieth century, but he was fascinated by the brilliant colors and geometric designs of Anatolian carpets, those produced during the time of the Ottoman Empire in what is today Asian Turkey. Apart from groups of early Anatolian carpets dealt with under other headings in this catalogue, a number of "singleton" early carpets from Anatolia together constitute a remaining group of early "classical"Anatolian carpets. These left an enduring mark on the weaving of subsequent centuries. They fall under three basic headings. The earliest, dealt with here, are two carpets with designs named after European painters.

The first of these is a handsome exemplar of a "small pattern Holbein" carpet. Like the "large pattern Holbein" carpets from Anatolia, a Spanish version of which is also in the Ballard collection, this carpet is geometric in design and utilizes bright primary and secondary colors. It features very small medallions formed of an interlaced strap or ribbon motif, repeating in stacked vertical rows. In overall design concept, this carpet also closely resembles the Syrian carpet of the so-called "chessboard" group in St. Louis. It reflects a period in western Anatolian weaving from the later fifteenth century onward, when geometric motifs arranged into repeated patterns predominated. A favorite border was composed of a geometric interlaced white ribbon, also seen in "Lotto" carpets. As we have noted, it was probably itself ultimately derived from borders echoing the angular kufic form of Arabic script. These carpet types include most of those we today conventionally name after European painters who depicted them: Holbein, Lotto, Bellini, Crivelli, Memling, Ghirlandaio, Foschi, Tintoretto. The general technique was very simple: all-wool Z-spun (and, when plied, S-plied) yarns, undyed two-ply warp on one level, single-ply red weft shot once in each direction, and symmetrically knotted two-ply pile on two warps, dyed in a range of six to eight colors.

This type, too, is named after a similar carpet depicted in an early sixteenth-century portrait by Hans Holbein of the German merchant Georg Gisze, now housed in the Berlin Museums [**FIG.13**]. Carpets with the same highly specific design and border type were woven in Anatolia from at least as early as the fourteenth century through the eighteenth, and descendants of the design continue to be popular down to the present day. Of all of the early carpet design types this one was probably depicted most frequently in European paintings, and the legacy of the design was immense. It is certain that, had this carpet been offered to the Metropolitan Museum before 1922, it would have been requested by that institution, which did not acquire its own first carpet in this design until 2010.

The other Ballard carpet included under this heading is a so called "Bellini" carpet. Once again the source of the name is a painting, this time a late fifteenth-century altarpiece by the Venetian painter Giovanni Bellini that shows a carpet with a design similar to this one under the feet of an enthroned Madonna. The design of Bellini carpets has long been a subject of controversy and speculation. But it is now generally agreed that the motif at each end of this carpet is derived from a medieval Spanish depiction of a gated walled city, with the upper and lower "re-entrant" motifs almost certainly depictions of horseshoe-arched gateways in a city wall. This interesting discovery shows, along with a few other recent discoveries, that the sharing of carpet designs from one end of the Mediterranean to the other was almost certainly a two-way street rather than an early case of artistic "westward-ho!"

Ballard collected a total of four Bellini-design carpets, a remarkable accomplishment. Three were given to the Metropolitan Museum of Art (22.100.109, 22.100.89, and 22.100.14). Despite its relatively poor condition the St. Louis double-ended or "re-entrant" version of the Bellini theme is arguably the most attractive, and probably the oldest of the four.

Further Reading: Denny 1999, Denny 2002

17

"Double-ended" or "Re-entrant" "Bellini" Carpet

Central or west-central Anatolia, late 16th–early 17th century

Gift of James F. Ballard, 130:1929

Large areas of this carpet have been restored, probably around 1900; the gradual fading of the restoration allows us to distinguish original from restoration without difficulty, while not detracting overly from the overall impact of the carpet; certain areas, such as the "hanging" ornaments inside of the two "re-entrant" motifs, still exhibit substantial original pile. Despite the condition, this is a very handsome example of an early Bellini carpet.

A number of "Bellini" carpets with this curious "keyhole" design have survived, of which all but one are products of Anatolian looms. The exception is in the Berlin Museums, a prayer carpet with the characteristic motif, which based on its coloration, minor motifs, and S-spun wool, was woven in Egypt. As with carpets with the various "Holbein" patterns, carpets such as this were in fact illustrated by many different European Renaissance painters.

Bellini carpets can be divided into in three principal groups: the first has a tall, narrow "keyhole" at the bottom only, and usually has a gable or arched form at the top that indicates the carpet was meant to be a *sajjadah* or prayer rug; a Ballard example in this design is found in the collection of the Metropolitan Museum of Art (22.100.109). A second version displays a far shorter and wider keyhole motif, again at the notional bottom of a carpet with a prayer rug layout; a Ballard example of this design is also in the Metropolitan (22.100.114). The third type, seen in this example, in effect turns the layout of the second group into a doubled-ended one, with a "keyhole" octagon at both the top and the bottom of the design. Given the name "re-entrant" by Charles Grant Ellis, numerous examples of carpets woven in this layout are known, including one from James Ballard (22.100.89) and two from Joseph V. McMullan (1974.149.26 and 1949.149.27) in the Metropolitan.

The design of Bellini carpets has long been a subject of controversy and speculation. It has been variously conjectured that the "keyhole" motif represents a Chinese stylized mountaintop, a mihrab niche from a mosque, or an octagonal pool of water in a formal Islamic garden. Based on recent scholarship, it now seems far more likely that the motif and the layout are derived from a medieval Spanish depiction of a gated walled city, with the upper and lower "re-entrant" motifs almost certainly depictions of horseshoe arched gateways in a city wall. A very striking depiction of Babylon in an early Mozarabic Beatus manuscript in the Morgan Library from around 940–45, illustrated by Maius, clearly shows the form as a horseshoe arched gateway. The lost carpet prototype probably represented in schematic form the holy enclosure of the city of Mecca, toward which all Muslims face during the salat or five canonical daily prayers. This interesting discovery forms part of a growing body of evidence that demonstrates that the sharing of carpet designs from one end of the Mediterranean to the other was almost certainly a two-way street.

Further Reading: Denny 1999, Denny 2002

Length: Approximately 213 cm

Width: Approximately 155 cm

Warp: Undyed white wool, two Z-spun yarns plied S, very slight depression of alternate warps

Weft: Dyed red wool, one Z-spun yarn, shot twice (1+1) between each row of knots

Pile: Wool dyed red, red-brown, orange, yellow, dark blue, medium blue-green, light blue, purple, light brown, corrosive dark brown, undyed white; all two Z-spun yarns plied S

Knot: Symmetrical, pulled slightly to left; 36V x 35H per decimeter

Edges: Stripped, rewoven, replaced

Ends: Stripped, extensively rewoven, especially at bottom of carpet

Detail

Reverse view

18

"Small-pattern Holbein" Carpet

Probably west or west-central Anatolia, early 16th century

Gift of James F. Ballard, 106:1929

Published: Indianapolis 1934, No. 78; Dimand 1935, pl. XIV;
Walker 1988, No. 1

Despite the wear and repairs, a handsome example of this famous carpet type, with most of its structure intact.

This small carpet is a handsome exemplar of what carpet scholars call a "small pattern Holbein." This type, too, is named after a representation of a similar carpet in an early sixteenth-century painting by Hans Holbein, this time a portrait of the German merchant Georg Gisze [**FIG.13**]. The carpet reflects a period in western Anatolian weaving from the later fifteenth century onward, when geometric motifs arranged into repeated patterns predominated. During this era knotted-pile carpets were woven in a very straightforward technique: undyed warp on one level, single-ply red weft shot twice, and pile symmetrically knotted on two warps, all of Z-spun wool.

The Ballard carpet uses a pattern composed of staggered rows of two motifs. One is a compact octagon with an interlace knot on each of its eight sides; the other is a larger but less obtrusive cruciform motif composed of split-leaf *rumi* elements. The latter is probably the most important, and in Europe after the Lotto carpets certainly the most popular, of early Anatolian carpet designs. The earliest carpets using these elements in this pattern, which have survived only as fragments, can be dated with some confidence to the later fourteenth century. Three of the most interesting are found in Istanbul (Museum of Turkish and Islamic Art 303), Berlin (Museum für Islamische Kunst I.6737), and in a private collection in Italy.

Numerous "Holbein" carpets are depicted in European paintings, most of them by Italian artists, but some are also included in works by British, German, Austrian, Spanish, Flemish, and French painters. On the basis both of stylistic analysis and of comparison with examples illustrated by European painters, scholars have generally concluded that the earliest and rarest of these carpets, probably dating from the later fourteenth century through the fifteenth, have what is known as an "open kufic" border. In this the vertical ligatures of the stylized but unreadable Arabic letters, with their crowning finials, are easily seen. An example of such an open kufic border can be seen in one of the St. Louis Lotto carpets [**CAT.7**]. The "closed" border seen here is probably a slightly later development first appearing in the later fifteenth century; it also characterizes the carpet depiction by Holbein giving the group its name.

Examples analogous to the St. Louis Ballard example include carpets in St. Margaret's Evangelical Lutheran Church in Media, Romania; the Museum of Applied Arts, Budapest; the Stefano Bardini Museum, Florence; and the Cathedral of St. Catherine in Sion, Switzerland.

Length: Approximately 198 cm

Width: Approximately 121 cm

Warp: Undyed white wool, two Z-spun yarns plied S; alternate warps slightly depressed

Weft: Wool dyed red, one Z-spun yarn, two shoots (1+1); occasionally discontinuous wefts are doubled back resulting in diagonal "lazy lines" visible on the back of the carpet and, because of extensive wear, on the front as well

Pile: Wool, dyed red, medium blue, dark blue, dark green, purple, corrosive brown, undyed white; all two Z-spun yarns plied S

Knot: Symmetrical, pulled to left, raising the right warp of each pair; approximately 36V x 31H per decimeter

Edges: Original edges stripped, overcast

Ends: Both stripped

Detail

Reverse view

A "Transylvanian" Carpet

We have mentioned the survival of large numbers of early carpets, most of them from Anatolian Turkey, in central European Protestant churches. Many of them are in the area known as Transylvania, today southern Hungary and northern Romania [**FIG.16**]. While these churches have given up their share of Lottos, Holbeins, Memlings, Ghirlandaios, Bellinis, Crivellis, and other early Turkish carpets named after European painters, the most numerous types to have emerged in central Europe have been dubbed "Transylvanian" in the carpet literature. For a brief time the idea was floated—notably by Charles Grant Ellis in his catalogue of the carpet collection of the Philadelphia Museum of Art—that some of them were woven in Eastern Europe, specifically Wallachia. Scholars from central Europe quickly noted that, in decades of searching, they have found no evidence that carpets were woven in Romania or Hungary. However, many documents attest to the importation of Turkish rugs to this area since at least the late fifteenth century. It is now generally agreed that these carpets were all woven in western Anatolia; their appearance in European and even in North American paintings suggests dates from the mid-seventeenth through the nineteenth centuries for most of them, and attests to their great popularity outside of Turkey.

There are two Ballard examples in St Louis. They are quite similar, not only in their structure but in their colors, field design, and borders. One of these carpets, which has been relegated to the appendix of the current catalogue because of its poor condition (93:1929, p. 218) is a classic example of a *sajjadah* or *seccade*, which literally translates as a "rug for prostration;" the term is usually translated into English as "prayer rug" or "prayer carpet". In size, it is appropriate for one individual to use as a ritually clean place to perform the five daily Islamic prayers that require an individual to kneel and briefly touch the forehead to the ground as a sign of submission to God. Its design is composed of an arch, symbolizing the gateway to paradise; the vase-like form at the top of the arch is a lamp that symbolizes the presence of God, who in Muslim scriptures is described as "the Light of the Heavens and the Earth," and whose illumination is likened to that of a glass oil-lamp hanging under an arch.

In the second Ballard carpet of this group [**CAT.19**], the design has been made symmetrical end to end, resulting in what has been termed a "double ended prayer carpet." In fact, the artistic result we observe is simply born of a wish for bilateral symmetry in both a vertical and a horizontal direction. In their design details, from the floral arabesques with lotus blossoms to the cartouche and roundel borders with stylized split-leaves, these carpets are very much in the classical tradition of Anatolian weaving. Countless village carpets of the nineteenth and early twentieth centuries woven in western Anatolia continued to follow the design layout of the so-called "Transylvanian" carpets.

There is a delicious irony in the use of such carpets in European churches. Many of the central European churches in which these carpets were found had been Roman Catholic until the time of the Reformation, after which many became Calvinist or Lutheran. Following Protestant practice, the original stained glass, frescoes, and statuary had been destroyed or removed. The interiors were then whitewashed, giving an austere but appealing effect recognizable to anyone familiar with the seventeenth-century Dutch paintings of Calvinist church interiors by Emanuel de Witte or Pieter Jansz Saenredam. Eventually, it appears that the simple human urge to make these somewhat forbidding structures more user-friendly and welcoming resulted in their redecoration, this time with colorful Turkish carpets. Because they had no images of crucifixes or saints, the carpets were acceptable to their Protestant clergy and congregations, who imagined them to have no religious meaning whatsoever.

Further Reading; Denny 1990, Ionescu 2005, Franses 2007

19

"Transylvanian" carpet

West Anatolia, late 17th century
Gift of James F. Ballard, 92:1929
Published: Dimand 1935, pl. XXIII; Walker 1988, No. 8

With small areas of reweaving, this is a good example of the so-called "doubled-ended prayer rug" design format found in west Anatolian rugs of this group; the vase-like motif at each end may possibly have been derived from the design of a hanging lamp in a niche. The abrupt ending of the side border design easily indicates the top end of the rug.

Another Ballard carpet in this group, which because of its poor condition has been relegated to the appendix of the present catalogue, is a classic example of a "prayer rug or "prayer carpet" (93:1929, p.218).

In this example, however, the original prayer rug schema has been given vertical symmetry, and a lamp "hangs" either up or down at either end under the notional "arches." A look at the border articulation in the corners clearly shows how the weaver worked. In beginning the rug, she seems to have conceptualized the bottom border from the center of the loom outward, meaning that the two eight-pointed stars in the lower corners each lost an outer point in order to fit in. After somewhat abruptly finishing the side borders at the level of the top trefoil guard border with a line of blue knots cutting off a white-ground cartouche, she then profited from her experience at the bottom border by reducing the size of the middle star in the upper border, so that the two stars in the upper corners could be intact, creating a top border of perfect horizontal symmetry.

In fact one of the most interesting aspects of these small and colorful masterpieces of early Turkish weaving is their suppleness of design, their avoidance of strict symmetry, and their implied story of the struggle of the artist with her attractive but intractable medium.

Further Reading; Bátari 1994, Denny 1990, Ionescu 2005, Franses 2007

Length: Approximately 160 cm

Width: Approximately 125 cm

Warp: Undyed white wool, upper and lower ends of warps apparently dyed yellow while on the loom, two Z-spun yarns plied S, alternate warps strongly depressed

Weft: Dyed red wool, one Z-spun yarn: shot twice (1+1)

Pile: Wool dyed light blue, dark blue, red, pink, dark yellow, beige (faded from light purple?), green, corrosive dark brown, and undyed white; all two Z-spun yarns plied S

Knot: Symmetrical, approximately 38V x 37–38H per decimeter

Edges: Original edges replaced with machine-made edges sewn on

Ends: Both stripped, with yellow-dyed warp showing

Detail

Reverse view

West Anatolian Carpets

shak, the greatest center of Anatolian commercial production, is in the western part of Anatolia, today only a few hours drive from the Aegean Sea. The uplands of west Anatolia provide excellent grazing for sheep, which produce wool that in spring can be washed and dyed in the abundant water of the region's rivers and streams. It is therefore not surprising that west Anatolia is even today a world-renowned center for village carpet weaving, thanks to the revival of traditional weaving and dyeing methods in the late twentieth century.

James Ballard's main interest in west Anatolian village weaving centered on the small cottage-industry carpets of Gördes (once spelled Ghiordes) and Kula, which in the early twentieth century were highly prized in the marketplace; each of these two weaving sites is to be discussed in a separate heading in this catalogue. Today, however, in a different atmosphere of taste, it is Ballard's interest in more traditional village weaving that we tend to find more impressive.

The enormous wealth of the more traditional west Anatolian weaving types, often reaching the marketplace under the designation "Bergama," attracted Ballard from the beginning. His gifts to the Metropolitan Museum of Art in 1922 were in effect the Metropolitan's own preferences from his collection. They included, in addition to three "Transylvanians" and

significant numbers of Gördes and Kula carpets, a Milas prayer rug (22.100.24), two Demirci carpets (22.100.78 and 88) and a "Kiz-Gördes" carpet (22.100.107).

Thomas Farnham has observed that the St. Louis Ballard gift of 1929, itself a reflection both of what the Metropolitan chose not to select, and what Ballard subsequently collected in the seven years between 1922 and 1929, may indicate an apparent change in Ballard's collecting interests. More-recent Transcaucasian carpets and Turkmen carpets became almost absent, while his abiding interest in Anatolian carpets continued to result in new and significant acquisitions.

Further Reading: Denny 1972, Markarian 1988, Denny 2002

20

Medallion Carpet with Depictions of Jewelry Pendants

Probably southwest Anatolia, 18th or early 19th century

Gift of James F. Ballard, 88:1929

Published: Dimand 1935, pl. XXX; Walker 1988, No. 21

The very soft and lustrous wool and brilliant colors of this well-preserved west Anatolian carpet create a strong impression. The border and overall layout are derived from the slightly earlier "Transylvanian" type carpets, and the depictions of *nazarlik*—triangular silver jewelry pendants with hanging beads at the bottom—are typical for this type of carpet, whose latter-day descendants in the nineteenth century are associated with the village of Dazkırı.

This impressive medallion carpet with jewelry depictions has a border type and corner-pieces of the central panel that are clearly related to the borders of the "Transylvanian" carpets. Indeed, the documented west Anatolian provenance of this and similar carpets is another strong argument, were any needed, for the attribution of carpets of the "Transylvanian" group to western Anatolia.

In many ways it epitomizes the genius of Anatolian village carpets at their best. It is in excellent condition, with the lush wool showing off a wonderful array of brilliant colors. The balance between highly ornamented spaces and the subtle horizontal abrash of the open red field is excellent. The highly skilled weaver has carefully adjusted the corners of the borders; and the symmetries of the field, while thorough, remain slightly irregular, thus enhancing the carpet's visual suppleness.

The hanging lamp symbolizing Divine Light has here metamorphosed into depictions of six hanging jeweled amulets. These traditional amulets, fashioned of silver, consist of triangles of various sizes, from each of which hang three small chains with beads and small bells. The tinkling and motion of the hanging elements was thought to ward off the jealousy of evil spirits. Given the vibrant colors and superb wool of this very beautiful carpet, one must suppose that the protective effort was well-advised.

The right-handed weaver apparently beat down the wefts with much more force on the right side of the carpet than she did on the left, resulting in the left side being longer than the right. In a village carpet, such asymmetries are best celebrated as part of the carpet's earthy appeal.

Further Reading: Denny 2002

Length: Approximately 246 cm

Width: Approximately 163 cm

Warp: Undyed white wool, uniform and very thin and delicate, two S-spun yarns plied Z, one level

Weft: Dyed red wool, uniform and regular, one Z-spun yarn, shot twice (1+1) and infrequently three times (1+2//)

Pile: Red, medium blue, light blue (abrash to very pale blue), green (abrash to yellow-green), purple, yellow, corrosive brown, and undyed white; all two Z-spun yarns plied S

Knot: Symmetrical, approximately 41V x 32–33H per decimeter

Edges: Both flat selvedges of three bundles of two warps wrapped in red wool

Ends: Both stripped

Detail

Reverse view

21

"Demirci" Carpet

West Anatolia, early 19th century
Gift of James F. Ballard, 90:1929
Published: Dimand 1935, pl. XXVIII

Ballard owned two of these rugs; an older but terribly worn example has been included in the Appendix (318:1972, see p. 226). Despite the wear in the central field, probably due to the corrosive presence of iron sulfate in the dark-red dye, the lush pile and brilliant colors of the border make this small rug, with its echoes of the west Anatolian "Transylvanian" rugs of the previous two centuries, a visual delight.

This small Demirji (modern Turkish: Demirci) carpet has a striking yellow border consisting of a meandering vine adorned with generic small blue flowers nd easily identifiable bright-red carnations, but its field is a perfect lineal descendant of the "Transylvanian" carpet [**CAT.19**] in the Ballard Collection. The motifs have been simplified, and the long pile and soft wool obscure some of the subtleties of the design, and the complicated border of the earlier rug has been abandoned, but the carpet otherwise plainly demonstrates its artistic DNA.

Despite the debt to the "Transylvanian" layout in the central field, the border of the Ballard carpet is entirely distinctive to the group of carpets produced in the nineteenth-century village of Demirci, in the Kula district of western Anatolia. On a vivid yellow ground, it consists of a meandering vine, from which spring trios of red carnations and blue cornflowers, each trio of flowers punctuated by small three-lobed hyacinths and larger three-petaled red tulips.

These flowers are manifestations of a floral style that began in Ottoman times in the middle of the sixteenth century, and whose floral elements became the virtual brand or trademark of Ottoman style.

Ballard's fascination with this group of Anatolian village carpets is reflected in his gift to the Metropolitan Museum of Art in 1922, which included both a pendant to the St. Louis carpet (22.100.88, identified by Dimand as "Bergama") and a seccade or prayer rug from Demirci, whose central field is filled with a flowering tree bearing a huge variety of classical Ottoman flowers (22.100.78, identified by Dimand as "Ghiordes"). In the George Hewitt Myers collection in The Textile Museum are another carpet similar to the St. Louis Demirci (R34.5.1) and another prayer rug with a flowering tree motif (1971.23.8), both exhibited there in a recent show devoted to the Ottoman floral style.

Further reading: Dimand 1973, Denny and Krody 2012

Length: Approximately 162 cm

Width: Approximately 130 cm

Warp: Very soft undyed white wool, two Z-spun yarns plied S, alternate warps moderately depressed

Weft: Undyed white wool, one Z-spun yarn, shot twice (1+1) and occasionally three times (1+1+1)

Pile: Wool, dyed dark corrosive red, red, brown-purple dark blue, medium blue, blue-green, green abrashed both light and dark, yellow, dark brown, and undyed white; all two Z-spun yarns plied S

Knot: Symmetrical, approximately 42–43V x 37H per decimeter

Edges: Both rewrapped

Ends: Both stripped

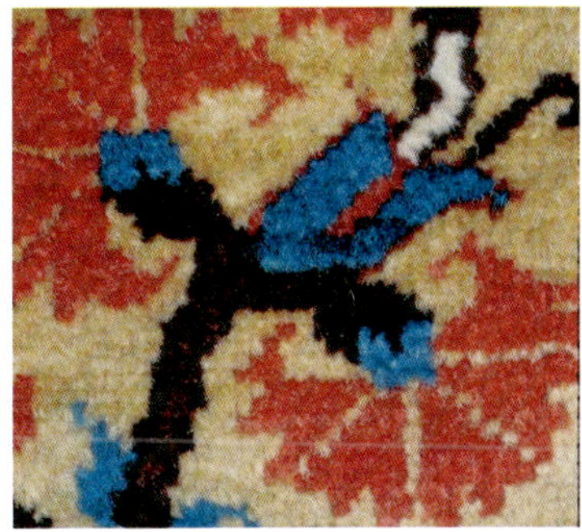

Detail

Reverse view

22

Small Carpet with Ottoman Saz Design or "Smyrna" Rug

West Anatolia, late 18th–early 19th century

Gift of James F. Ballard, 114:1929

Published: Dimand 1935, pl. LII, attributed to "Smyrna, early XVIII century"

Despite this carpet's irregular weft pattern and packing, resulting in a vertically stretched design, and the different palette of pile colors, a comparison of its back with the back of cat. 23 shows striking similarities. It is likely that both of these carpets belong to a similar village production that used designs adapted from earlier carpets woven in distant places; this would explain the adaptation of a sixteenth-century Ottoman design seen in this carpet, as well as the adaptation of an early Transcaucasian design seen in cat. 23. Both carpets exhibit typically west Anatolian materials and structure.

In the nineteenth century, somewhere in the vicinity of Izmir (formerly Smyrna), there was a small production of village carpets that self-consciously reproduced the designs of sixteenth-century Ottoman examples, but in a characteristic west Anatolian weave structure and with a distinctive coloration including a great deal of red and yellow. James Ballard's example in St. Louis is in its field, color apart, a quite literal copy of an Ottoman court carpet of the late sixteenth century, but its border is a typical village design from west Anatolia.

Relatively late carpets with a clear relationship to examples from centuries earlier are of course common if not overwhelmingly prevalent in Anatolian weaving. They form part of an unusual artistic continuum in which innovation and tradition are involved in a perpetual sort of artistic *pas de deux*. More often than not the later examples may today easily be regarded as the artistic equals of their older, and today much rarer, forebears.

The large complex floral palmettes seen as the major elements in the design of this carpet, together with the bi-color curved leaves are, color apart, very carefully adapted from designs found in sixteenth-century Ottoman court carpets.

Length: Approximately 175 cm

Width: Approximately 122 cm

Warp: Undyed white wool, uniform, two Z-spun yarns tightly plied S, alternate warps mildly depressed

Weft: Dyed red wool, uniform, irregular, one Z-spun yarn, shot twice (1+1) and three times (1+1+1, 1+2//); discontinuous wefts that double back create diagonal "lazy lines" easily visible on the back of the carpet

Pile: Wool, dyed red, pink, blue, white, yellow, corrosive brown, beige, dark purple-brown, and undyed white

Knot: Symmetrical, approximately 37V x 41H

Edges: Machine-serged edges replace original selvedge

Ends: Stripped

Detail

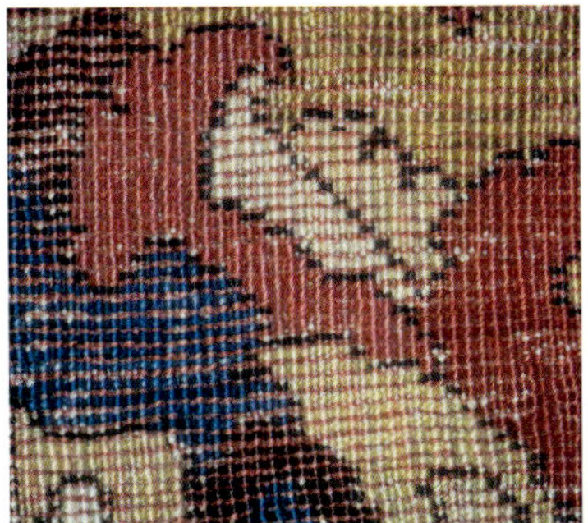

Reverse view

23

Small Carpet with Geometric Blossom Design

West Anatolia, late 18th–early 19th century

Gift of James F. Ballard, 91:1929

Published: Dimand 1935, pl. XXXI, where a Gördes
provenance is proposed; Walker 1988, No. 15

Dimand first commented on the strong resemblance between the designs of west Anatolian village carpets such as this and commercial carpets woven in the Kuba district of Transcaucasia in the 18th century. The corrosive dark-red dye used in these Anatolian carpets is reminiscent of that found in the carpets attributed to the Demirci area (see cat. 22). The structure of this carpet is certainly much different from that of Gördes production (compare with the entries for the Ballard Gördes carpets, cats. 24–27).

This nineteenth-century west Anatolian carpet is clearly inspired by earlier carpets from Transcaucasia more than 1,400 kilometers to the east [**CAT.45**] but the actual mechanics of the connection remain murky. We do know that there are nineteenth-century village carpets from northwest Anatolia in the so-called "large-pattern Holbein" layout that look very much like nineteenth-century Kazak carpets from south Transcaucasia, and there is speculation that Turkic weavers from the southern Lesser Caucasus mountains may have migrated to the shores of the Aegean as Russian power expanded into their traditional homelands in the nineteenth century.

A similarly interesting puzzle is presented by a "Smyrna" carpet in the Ballard collection, part of his gift to the Metropolitan Museum of 1922. It too has craggy serrated hooked geometric leaves and large geometric blossoms that also owe a stylistic debt to the Transcaucasian weaving tradition (22.100.87).

Length: Approximately 165 cm

Width: Approximately 137 cm

Warp: Undyed white wool, uniform, two Z-spun yarns plied S, alternate warps moderately depressed

Weft: Dyed red wool, uniform, one Z-spun yarn, shot twice (1+1)

Pile: Wool; corrosive dark red, medium red, dark blue, medium blue, light blue, dark yellow, brown-purple, light green, corrosive brown-black, and undyed white; all two Z-spun yarns plied S

Knot: Symmetrical, approximately 41V x 35–36H per decimeter

Edges: Rewrapped

Ends: Stripped and/or restored by large reweaves

Detail

Reverse view

Gördes Carpets

In James Ballard's day, the west Anatolian carpets that we call Gördes weavings, and he and his dealers knew as Ghiordes, were the Holy Grail of later Anatolian carpet production. Many examples that we now date to the nineteenth century were imagined to date from the eighteenth or even from the seventeenth. Ballard's great disciple, Joseph V. McMullan, followed his taste and interests in every way, except for a more "modern" disdain for Gördes and Kula weavings. He thought their designs fussy and found their colors for the most part disappointingly weak and "un-Turkish." Today we can appreciate the best of Ballard's Gördes carpets, those that were not bleached to conform to their role as decorative adjuncts to Victorian parlors. A nineteenth-century cottage industry produced products that were intended to appeal to European and North American markets—bringing the exotic persianate prayer rug to Peoria, as it were, while offering patterns and colors thought to be more "refined" than those of the often more powerful and even boisterous typical Anatolian village products.

The cream of Ballard's Gördes prayer rugs in St. Louis are the white-ground and red-ground examples; the esteem in which the latter was held is in some ways indicated by the enormous expense Ballard endured to have a substantial part of the field rewoven. Heavily compacted in weave, these carpets have very finely detailed complex multiple borders and highly detailed designs, for which the open field gives a welcome visual relief. Many of the motifs are clearly descendants of sixteenth-century Ottoman prototypes.

In addition to a precise, compact weave, Gördes rugs often exhibit two very interesting technical features. First, in common with many west Anatolian rugs, they show "lazy lines." These occur when the weaver, instead of sliding all the way across the weaver's bench as she ties each row of knots, may complete only half the width of a row, and then double the weft back. On the next row, she doubles back again, but at a distance one knot less (or two warps less) than the first time, to avoid having a vertical slit in the finished rug. After continuing this process for ten to thirty rows of knots, she then moves to the other end of the bench and completes that side of the rug. There is a resultant line of tiny holes in the structure, where each row of wefts doubles back rather than continuing across the rug (thus the term discontinuous wefts). It is easy to see on the back of a rug and, if the rug is worn, equally easy to see on the front.

On some white-ground prayer rugs (but not on this example) the weaver may use the discontinuous weft technique to insert a white weft under the central field (making wear less obvious) while preserving a red weft under the darker borders. This gives both the rug, and the seat of the weaver's *shalvar*, extra life.

The second Gördes technical feature, also found in other west and central Anatolian prayer rugs, is the practice of starting the weaving of the rug at the top of the design. When the rug is hung for display, the pile points upward, creating problems for museum lighting designers; otherwise this fact usually goes unnoticed. It too has a practical purpose: the weaver uses a small loom, and to earn her piecework rate must fill the loom completely with a woven carpet. Calculating where the complex arch end of the rug must be started in order to fit the complete design into the loom is very difficult. It is far simpler to calculate at the simpler "bottom" end of the design, which is thus saved for last, and becomes technically the "top" of the rug.

The double-ended so-called "Kiz-Gördes" carpets [CAT.26] and "Mejidiye" [CAT.27] carpets are probably produced in the same region as the prayer rugs. The former was often marketed as a "dowry rug," just as the arched-design carpets were marketed as "prayer rugs," although both may have been destined in the main for foreign rather than domestic Turkish markets. The vaguely Second Empire colors of the "Mejidiye Gördes" rugs, of which the Ballard example is one of the very best, show the powerful influence of European taste in nineteenth-century Anatolia. But the arrow-head-shaped cypress tree forms are the descendants of the same motifs in the Syrian and Egyptian carpets in the Ballard Collection.

Further reading: Markarian 1988

24

Prayer Carpet with Red Ground Field

West-central Anatolia, Gördes District, late 18th–early 19th century

Gift of James F. Ballard, 80:1929

Published: Dimand 1935, pl. XXXVI; Walker 1988, No. 12

This handsome carpet woven in western Anatolia, probably during the later eighteenth century, represents the best in Gördes weaving that has come down to us. Rightly recognizing the carpet's beauty, Ballard apparently invested a considerable sum in having a broad horizontal band at the bottom of the field (as illustrated) completely restored. The design we see is complicated: there are horizontal panels both above and below the central field with its niche or portal design, both of which incorporate what are essentially fragments of standard Gördes border designs. The spandrels of the portal arch show sprays of floral vines in white against a dark blue background; this carpet is early enough in the process of stylization that many standard Ottoman floral motifs, among them hyacinths and tulips, are still identifiable by type.

At the notional top of the portal arch is a "hanging" ornament. In early Ottoman prayer carpets that served as the original prototypes for this carpet—such as the famous later sixteenth-century Ballard triple-arched coupled-column prayer rug in the Metropolitan Museum of Art [**FIG.14**] (22.100.51), or a quite similar single-arched carpet in the al-Sabah collection in Kuwait (LNS 29 R)—this motif was a lamp, symbolizing the Divine Presence and underlining the carpet's religious use. In the Ballard Gördes it has metamorphosed into a vaguely floral ornament.

Despite the long-term effects of stylization, on close examination the border of the Ballard carpet shows a close resemblance to the sixteenth-century original. It consists of eight-lobed rosettes (each flanked by a pair of white lanceolate leaves) alternating with complex stylized floral palmettes (also flanked by similar leaves); in the interstices we can see small sprays of light blue hyacinths, fan-shaped carnations, and the vestiges of three-petaled tulips, all of them simplified from their original form but still easily identifiable.

It was undoubtedly this sense of familial artistic lineage that served as one of James Ballard's principal collecting motivations. In his own time he saw, perhaps more clearly than anyone else, the broad, centuries-long span of artistic kinships and inheritances that unites some of the humblest and simplest of Anatolian village weavings with the great imperial traditions of the Ottoman empire at its zenith.

Further Reading: Dimand 1973, Spuhler 2012, Denny 1990 and 1991 (on the imagery and symbolism of prayer rugs)

Length: Approximately 170 cm

Width: Approximately 125 cm

Warp: Undyed white wool, 2 Z-spun yarns plied S, alternate warps slightly depressed

Weft: Dyed red wool, one Z-spun yarn shot twice (1+1)

Pile: Wool, dyed dark blue, light blue, bright green, pale blue-green, dark purple-red, medium red, pinkish red, yellow, slightly corrosive black-brown, and undyed white, all two Z-spun yarns plied S

Knot: Symmetrical, approximately 62V x 44H per decimeter

Edges: Both reconstructed

Ends: Both stripped

Detail

Reverse view

25

Prayer Carpet with White Ground Field

West-central Anatolia, Gördes District, late 18th–early 19th century

Gift of James F. Ballard, 79:1929

Published: Dimand, 1935, pl. XXXVI; Walker 1988, no. 14

Finely and very regularly woven, with knots and weft strongly packed down, this very typical Gördes prayer carpet has excellent colors, having escaped the bleaching "wash" often given to such carpets before they reached European or American retail markets. Weaving was begun from the top as illustrated, allowing the weaver to complete the more complicated half of the central panel first. The rug has a typically stiff and dry handle.

Ballard's white-ground Gördes carpet in St. Louis has survived in an almost miraculous state of preservation, especially as the white-ground central field was particularly fragile and prone to staining or showing wear. The dramatic contrast between the single-color ivory field under the portal arch and the extremely complex spandrels, top and bottom panels, and borders, adds to the visual impact of this carpet.

The central field incorporates two vertical lateral bands that are the vestiges of columns from an architectural depiction of the gateway to heaven found in the sixteenth-century Ottoman court carpet prototype [**FIG.14**]. Four carnations, each flanked by a pair of lanceolate leaves, at the "bottom" of the field, symbolize the flowers of paradise promised in the Qur'an, while another ornament in the white field under the arch is the vestigial shadow of the original hanging lamp. The spandrels of the arch show easily identifiable hyacinths and carnations from the Ottoman classical past as part of their overall decoration of flowers and vines. The top and bottom panels, above and below the field, incorporate elements of standard Gördes borders from this period in the same manner as seen in **CAT.24**. The main border is also based on exactly the same prototype as **CAT.24**.

The extremely rich and complex impression made by this small prayer carpet is due in the main to its profusion of minor borders. A group of three minor borders, in each case consisting of inner and outer guard stripes flanking a distinctive guard border, is found on either side of the main border. A different light-blue border frames the central panel consisting of a white ground under the portal arch. Still another unusual border frames the panel "above" the portal arch, while a narrow red-ground strip underlines the bottom panel. These small borders are colorful, imaginative, and diverse; they represent the original creations of Gördes weavers, and may be considered as one of the supreme artistic contributions of the Gördes carpet designers and weavers to the overall history of Anatolian carpet design.

Further reading: Dimand 1973 (a similar Ballard Gördes carpet in the Metropolitan, 22.100.129)

Length: Approximately 185 cm

Width: Approximately 137 cm

Warp: Undyed white wool, two Z-spun yarns plied S, slight depression of alternate warps. Warps at ends appear slightly blue due to color rub-off from subsequently stripped blue tapestry weave elem

Weft: Mostly dyed red wool and some undyed white wool, one Z-spun yarn, shot twice (1+1), discontinuous wefts that double back create diagonal "lazy lines" easily visible on the back of the carpet

Pile: Wool dyed dark blue, medium blue, light blue, dark red, dark purple-red, pinkish red, dark yellow, pale green, slightly corrosive dark brown, and undyed white, all two Z-spun yarns plied S Undyed white cotton, two Z-spun yarns plied S

Knot: Symmetrical knot, approximately 80V x 43H per decimeter

Edges: Original edges missing; all of the present edge finish is a later repair

Ends: A few millimeters of light-blue tapestry weave at each end; cotton warps projecting from the bottom (illustrated as top) of the rug are from restoration

Detail

Reverse view

26

"Kiz-Gördes" Carpet

West Anatolia, Gördes district, 19th century
Gift of James F. Ballard, 76:1929
Published: Dimand 1935, pl. XXXVII, as "Betrothal Rug, Turkish,
Asia Minor, Kis-Ghiordes, XVIII Century"; Walker 1988, No. 14

The 7/4 knot ratio is easily seen in the difference in width of the side and end borders; the vertical density increases toward the top of the rug, which makes the top horizontal border narrower than the bottom. Because the design of the carpet is driven by the central field, the side borders are arbitrarily interrupted at the top.

Among the many fictions of the rug market that have emerged as "fact" in rug literature is the story that late Gördes carpets such as these double-ended so-called "Kiz-Gördes", with their white ground, very detailed,w even ornate designs, and characteristic borders and purple-red motifs, were a special type woven by young girls for their dowries—hence the appellation "Kiz-Gördes or "young-girl-Gördes." They are legitimately attributed to Gördes, because their colors and motifs are found in a large group of late Gördes prayer carpets, and because of their structural similarity to other Gördes weavings. These carpets were especially coveted by collectors of Ballard's era.

The typical design found in the St. Louis carpet incorporates a central panel graced by a medallion with a classical Anatolian quatrefoil ornament. Some see this central panel as a doubled-ended prayer rug; certainly the pendant motif recalling the hanging lamp, the floral designs of the spandrels with their large carnations, and the horizontal panels above and below, recall the two Ballard Gördes prayer rugs already discussed. The small-scale repeating pattern of the field and the diagonal stripes in the borders remains an enigma; some see it as a descendent of an early Anatolian carpet type thought to represent the pelt of a snow leopard, but in all likelihood it is yet another original creation of the enterprising Gördes commercial workshops in the nineteenth century.

Further reading: Dimand 1973 (the Metropolitan's Ballard carpet 22.100.107 is quite similar); Markarian 1988; Denny 2002 (for the quatrefoil medallion and classical survivals)

Length: Approximately 147 cm

Width: Approximately 129 cm

Warp: Dyed light-orange wool, two Z-spun yarns plied S, alternate warps slightly depressed

Weft: Undyed white wool, uniform, regular, one Z-spun yarn plied S; shot twice (1+1)

Pile: Wool dyed dark blue, light blue, yellow-green, purple-red, orange, yellow, dark brown and undyed white, all two Z-spun yarns pied S

Knot: Symmetrical, pulled slightly to left; approximately 70V x 40H per decimeter

Edges: Original edges have been rewrapped

Ends: Both have been stripped

Detail

Reverse view

27

Mejidiye (Mecidiye) Prayer Carpet

West Anatolia, probably Gördes district, mid 19th century
Gift of James F. Ballard, 75:1929
Published: Dimand 1935, pl. XXXVIII

The faded green color is problematic; it is probably an early synthetic dye, made by treating indigo with a sulfur compound to produce a one-step green instead of the usual two-step Anatolian green, in which wool was dyed in both weld and indigo.

Carpets such as these, named after the mid-century Ottoman sultan Abdulmecid I (r. 1839–1861), are a bizarre footnote to the history of western Anatolian weaving. They reflect the Europeanizing style of the times, greatly influenced by the neo-baroque style of Second Empire France. In acquiring this carpet, Ballard was no doubt attempting to collect a representative of almost all of the well-known types of Turkish carpets then known to dealers and collectors.

The vaguely Second Empire colors of the "Mecidiye Gördes" rugs, of which the Ballard example is one of the very best, show the powerful influence of European taste in nineteenth-century Anatolia. However, the arrow-head shaped cypress tree forms are the descendants of the same motifs that appear in the Syrian and Egyptian carpets in the Ballard Collection [CATS.3-5].

Much more interesting than the vocabulary of motifs is the syntax of the carpet; the notion of a border is maintained by the shift in the ground color, but there is no outlining at all in the design. Carpets such as these were clearly invented at the behest of an entrepreneur who felt their coloration would fit better with European taste, and it is difficult to imagine anything further from the traditional Anatolian carpet aesthetic. At the same time, however, the design of the carpet reflects the almost boundless inventiveness, as well as the highly eclectic approach to taste, of nineteenth-century Gördes entrepreneurs.

Further reading: Dimand 1975 (a similar carpet, 22.100.94, was given by Ballard to the Metropolitan Museum of Art)

Length: Approximately 188 cm

Width: Approximately 112 cm

Warp: Undyed white wool, two Z-spun yarns plied S, alternate warps slightly depressed

Weft: Undyed white wool, variable thickness, irregular, shot twice (1+1), three times (1+2//), four times (2// + 2//), five times (2//+3//); discontinuous wefts cause diagonal lazy lines in the structure

Pile: Wool dyed dark blue, dark purple-red, pink, very pale green, salmon-tan and undyed white; all two Z-spun yarns plied S

Knot: Symmetrical, pulled slightly to left, 57V x 30H per decimeter

Edges: Both have a selvedge of one warp wrapped in white weft wool

Ends: Both stripped

Detail

Reverse view

Kula Carpets

It is easy in hindsight to find some fault with Ballard's echoing of contemporary values in Anatolian carpets with his collecting of Gördes and Kula examples in large numbers. Certainly by the middle of the twentieth century the American collector most inspired to follow Ballard's broad historical approach toward collecting, Joseph V. McMullan, had come to disdain the commercially produced west Anatolian prayer carpets from these two centers. As mentioned, he found their designs obsessively fussy, their colors often pale and anemic, and their visual impact somehow "un-Turkish" by the then-prevailing standards of collecting.

Ballard collected many different types of Kula carpets, including several variations on the coupled-column theme (four of them in St. Louis), a few carpets utilizing multiple narrow borders, and a single carpet of the "cemetery rug" type, depicting small houses and cypress trees over and over in a pattern in the central field. The four Ballard Kula carpets in St. Louis all have good colors, considerable artistic impact, and are in exceptionally fine condition; looking at them, it is interesting to ponder the Metropolitan's choice from the Ballard collection in 1922. Two of these were miscatalogued as "Ghiordes" (22.100.83 and 22.100.84), and three others were of a "busy" multi-bordered type not found in St. Louis (22.100.79, 22.100.80, and 22.100.81). One (22.100.79) was of the "cemetery rug" design type. By the standards of the early twentieth century, the Metropolitan probably chose well; but, with historical hindsight, the Kula rugs in St. Louis are by far the more attractive and artistically pleasing by the standards of the early twenty-first.

Further reading: Dimand 1975

28

Prayer Carpet with Red-ground Field and Pendant Ornament

West Anatolia, probably Kula, 18th century
Gift of James F. Ballard, 82:1929

At the time the restoration work was performed, the extensive re-napping in the central field matched the red of the original pile, but the original colors have remained strong while the ca. 1900 repairs have faded. Weaving of the rug was begun at the top end above the niche as illustrated.

Rugs of this sort have been attributed to two different west Anatolian districts, Gördes and Kula, which wove superficially similar but technically quite different types of small prayer carpet. Because of the two-level warp, and the almost 1/1 knotting ratio, this carpet is in all probability a product of the Kula district. Were it of the Gördes district, we would expect warps on one level, red or white weft with a very regular structure, marked packing of the knots, giving an almost 2/1 vertical/horizontal ratio, and weaving that began at the top of the design.

This carpet is clearly inspired by Ottoman court carpets in *seccade* or prayer-rug format woven in Egypt in the sixteenth and seventeenth centuries. The shape of the niche and spandrels, the vine arabesques of the spandrels and the major border with palmettes and cockaded lotus-blossoms, all relate directly to the earlier classical prototypes. The colors are in the main highly saturated, and there is little of the palette of browns, beiges and tans found in later Kula carpets. The result, despite the fading of the field repairs, is one of brilliant colors and a complex design that is given visual focus and stability by the simple and ornamented central field.

Length: Approximately 178 cm

Width: Approximately 122 cm

Warp: Undyed white wool, two Z-spun yarns plied S, alternate warps moderately depressed

Weft: Undyed dark brown wool, one Z-spun yarn; shot twice (1+1), three times (1+1+1) and four times (2// + 2//); discontinuous wefts that double back create diagonal "lazy lines" easily visible on the back of the carpet, and in the lower part of the worn central field

Pile: Wool dyed red, dark blue, light blue, yellow, light-green faded to ecru, corrosive dark brown, and undyed white; all Z-spun yarns plied S

Knot: Symmetrical, approximately 35–36V x 35–36H per decimeter

Edges: Both restored, rewrapped

Ends: Both stripped and rewoven

Detail

Reverse view

29

Coupled-column Kula Prayer Carpet (*seccade*)

West Anatolia, Kula district, early 19th century
Gift of James F. Ballard, 83:1929

The general condition of this carpet is very good; the array of tans and beiges is indicative of a later date than the previous example, and it appears some of these colors have faded from their originally intended hues.

This is an archetypal Kula carpet in quite good condition with harmonious colors. The bottom of the carpet as woven is at the top of the carpet as illustrated. There have evidently been changes in some of the original coloration due to dyes that were not color-fast in water and/or light. This carpet is closely related to a sister carpet Ballard gave to the Metropolitan Museum of Art (22.100.83), but the St. Louis carpet is far more faithful to the coupled-column Ottoman prayer rug that served as its prototype [FIG.14], the only surviving complete example of which is likewise in the Ballard Collection in the Metropolitan (22.100.51).

This carpet exhibits a rich variety of border and guard-border designs, and equally original panels below and above the central field. The interest—sometimes apparently bordering on artistic obsession—in borders seen in Kula weavings explains the decision to turn the spaces between each pair of coupled columns into borders as well.

Length: Approximately 183 cm

Width: Approximately 122 cm

Warp: Undyed white wool, two Z-spun yarns plied S, alternate warps moderately depressed

Weft: Undyed white wool; dyed red wool; all one Z-spun yarn, shot twice (1+1) and three times (1+2//); discontinuous wefts that double back create diagonal "lazy lines" easily visible on the back of the carpet

Pile: Wool dyed red, dark blue, medium blue, dark brown/black, medium brown, tan (the tan may originally have been yellow-green from an indigo sulfonic dye), and undyed white; all two Z-spun yarns plied S

Knot: Symmetrical, approximately 39V x 36–37H per decimeter

Edges: Both have been re-selvedged

Ends: Both are stripped, with some reweaving

Detail

Reverse view

30

Two-column Kula Prayer Carpet (*seccade*)

West Anatolia, Kula district, mid-19th century
Gift of James F. Ballard, 85:1929
Published: Dimand 1935, pl. XLI

The process of making a single ornamented border out of two discrete thin columns seen in the previous Kula example [CAT.29] has now in this Kula prayer carpet run its course. The columns have effectively disappeared. They no longer have any bases or capitals, and represent instead abstract "downward" extensions of the light-blue spandrels with their small repeated ornaments. A row of carnations at the "bottom" of the niche is a vestigial indication of the flowers of paradise, while an elaborate pendant at the "top" of the central arch contains an elaborate floral bouquet springing from a small water ewer. This, in the weaver's view, was of course right side up; but it hangs upside-down if we attempt to recognize the original architectural origins and symbolism of the portal to paradise that originally inspired prayer rugs of this type.

The splendid condition of this carpet gives us a vivid idea of the impression that Kula rugs once made, an impression all too frequently lacking in surviving examples that were chemically bleached to soften their colors, or beaten into oblivion under shod feet in North American interiors.

Length: Approximately 191 cm

Width: Approximately 130 cm

Warp: Undyed white wool, two Z-spun yarns plied S, alternate warps moderately depressed

Weft: Undyed white, light brown and dark brown wool, all one Z-spun yarn, shot twice (1+1) and three times (1+1+1)

Pile: Wool dyed dark purple-red, dark blue, light blue, rich purple-brown, yellow, tan (the tan may originally have been yellow-green from an indigo-sulfonic dye), corrosive brown-black, and undyed white; all two Z-spun yarns plied S

Knot: Symmetrical, approximately 42–43V x 33–34H per decimeter

Edges: Both exhibit narrow selvedge of tan wool over two single warps

Ends: Both are stripped

Detail

Reverse view

31

Two-column Kula Prayer Carpet (*seccade*)

West Anatolia, Kula district, early 19th century
Gift of James F. Ballard, 186:1929
Published: Dimand, 1935, pl. XL; Walker 1988, No. 17

By today's standards this is an archetypal Kula carpet, which despite a few repairs is in quite good condition, and displays uncharacteristically unfaded and harmonious colors.

This final Ballard Kula carpet in St. Louis is very much of the same type as **CAT.30**. It exhibits a number of design similarities with its mate, while showing the individuality of detail that ensures that no two Turkish prayer rugs are ever identical.

Further reading: Dimand 1975

Length: Approximately 162 cm

Width: Approximately 114 cm

Warp: Undyed white wool, occasionally one ply each of undyed white and undyed brown wool; two Z-spun yarns plied S, uniform; painted yellow at each end while on the loom; alternate warps moderately depressed

Weft: Undyed white wool; dyed pinkish-red and rarely blue wool; all one Z-spun yarn, shot twice (1+1) and three times (1+1+1); discontinuous wefts that double back create diagonal "lazy lines" easily visible on the back of the carpet

Pile: Wool dyed dark red, dark blue, light blue, green, light and dark tan (the light tan may originally have been yellow-green), corrosive dark brown, and undyed white; all two Z-spun yarns plied S

Knot: Symmetrical, approximately 44V x 31H per decimeter

Edges: Both have a selvedge of two warps very tightly wrapped with dark and light tan and green pile yarn

Ends: Both are stripped

Detail

Reverse view

Southeast Anatolian Carpets

Carpet studies are still developing rapidly in knowledge and sophistication. Before we look down on the silly mistakes of earlier generations of scholars it is instructive to ponder how our own hypotheses may look fifty years hence. These two carpets, here attributed to Kurdish weavers in southeast Anatolia, may serve us as a useful proving ground both for art-historical reasoning and art-historical humility.

The entire question of Kurdish carpets is fraught with political implications, born of a situation in which substantial Kurdish ethnic minorities form a significant population element in Iran, Syria, Iraq and Turkey, but have no state of their own. For decades the Turkish government denied the existence of Kurds as a separate group. They sought to prove that the Kurds' two languages were Turkic dialects when in fact they are manifestly of the Indo-European family and allied to Farsi. These efforts were compounded by some Turkish publications attempting to subsume ethnic Kurdish weaving in Anatolia under the generic rubric of "Yürük"—that, is "nomadic"—weaving. It all had the opposite of the intended effect, ultimately exposing some of these protagonists to ridicule and relegating many of their "scholarly" efforts to oblivion.

There is however a vast spectrum of carpet weaving by ethnic Kurds across the Islamic world that makes easy identification of their many subgroups impossible. After all, in two towns close to each other in the Kurdish-speaking area of Iran, Bijar and Sanandaj, we find two traditions of pile carpets that are perhaps the most extreme opposites in modern carpet history. The effort to pursue Kurdish weaving backward in time is even more difficult.

One supposed indication of Kurdish weaving is the phenomenon of offset knotting, in which successive horizontal rows of knots in a pile carpet are tied are one warp offset from the previous row, instead of each row of knots sitting exactly on top of the previous row. A well-known group of small Kurdish pile bag faces with a central design of diamond-shaped rectangles is famous for employing this technique in the central field, but in the borders continuing the traditional knotting structure of orderly vertical as well as horizontal rows of knots. There is a reason for offset knotting in this group of small carpets, and in other groups of supposed Kurdish weaving employing hexagonal motifs rather than octagonal ones (typified by **CAT.32**): it makes possible much steeper diagonal lines in the design, suitable for hexagons and for the vertically elongated diamond shapes of the small bags. The weaver and carpet scholar Marla Mallett, in "Offset Knotting: Where and Why?" (*http://www.marlamallett.com/offset_knotting. htm*), has discussed this matter in some detail.

The question then arises as to whether offset knotting found in carpets such as **CAT.33**, which do not have geometric designs of diamonds or hexagons, is also an indication of Kurdish provenance. Given the insecurity of attribution of origins to many early carpets, scholars are tempted to rely on rules of thumb. *Jufti* knots (knots tied over four rather than two warps) are thought to be an indication of carpets woven in Khurasan, northeastern Iran. Large floral and medallion carpets of Persianate design with four-ply cotton warps are thought to be from Iran, while those with six or more plies are thought to be from India. And carpets with offset knotting are thought to be Kurdish, from southeastern Anatolia or northern Syria and Iraq. The long-term efficacy of these rules of thumb may or may not turn out to be valid. At present, however, the prevailing opinion is that **CAT.33** may well be one of the earliest Kurdish carpets known to have survived.

Further reading: Beattie 1970; Bruggemann and Böhmer 1980; Franses 2004

32

Carpet with Hexagonal Compartments

Southeast Anatolia, early 19th century

Gift of James F. Ballard, 89:1929

Published: Dimand 1935, pl. LXII (where it is called a Kazak carpet from the Caucasus); Walker 1988, no. 25

A carpet of a type that is typically assigned to Kurdish weavers because of the offset knotting used to make the steep diagonals of the hexagonal compartments. This example has incredibly soft wool in a very long and lustrous pile, and is very beautifully woven despite the variations in wefting. The faded colors may have resulted from extensive exposure to sunlight, or more likely to the effects of local water on the dyeing process; the carpet is highly typical of works from southern and southeastern Anatolia.

Happily none of the doubts about age and provenance mentioned above exists for the more recent of the two carpets in this southeast Anatolian grouping. It is roughly designed, with extremely long pile, but with tight and precise knotting despite the irregular wefting visible on the back. Ballard's Yürük carpet (a generic term for rugs woven by nomads in Anatolia) probably comes from a Kurdish tribal weaver in south-central or southeast Anatolia, and was woven in a winter pasture (*kishlak*) close to the Syrian border, before she migrated north to central Anatolia's *yayla* or alpine pastures with her flocks in the summer. With beautiful colors, beautiful wool, and beautiful construction, this powerful work of art was a complete enigma to James Ballard as to its origins and history. But whereas the conventionally minded collector values only that to which he can attach a name, Ballard knew it was beautiful, and he bought it; he knew it was important, and gave it to the Saint Louis Art Museum. Do we encounter this kind of assurance and disregard for market value (or is it simply raw courage?) among the top rank of collectors today?

Further Reading: Beattie 1970; Brüggemann and Böhmer 1980; Franses 2004

Length: Approximately 185 cm

Width: Approximately 122 cm

Warp: Undyed white wool, two Z-spun yarns plied S, one level

Weft: Dyed red wool, one Z-spun red yarn shot twice (1+1), three times (1+2//) and four times (2//+2//, 1+1+1+1)

Pile: Wool dyed pale red-orange, brown-red, darker purple, pale purple, pale blue-green faded almost to white, unfaded pale-green, medium blue, yellow, corrosive dark brown-black, and undyed white; all two Z-spun yarns plied S

Knot: Symmetrical, approximately 44V x 27H per decimeter

Edges: Each two bundles of two warps wrapped in varicolored one-ply wool yarn in pile colors

Ends: Top: approximately one centimeter red tapestry weave

Bottom: Stripped

Detail

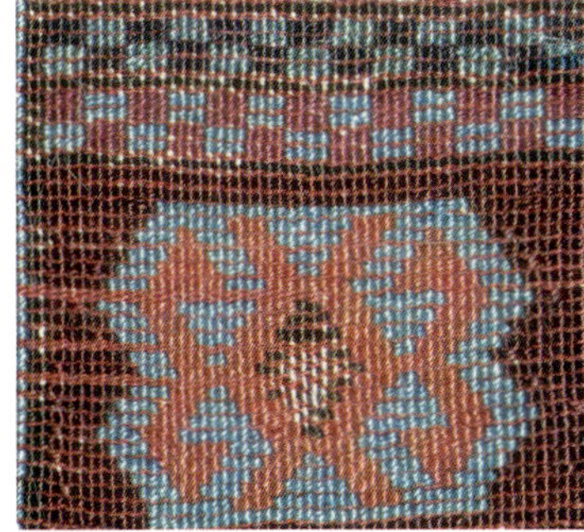

Reverse view

33

Medallion Carpet with White-ground Border

Probably southeast Anatolia, late 17th–mid 18th century

Gift of James F. Ballard, 116:1929

Published: Dimand 1935, pl. LXII (where it is called a
Kazak carpet from the Caucasus); Walker 1988, no. 25

The offset knotting of this carpet argues for a southeast Anatolian provenance in an area of ethnic Kurdish weavers. The almost complete absence of a single line of dark-brown wool outlining colored areas is a characteristic of this group of carpets. Because the back of the carpet is flat, one can easily see that the individual knots are much wider than they are high. Despite the triple wefting, this results in a knot count that is much higher in the vertical direction. In order to achieve the very steep diagonals of the design, the weaver had to use offset knotting, visible in the detail illustration. The inclusion of a few knots of silk pile serves as a *nazarlik,* an amulet guarding against the evil eye. This carpet is widely regarded as one of the most important and beautiful in the Ballard collection.

This medallion carpet with offset knotting throughout its structure is one of the most important, most beautiful, and most intriguing rugs in James Ballard's collection. With its intense coloration, dark purple dye, and absence of outlining between color areas, it shows many characteristics of what some now call Karapinar carpets. These were woven in Konya province in central Anatolia, recognized first by May Hamilton Beattie and now by many scholars as the site of some of the most powerful, original, and beautiful Anatolian carpet weaving. Two factors, however, militate against the Karapinar attribution. One is the extensive and sometimes almost random use of offset knotting throughout the carpet. Offset knotting is a hallmark of Kurdish nomadic weaving from southeast Anatolia. It is seen in the powerful carpet with a design of staggered rows of octagons with quatrefoil medallions [**CAT.32**] that Dimand had thought in 1935 to have been woven in the Kazak district of the Lesser Caucasus. The second factor is the complete absence in the design of any stylized Ottoman flowers, which we have come to expect in most Karapinar rugs, a feature that has led the present writer to dub such carpets "Kara Memi" rugs, after the sixteenth-century Ottoman court artist who invented the floral vocabulary. There is one carpet that may be a close sibling to the Ballard medallion carpet: a much larger two-medallion carpet at one time in the possession of The Textile Gallery in London. Consensus among scholars on the origins and the age of these two carpets is, however, still elusive.

Length: Approximately 229 cm

Width: Approximately 164 cm

Warp: Undyed white wool, uniform, two Z-spun yarns plied S, one level

Weft: Dyed dark purple-red wool, one Z-spun yarn; shot mostly three times (1+2// or 2//+1) and rarely twice (1+1)

Pile: Wool, dyed dark red, pink, purple-brown, blue with marked abrash between medium and light values, blue-green, salmon pink-orange, dark brown-black and undyed white; all two Z-spun yarns plied S Silk, dyed magenta, apparently two Z-spun yarns plied S, found in two tiny blue-bordered rectangles in the top left-hand corner of the white border

Knot: Symmetrical, almost random mixture of stacked and offset knotting throughout the carpet; approximately 38–40V x 25–26H per decimeter

Edges: None original, various repairs

Ends: Both stripped, restored and/or reconstructed

Detail

Reverse view

Central Anatolian Carpets

arpets conventionally attributed to central Anatolia—a broad geographic area from Konya and Ankara provinces in the west to Sivas and Kayseri provinces in the east—have been historically under-represented in museum collections in Europe and North America. There are several reasons for this. First, unlike their western Anatolian counterparts, early carpets from this region were less frequently exported to Europe, and as a consequence also appear far less often in European paintings of the fifteenth through the eighteenth centuries. Second, as a direct result of their relative isolation from Mediterranean marketplaces, they appear to have been less frequently produced in the larger sizes and formats that European buyers wanted. The true richness of the central and eastern Anatolian traditions has only begun to be recognized since the 1970s: as access for study of carpets in the Turkish and Islamic Art Museum in Istanbul began to open up; as the new Vakıflar Museum in Istanbul began surveying and collecting mosque carpets under its then curator Belkis (Acar) Balpınar; and in particular as the unusually rich collections of the Great Mosque of Divriği, first carefully studied in 1973, became known to carpet scholars.

The richness of central and eastern Anatolian carpet designs has been a revelation. It was once thought that Turkish village weavers avoided the medallion format in their carpets. The Divriği carpets revealed an amazing variety of carpets in the medallion layout. It was once thought that central Anatolian carpets tended to follow deep-rooted and highly localized stylistic traditions. We now see an amazing variety of stylistic links that testify to widespread carpet commerce and an active interchange of artistic ideas. From sometimes enigmatic early documents mentioning the wonderful carpets of Konya province, and in particular those of the market town of Aksaray situated on the intersection of two major trade routes, we have long been aware that central Anatolia produced important carpets. But it has taken a long time for us to begin to identify these carpets and their historical development.

Today, four major world museum carpet collections allow one to assess the true variety and richness of the historical spectrum of Anatolian carpets in general, and central Anatolian pile carpet weaving in particular. Two of them, the Turkish and Islamic Art Museum and the Vakıflar Carpet Museum, are in Istanbul. One is in Europe, housed in the Museum für Islamische Kunst on the Museum Island in the Spree River, in the heart of Berlin. And one is divided between the Metropolitan Museum in New York and Saint Louis Art Museum.

The four central Anatolian carpets in the Ballard collection form another example of Ballard's prescient collecting. James Ballard's "Anatolian eye" even worked when one of the carpets in question [CAT.35] was attributed by experts—in this case the capable and renowned Maurice Dimand—to Central Asia.

At first glance these four carpets might not look as if they had anything much in

common, except that three of them were obviously woven by right-handed weavers (whose more powerful right arm, wielding the weft beater, was more effective on the right side of the carpet than on the left, thus making the right side of three of these carpets shorter than the left side). One is the work of a left-handed weaver. In fact, all were probably woven in central Anatolia, in Konya province (modern Turkey's largest in area), but in remarkably diverse techniques. Three utilize a centralized medallion format, and one was inspired by, of all things, a fifteenth-century Venetian silk velvet.

The oldest of the four medallion carpets [CAT.36], beautifully designed and woven and marvelously preserved, represents the summit of what many scholars have called early Karapinar weaving in Konya province, and may be for many the crown jewel of the St. Louis collection. The harmonious medallion design traces its origins to fifteenth-century Islamic bookbinding, but the sprays of hyacinths attached to each pendant are purely sixteenth-century Ottoman in their origin. For this artist, the field was the important thing: the border is relegated to the role of a picture frame. The symmetry of the field is precise, but the "lappet" knotted-pile elem panels, partially stripped at the bottom end, with their stylized tulips, are completely random in coloration.

The Karapinar carpet's alter ego is from Karaman, further to the south [CAT.35]. With incredibly long pile and limited colors without white pile at all, this shorted version of a type normally seen as a long runner was probably woven as a *yatak*, or mattress rug.

Sharing a layout with the Karapinar rug, it is otherwise its direct opposite.

Far more complex in design and layout is the Karapinar rug with a white-ground border [CAT.34]. This unusual design is also based on the bookbinding medallion layout, but it has been put together as a work of art with immense originality and little regard for the delicate niceties of the prototype. It incorporates the ancient symbol of three dots and two wavy bands known as *çintemani*, originally of Buddhist origin, that permeates Ottoman Turkish art from the fifteenth century onward and serves as the ultimate good luck symbol.

A fourth Ballard rug from central Anatolia [CAT.37] has at first glance perhaps the most incomprehensible design, but belongs to a fairly well-known group of central Anatolian carpets whose field design was inspired by Italian velvets, probably from Venice, that were evidently imported into the Ottoman empire as early as the first half of the sixteenth century.

Further Reading: Paquin 1992, Paquin 1996, Klose 2000, Denny 2002

34

Small Medallion Carpet with *Çintemani* Border

Central Anatolia, Konya province, Karapinar district, late 17th–18th century

Gift of James F. Ballard, 107:1929

Published: Dimand 1935, pl. LV, where it is called a "Rager" rug

Despite the faded re-napping, this carpet is one of the most interesting Karapinar rugs to have come down to us. The Ballard rug is distinguished by its white ground *çintemani* border of three dots and a wavy band. A similar carpet in two fragments is in the Turkish and Islamic Art Museum, Istanbul, Nos. 399 and 445; see Ölçer and Denny 1999, pl. 4 and p. 7.

This carpet, loosely based on a medallion layout seen in bookbinding, is a work of art of immense originality with little regard for the delicate niceties of the prototype. The leaf arabesques in the corner-pieces are symmetrical side to side and end to end, but their forms have become almost completely abstract. And the weaver has created a border and end "calipers" to the central field that repeat one of the most emblematic of all Ottoman Turkish motifs, called *çintemani* (originally a Sanskrit term meaning "auspicious jewel").

These groups of three circles and wavy lines originally stem from Buddhist iconography, where they were depicted as three flaming pearls in the headdress of religious figures. The apotropaic symbolism of the motifs ended up being diffused far to the West, where as early as the tenth century we see the motif appearing in the pottery of Abbasid Samarra. In the Timurid Empire in Iran and Central Asia after the late fourteenth century, the motif was included on the coinage. By Ottoman times, while its origins had been entirely forgotten, the design of "balls" or "spots," mentioned in Ottoman documents as "*benekli*," had been adopted in most artistic media. The most popular motif in fifteenth-century Bursa velvets, by the sixteenth century it was found on a variety of Ottoman silk textiles, and was used extensively in the polychrome pottery of Iznik. It was also used by the commercial carpet weavers of Ushak in west Anatolia. A medallion carpet in the Metropolitan Museum, and several others in Istanbul, use the design of three spots and pairs of wavy lines as a field motif. It also appears in a few Ottoman court carpets woven in Cairo; the wavy flame motifs, used in vertical pairs in their original form, also appear as flames in a brazier in the famous *parokhet* or Torah cover from the Padua synagogue, woven in Cairene technique with Cairene materials in Egypt or even possibly Italy sometime in the sixteenth century.

A prime characteristic of the so-called "Karapinar" group is the frequent absence of a black outlining between colors in certain motifs. This is most easily seen in the spandrels of the Ballard carpet, where vaguely vegetal shapes in various colors are juxtaposed without outlines. The central field does not take its shape in the negative space defined by the four corner-pieces, as in most central Anatolian medallion carpets of this time. Instead, it appears to echo a large octofoil medallion of a type known from early medallion carpets of northwest Persia that was often incorporated into Anatolian carpets (see Kirchheim 1993, No. 178). The central pendant motif, complete with vertical "chain", and the small sprays of flowers that dot the field, almost seem to be artistic afterthoughts.

Despite the extensive repairs, this carpet makes a powerful artistic impression. It is worthwhile remembering that at the time Ballard purchased it from the Berlin dealer Heinrich Jacoby, carpets such as this were virtually unstudied and unpublished; one must imagine that Ballard's acquisition of the piece was based almost entirely on his visual response to its power and quirky originality.

Length: Approximately 241 cm

Width: Approximately 137 cm

Warp: Undyed white wool (with some brown fiber), two Z-spun yarns plied S, one level

Weft: Dyed red wool, one Z-spun yarn shot twice (1+1), three times (1+1+1 or 1+2//), four times (1+1+1+1 or 1+2//+1)

Pile: Wool dyed red, blue, purple, pinkish-tan, green, (possibly undyed) light brown, dark brown, and undyed white; all two Z-spun yarns plied two

Knot: Symmetrical, pulled to left, approximately 32V x 24–25H per decimeter

Edges: Each one warp wrapped in red wool

Ends: Both stripped and rewoven

Detail

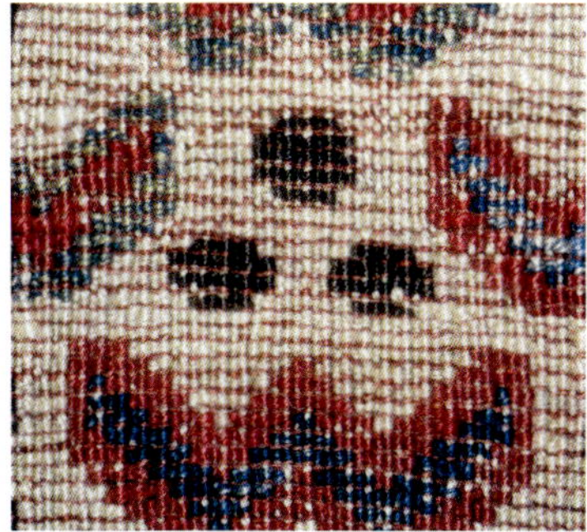

Reverse view

35

Small Quatrefoil Medallion Carpet

Central Anatolia, Karaman district, early 19th century

Gift of James F. Ballard, 123:1929

Published: Dimand, 1935, pl. LXVI, where it is identified as
"Central Asiatic, Afghan, XIX century"

A very thick and heavy carpet with long pile; heavy restoration at the top end is knotted on a soft wool warp. Restoration aside, this rug is in marvelous condition with pile close to its original length.

This example from the district of Karaman to the south of Konya is the rough-hewn alter ego to Ballard's elegant medallion carpet [CAT.36]. With no white pile at all, a limited range of colors, and incredibly long pile, it is a short version of a type normally seen as a long runner, which was probably woven for use as a *yatak*, or mattress rug.

It is interesting to note that the only carpets that can positively be assigned to Karapinar, although quite different in weave from this example, also employ the same quatrefoil medallion, and were woven on similarly narrow looms, often in the long rug or *kenareh* format.

Length: Approximately 175–85 cm

Width: Approximately 120 cm

Warp: Undyed hard white wool, irregular thickness, two Z-spun yarns plied Z, one level

Weft: Apparently undyed brown wool, one Z-spun yarn, shot twice (1+1)

Pile: Wool dyed dark red, light red, green, purple, light blue, slightly corrosive black-brown; all two Z-spun yarns plied S; very long pile length (around 2 cm)

Knot: Symmetrical, pulled very slightly to the right; approximately 26–27V x 23–24H per decimeter

Edges: Four cables of two warps each, wrapped in red, white, and brown wool

Ends: Both stripped

Detail

Reverse view

36

Small Medallion Carpet

Central Anatolia, probably Konya province, 17th century
Gift of James F. Ballard, 129:1929

Typically stiff handle due to the thick foundation, with lustrous but very hard wool; very regularly woven; despite wear and repairs, a carpet with stunning presence.

This is probably the oldest central Anatolian medallion carpet in the Ballard collection, and it is certainly one of the finest, if not the finest, of its type known today in terms of its artistic quality and overall fine state of preservation. The design has its roots in the classical International Style shared by Anatolia, Greater Iran (Samarkand to Tabriz), Mamluk Egypt and Syria in the fifteenth century. The proportions and general layout suggest a relationship with illumination and bookbinding, where the central medallion and four corner pieces were a standard layout, and architectural decoration, where the medallion with vertical pendants was a favored design.

Two elements of the design show us the impact of the style of the far-away court design atelier in Istanbul: the eight sprays of stylized hyacinths in the field; and the compartmented end-panels of lappets decorated with stylized tulips in random color combinations. The latter echo a famous and highly influential type of Ottoman velvet cushion-cover that was widely known and copied in rugs of the Ottoman empire from the mid-sixteenth century onward. One other design element, with a far more venerable pedigree, recalls the much older geometric tradition of central Anatolian weaving: the pair of simple strap-work stars at either end of the carpet.

The main border is an elegant meandering vine with simple floral elements that clearly demonstrates that the carpet was both conceptualized and knotted beginning from the lower right corner. The outermost orange-ground guard border, which would have been identical to the innermost one, was eliminated when the carpet was narrowed; when presented with ragged edges, many carpet dealers preferred the simpler and cheaper expedient of simply stripping away the edges of a carpet, rather than the expensive alternative of reknotting all the missing areas.

Carpets such as this were designed with fairly finely drawn elements, often outlined in a dark brown, constructed in a reasonably fine weave, and with a pile clipped short enough to showcase the elegant floral and geometric design elements. Thanks to the good state of preservation, the highly saturated dyes and the shiny and hard wool of the Karaman or central Anatolian fat-tailed sheep, together with the density of the knotting and optimum pile length, have produced a vibrant and lustrous surface. It allows us to imagine the original appearance of many examples that have not survived in such excellent condition.

Carpets of this type are often attributed to the region of Karapinar in Konya province. While such carpets do have a number of common artistic and technical characteristics, the attribution of manufacture to Karapinar location itself is much less reliable.

Further reading: Oakley 2010

Length: Approximately 172 cm

Width: Approximately 116 cm

Warp: Undyed white wool, two Z-spun yarns plied S; alternate warps strongly depressed

Weft: Dyed dark red wool, one Z-spun yarn, shot twice (1+1)

Pile: Wool dyed red (strongly abrashed), red-brown, pink-red, purple, orange, dark blue, light blue, blue-green, yellow, corrosive very dark brown, undyed white; all two Z-spun yarns plied S

Knot: Symmetrical, pulled to left; approximately 43V x 39H per decimeter

Edges: Both missing, replaced with sewn-on mercerized cotton selvedge

Ends: Both stripped

Detail

Reverse view

37

Carpet with Design Taken from a Silk Velvet

Central Anatolia, 18th century

Gift of Nellie Ballard White, 304:1972

This rug has a typically robust and solid handle; its design is derived from that of a fifteenth-century Venetian silk velvet, and several parallel examples are known; see Denny 1999, pls. 90 and 91, for two in the Museum of Turkish and Islamic Arts, Istanbul.

This central Anatolia carpet has by far the most complex border—a zigzag progression of fringed floral forms in many colors on a corrosive brown field—and what is certainly the most complex and difficult-to-read field design. In fact this Ballard carpet was the first of what is now a larger group to meet the public eye; several other examples in Istanbul exhibit the same design (Museum of Turkish and Islamic Art, nos. 254, 443 and 483), which has been shown to be a paraphrase of an early Venetian silk velvet. Examples of this velvet were exported from Italy to Turkey in the fifteenth century and are still retained in the collections of the Topkapı Palace Museum.

It may seem far-fetched that comparatively small-scale European silk velvet fabrics of very fine weave would serve as the inspiration for large-scale knotted-pile wool carpets of robust construction and colorful designs made far to the east in central Anatolia. In fact the carpet medium has a long history of adapting designs from silk textiles, beginning at least as early as the fourteenth century, when a carpet of the so-called Konya group in the Museum of Turkish and Islamic Arts, Istanbul, was knotted in bright colors in a pattern inspired by a Yuan damask fabric from China (see Geijer 1963).

Further reading: Geijer 1963, Paquin 1996, Denny 1999, Klose 2000, Denny 2002

Length: Approximately 152 cm

Width: Approximately 126 cm

Warp: Undyed white wool, some undyed brown wool mixed in, two Z-spun yarns plied S; alternate warps moderately depressed

Weft: Dyed red wool, one Z-spun yarn shot twice (1+1) or three times (1+2//)

Pile: Wool dyed red, yellow, green, dark-blue, light-blue, corrosive dark brown and undyed white; all two Z-spun yarns plied S

Knot: Symmetrical, pulled slightly to left; approximately 38–40 V x 29–30H per decimeter

Edges: Original edges both replaced

Ends: Top end has approximately 2.5 cm red tapestry weave; bottom end has the same

Detail

Reverse view

Central Anatolian Prayer Rugs

The prayer rug genre has for centuries been a highly favored one in Anatolian weaving. It is ideally suited to the small vertical looms used under the low roofs of Anatolian village homes. Given the power of the classical carpet-weaving tradition in Anatolia, and the existence of beautiful and influential models in court weaving of the sixteenth century, the environment for the weaving of such small carpets was a good one. The market is a different matter; in our discussion of Gördes and Kula rugs we suggested that a nineteenth-century European market for these somewhat atypical Islamic prayer rugs might have been an Orientalist phenomenon, explaining why relatively so very few rugs of this production have turned up in Turkey itself. In the case of central Anatolian prayer rugs stemming from the classical tradition the situation is quite different, with many examples having been given to mosques as votive gifts protected in perpetuity under the terms of religious endowments (*vakıf* in modern Turkish).

The white-ground coupled-column prayer rug from the Konya area [CAT.40] is a type found in significant numbers in central European churches where its powerful Islamic religious significance was probably not understood. Strongly influenced by the sixteenth-century prototype, the carpet demonstrates two areas where the central Anatolian weavers departed from the classical formula: the border and the spandrels of the arches. In the prototype, the border had a very complex, delicate, curvilinear composition of feathery leaves, tulips, complex lotus palmettes, and tiny sprays of hyacinths; the arch spandrels had an equally complex arabesque of split leaves. Such complexity cannot be supported by the relatively coarser weave of the Konya-area tradition, nor is it appropriate for the vivid colors favored in central Anatolia. Thus even the early copies of court rugs from Konya simplify the border, using small medallions decorated with stylized tulips, which are also seen in a row above the crenellated parapet at the top of the composition.

Two further Ballard red-ground prayer rugs from central Anatolia have the same general layout, without the architectural specificity of the first. The older of the two [CAT.39] keeps the same border with its small eight-lobed medallions, but the spandrels are filled with forms that must have had some sort of protective function. The more loosely woven Mujur prayer rug shows echoes of the architectural parapet, while the depictions of water-ewers in the spandrels may refer to the ritual ablutions—the washing of face, hands and feet—required of Muslims before the five daily prayers [CAT.38]. Unlike the other two examples, Mujur rugs are almost invariably woven beginning at the top of the carpet as illustrated. The precise corner articulation of Mujur rugs is often achieved by "spacers"—partial motifs—inserted at the top of each side border (at the bottom as illustrated) and somewhere in the middle of each end border.

Further reading: Ettinghausen 1974, Denny 1990, Denny 2002

38

Prayer Rug (*seccade*)

Central Anatolia, Mujur (Mucur), 19th century
Gift of James F. Ballard, 108:1929
Published: Dimand, 1935, pl. LVII; Walker 1988, No. 23

A very handsome example of this well-known type of Anatolian prayer rug. Typically for Mujur rugs, it was woven beginning from the top as illustrated, so that the complicated part of the field could be woven first. The final vertical adjustments made by the weaver to ensure a good corner articulation can be seen at the "bottom" of the yellow-ground border, while similar horizontal adjustments have been made just to the right of center of each horizontal border.

Although missing its "bottom" (actually the top) guard border, Ballard's St. Louis Mujur prayer rug is a splendid example of the type, exhibiting the typical "spacers" used on all four borders to ensure that each corner of the border contains a major motif. Those on the side borders, occurring at the end of the weaving process (at the bottom as illustrated) are simply cut-off versions of the major motif, while those on the end borders consist of three small octagons. The water pitchers in the arch spandrels are typical of Mujur prayer rugs, as is the abbreviated parapet panel "above" the arch. This carpet exhibits the typically brilliant coloring and soft wool of Mujur carpets.

Ballard gave another quite similar Mujur carpet to the Metropolitan Museum of Art (22.100.22); the Metropolitan carpet, which is one of the rare Mujur prayer carpets that has perfect corner articulation without any spacers, is otherwise not quite as impressive in either design or color as the St. Louis example.

Further reading: Dimand 1973

Length: Approximately 193 cm

Width: Approximately 132 cm

Warp: Undyed white wool, uniform, two Z-spun yarns plied S; alternate warps slightly depressed

Weft: Dyed red wool, one Z-spun yarn, shot twice (1+1)

Pile: Wool, dyed red, pale purple, medium blue, light blue, dark yellow, yellow, pale green, dark green, light brown, corrosive dark brown, undyed white; all two Z-spun yarns plied S

Knot: Symmetrical, pulled to left; approximately 39V x 33H per decimeter

Edge: Two bundles of two warps wrapped in green wool

Ends: Both stripped

Detail

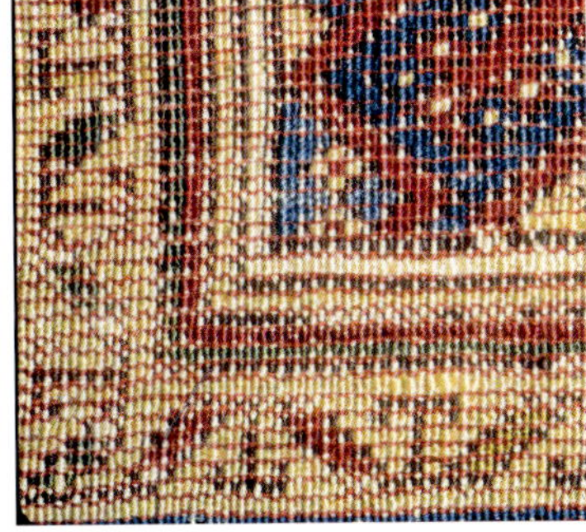

Reverse view

39

Prayer Rug (*seccade*)

Probably central or west-central Anatolia, late 18th–early 19th century
Gift of James F. Ballard, 109:1930
Published: Dimand 1935, pl. LVI; Walker 1988, No. 23

Despite very large areas of reweaving, this is a powerful example of an important type of Anatolian prayer rug. Dimand felt that, because the triangular intrusions into the field on either side of the top of the niche are also found in Milas rugs (his spelling was "Melas"), this carpet should be assigned to that district, very near the Aegean Sea. Milas rugs are almost invariably woven "right side up" as this example, but characteristically have very soft white wool in the warp, a red weft, and exhibit an entirely different repertoire of borders and spandrel designs.

A simple and exceptionally powerful design is found in this much-restored but still visually compelling prayer rug of a highly unusual design type that probably comes from central Anatolia. The small floral medallions of the border are found in many different types of Anatolian weaving. The two triangular indentations on each side of the field may represent a false start at completing the triangular arch, followed by the actual attempt. The wavy lines of the sides of the top triangle in the field indicate that the weaver wanted a steep diagonal that would use up the entire set of warps on her loom. Thus it is steeper than the technical diagonal of the carpet, but also gives a very peculiar wobbly contour to the arch. Finally, the very large finial or *alam* at the top of the arch probably is another indication that the weaver was determined to use every single inch of the warped loom.

The fanciful horizontal forms in the arch spandrels are among the compelling details of this highly original and highly eccentric carpet. Once again, condition notwithstanding, Ballard recognized the aesthetic power and merit in something that was otherwise totally unknown in his own time.

Length: Approximately 142 cm

Width: Approximately 97 cm

Warp: Undyed coarse white wool, two Z-spun yarns plied S, one level

Weft: Undyed light-brown wool, one very finely Z-spun yarn; shot twice (1+1), three times (1 + 2//) and four times (2// plus 2//)

Pile: Wool dyed dark red, red, purple, pale purple, dark blue, medium blue, blue-green, yellow, dark brown, undyed white; all two Z-spun yarns plied S

Knot: Symmetrical, pulled sharply to left, approximately 47V x 39H per decimeter

Edges: Both cut and re-selvedged

Ends: Both stripped

Detail

Reverse view

40

Coupled-column Prayer Rug

Probably west-central Anatolia, Kula district, 18th century

Gift of James F. Ballard, 113:1929

Published: Dimand 1935, pl. L, where it is described as "Ladik";
Walker 1988, No. 9

Charles Grant Ellis worried about the precision of weave and rather strident colors of this carpet; in fact, it is in reasonably good condition, probably had little exposure to light, and the precise weave is not atypical of carpets in this group.

Coupled-column prayer rugs of this type all trace their origin back to the later sixteenth century, where the most important surviving prototype is the famous Ballard prayer rug in the Metropolitan Museum of Art (22.100.51), probably woven in Cairo of S-spun wool from Ottoman court designs [**FIG.14**].

Countless examples have survived, many of them in Transylvanian churches in central Europe, many others in Turkish and western museums. There are endless speculations on the original roots of the design, the most recent being my own attempt to solve the riddle (Denny 2002, 5–52 and 107 ff.). The St. Louis carpet has a conventional border of small floral medallions, and a rather well-drawn series of six columns with faceted bases and abbreviated capitals. It has given up any attempt to reproduce the complex vegetal arabesques in the spandrel arches of the original, using instead a simple overall network pattern. Above the parapet are seven tulips and six carnations, while three more tulip blossoms are found at the bottom of the field.

The Ballard gift to the Metropolitan Museum included another carpet of this general type (22.100.62) with a red field. That gift was later augmented by a McMullan carpet that is almost identical to the St. Louis coupled-column rug and was undoubtedly woven in the same village (1974.149.19). The McMullan gift to the Metropolitan also included three other carpets with variations on the coupled-column theme (1974.149.18, 1974.149.20, and 1974.149.21). Another related carpet is in the Joseph Lees Williams Memorial Collection Philadelphia Museum of Art (1955-65-32).

Further reading: Dimand 1973, Ionesco 2005, Denny 2012

Length: Approximately 182 cm

Width: Approximately 121 cm

Warp: Undyed white wool, uniform, two Z-spun yarns plied S, alternate warps moderately depressed, tips at either end possibly dyed pink on the loom

Weft: Undyed white wool, uniform and highly regular, one Z-spun yarn shot twice (1+1); discontinuous wefts that double back create diagonal "lazy lines" easily visible on the back of the carpet

Pile: Wool dyed red, light red, dark blue, medium blue, orange-tan, strong yellow, corrosive dark brown, undyed white; all two Z-spun yarns plied S

Knot: Symmetrical, pulled to left, approximately 34-35V x 38-40H per decimeter

Edges: Both two single warps wrapped in various colors of pile yarn

Ends: Stripped, replaced with machine-made cotton and metal-thread fringe

Detail

Reverse view

Ladik Prayer Rugs

The best-known prayer rugs of Konya province come from the small town of Ladik and its environs. In addition to their distinctive construction, with a characteristic two-level warp easily visible from the back, Ladik prayer rugs tend to be narrower with respect to their length than most Anatolian prayer rugs. Many Ladik prayer rugs share a common border of flattened rosettes (a result of a vertical-horizontal knot ratio that may approach 3/2, or even 2/1) and tiny tulips flanked by small curved leaves, a direct if simplified descendant of the most common border found in sixteenth-century Ottoman court prayer rugs; this underlines the profound historical debt that these beautiful village rugs owe to the Ottoman classical tradition. The best Ladik rugs show an attractive range of highly saturated colors, and are constructed out of tightly spun and twisted yarns of very lustrous wool. One of the earliest types of Turkish prayer rug to gain the attention of Western collectors, Ladik prayer rugs have been highly prized for well over a century. A few Ladik carpets in other formats have survived; including small bolster covers (*yastık*) and long rugs (*kelley*). A very few rare early tapestry-woven kilim rugs from Anatolia, with a design of horizontal stripes and depictions of easily recognizable tulip blossoms, have also been attributed to Ladik (Denny 2012, 128–29).

The central niche panel in Ladik prayer rugs, commonly found under a triangular "arch" form, undoubtedly symbolizes the gateway to paradise. Some early examples show the tripartite gateway motif found in its original form in the famous Ballard Ottoman coupled-column prayer rug in the Metropolitan Museum of Art [**FIG.14**]. In some examples the columns have disappeared, while the triple arch form remains at the "top of the field" design. In addition to recalling the gateway to paradise, the arched form in Anatolian prayer rugs also echoes the form of the *mihrab*, the flat niche found on the *qibla* or Mecca-facing wall of a mosque that indicates the direction one faces during prayer. Indeed, the stepped forms seen on the sides of the triangular "arch" in Ladik prayer rugs has close parallels in mihrabs found in some Anatolian mosques.

While the great majority of Ladik prayer rugs show a single-color plain field under the arch or arches, in some examples we see a field decorated with shrub- or flower-like forms, symbolizing the verdure of paradise as described in the *Qur'an*. A few examples also show a hanging lamp in the middle of the field that refers directly to the passage from the *Qur'an*, chapter 24 verse 35, where a visual metaphor for the unseeable and unimaginable God is offered as the image of a glass oil-lamp hanging in a niche (Denny 1991). The most common field color in Ladik prayer rugs is red; examples in green are also known; more rarely, blue and yellow, as well as white, are also employed.

The design of the majority of Ladik prayer rugs also incorporates a panel of long-stemmed tulips, usually found with crenellations at their base, "above" the arch or arches of the portal of paradise that defines these prayer carpets. The relationship between the panel of tulips and the niche panel in the center of Ladik rugs is quite fluid; most examples show the arched panel below, and the tulips growing upward from the crenellations above it, echoing the Ottoman court prototypes. Some examples have the flowers "growing" in the opposite direction to that of the arch, and in some the floral panel is placed below rather than above the arch.

Ladik rugs are also often woven "upside-down"—that is, the weaver begins the rug at the end that is the top when we display the rug with the arch pointing upwards. The reason for this was the practical advantage of finishing the most complex part of the design, the top (with arches and floral panels) first. The much simpler open field "under" the arch could be created last, where it could be finished in a manner more likely to result in a completed design that took up the largest amount of space on the small vertical loom used by the weaver (Denny 2015).

In the St. Louis Ladik group, the two carpets with vestigial triple arches (without the coupled columns) were woven beginning at the top as illustrated; while the other two, with a single steep and stepped arch at the top, were woven from the bottom as shown.

As a result of field research in the Ladik area, the distinguished Turkish carpet scholar Belkis Balpinar found that a subgroup of Ladik prayer rugs with a distinctive meandering vine border, typified by **CAT.44**, were associated with the village of Innice, a few kilometers from the market town of Ladik. Most Innice rugs have been woven "right side up", from the bottom as illustrated.

fig. 17
Ladik prayer rug, central Anatolia,
late 18th century. 117 x 183 cm.
Metropolitan Museum of Art,
New York, Gift of James F. Ballard,
1922.100.63

The popularity of Ladik prayer rugs such as these as gifts to mosques is best illustrated by the fact that well over a dozen were found in the Alaeddin Mosque in Konya in the early twentieth century; this group is now in the Museum of Turkish and Islamic Art in Istanbul (Denny 1999, cat. 127–34). Another very large group of Ladik carpets is today in the Museum of Pious Foundations (Vakıflar Müzesi) in Istanbul (Balpinar 1988). In addition to the common red field, some of these Ladik carpets have fields in blue, green, and yellow. While most show designs oriented similarly to those in all four Ballard rugs—the row of tulips growing "up" over the top of the gateway arch—some, as mentioned, have the gate arch and the tulip panel "pointing" in opposite directions. This suggests that many weavers were oblivious to the architectural meaning of the design. With the exception of the Innice group, nearly all of which seem to have been woven with the same orientation as the design, beginning at the end with the bottom of the arched doorway, the bulk of Ladik rugs seem to have followed no set pattern of relating the direction of weaving to the top and bottom of the design, the matter apparently having been left up to the choice of the individual weaver.

It is believed that the earliest rugs of the Ladik type were woven in the triple-arched coupled-column design. A large number that have survived as votive gifts to Protestant churches in Hungary and Romania have been dated on the basis of comparative examples depicted in European paintings. They may have been woven as early as the seventeenth century. However, most early coupled-column village prayer rugs from Anatolia do not exhibit the highly characteristic two-level warp we associate with Ladik rugs from the late eighteenth century onward, and their actual place of weaving is far from certain.

A substantial number of Ladik rugs with dated inscriptions have survived. All of these are quite similar in coloration and weave to the Ballard rugs, and the dating of all of them is within a decade and a half of the Common Era year 1800. Later in the nineteenth century Ladik weaving was particularly afflicted by the introduction of aniline colors, and these later examples are often as unpleasant as their earlier forebears are beautiful.

Ballard's 1922 gift to the Metropolitan Museum of Art included three Ladik carpets: a white-ground piece (22.100.61) dated 1210 (1795/96), a rather late example with a flowering tree in the field (22.100.64), and a "classic" example with a red ground [**FIG.17**]. Two other Ballard rugs attributed to Ladik in the Metropolitan's 1975 catalogue (22.100.62 and 22.100.65) are probably from other central Anatolian locations.

Further reading: Ettinghausen 1974, Dimand 1975, Bailey 1985, Denny 1999, Denny 2015

41

Ladik Prayer Rug (*seccade*)

Konya Province, Central Turkey, ca. 1800
Gift of James F. Ballard, 94:1929
Published: Dimand 1935, pl. XLVII

Typically substantial and tightly woven. Bottom of rug as shown is top of rug as woven (the weaver began with the complex half of the field and finished with the simple half). The greater length of the rug on the right side, as woven, results from less force having been applied to packing the wefts and knots on the right side, as opposed to the left, during the first twenty percent of the weaving process.

This attractive Ladik carpet is remarkably similar to CAT.43, but with a blue-ground border instead of a yellow-ground one, and coming into our time with more intense colors. It shows the remarkable combination of traditional cohesiveness and individual variation that makes each and every prayer rug from the same village or district both a full-fledged member of its typical group, and at the same time an individual work of art.

Length: Approximately 188 cm

Width: Approximately 117 cm

Warp: Undyed white wool, two Z-spun yarns plied S, alternate warps moderately depressed

Weft: Undyed white, dyed red and undyed light-brown wool, all one Z-spun yarn; usually shot twice (1 straight + one sinuous), sometimes three times (1 straight + 1 sinuous + 1 straight)

Pile: Wool, red, red-pink, red-orange, dark blue, medium blue, pale green, eggplant-purple, pinkish-tan, corrosive dark brown, undyed white; all two Z-spun yarns plied S

Knot: Symmetrical, pulled sharply to the left (raising the right warp of each knot pair); approximately 51–52V x 29–30H per decimeter

Edges: Re-selvedged

Ends: Stripped

Detail

Reverse view

42

Ladik Prayer Rug (*seccade*)

Konya Province, Central Turkey, c. 1800
Gift of James F. Ballard, 96:1929
Published: Dimand 1935, pl. XLVIII

Compared to cat. 41 the colors are somewhat stronger, suggesting less exposure to light over the life of the carpet. This carpet is woven right side up as pictured.

The most archetypal of all of the St. Louis Ballard Ladik carpets, this example has the tall single niche found in most early Ladik prayer rugs. An individual variation of some importance is the insertion in both side borders of horizontal "bars" of decoration between the two major motifs of elongated rosette and tulip between two curved leaves.

Unusually—and unlike the first two Ladiks with vestigial triple arches already discussed—this carpet with its very tall single niche is woven entirely "right side up." Also unusual is the double depiction of water ewers in the two spandrels of the arch, a device frequently found in Mujur prayer rugs but less common in Ladik examples.

Again typical of Ladik weaving, the 58/28 vertical/horizontal knot ratio is echoed in the relative width of the side and end borders. Both have the same number of knots in their width, but the vertical compacting of the weave results in end borders that are only slightly more than half the width of the side borders.

Length: Approximately 206 cm

Width: Approximately 127 cm

Warp: Undyed white wool, two Z-spun yarns plied S, alternate warps moderately depressed

Weft: Dyed dark-brown wool, all one Z-spun yarn; shot twice (one straight + one sinuous)

Pile: Wool, red, red-orange, pale orange, pale yellow, medium blue, light blue, pale green, corrosive dark brown, undyed white; all two Z-spun yarns plied S

Knot: Symmetrical, sharply pulled to the left (raising the right warp of each knot pair); approximately 58V x 28H per decimeter

Edges: Flat selvedge of one-ply Z-spun yarn over three bundles of two warps

Ends: Stripped

Detail

Reverse view

43

Ladik Prayer Rug (*seccade*)

Konya Province, Central Turkey, late 18th–early 19th century

Gift of James F. Ballard, 97:1929

Published: Dimand 1935, pl. XLVI

The rug was woven upside down as illustrated; the weaver began with the complicated half of the field and finished with the simple half. In handle and in construction this rug is similar to the other Ladik prayer rugs in the Ballard collection.

This handsome carpet exhibits the most typical of Ladik borders and a coherent adaptation of the Ottoman prototype, with the parapet and flowers rising vertically above the triple-arched niche. It betrays its upside-down weaving history with the exceptional narrowness of the bottom (as illustrated) border, the last part of the rug to be woven. Although the coupled columns of the prototype have disappeared, the triple arch with its three alem, or crescent-shaped, finials clearly recalls the architecture of the Ottoman prototype.

The border of this carpet has two main elements. One is a somewhat diamond-shaped small serrated medallion, the descendant of the complex round rosette from the late sixteenth century found in the prototype. The other is a tulip flower, ornamented with two tiny carnations, in the embrace of two curved leaves. Again this is a direct adaptation of the original tulip and leaves from the sixteenth century.

Further reading: Ettinghausen 1974, Bailey 1985, Denny 1999

Length: Approximately 183 cm

Width: Approximately 112 cm

Warp: Undyed white wool, two Z-spun yarns plied S, alternate warps moderately depressed

Weft: Dyed dark-red, pink, and (probably undyed) brown wool, all one Z-spun yarn; shot twice (one straight + one sinuous)

Pile: Wool, red, dark blue, medium blue, pale green, pale purple, corrosive dark brown, undyed white; all two Z-spun yarns plied S

Knot: Symmetrical, sharply pulled to the left (raising the right warp of each knot pair); approximately 57V x 32H per decimeter

Edges: Single-ply red weft wool wrapped around two bundles of two warps each

Ends: Bottom as woven: stripped and restored

Top: As woven: A few remains of pale-purple tapestry weave

Detail

Reverse view

44

Ladik Prayer Rug (*seccade*)

Konya Province, Central Turkey, c. 1800
Gift of Nellie Ballard White, 311:1972
Published: Indianapolis 1924, No. 53; Walker 1988, No. 19

Rugs of this "Innice" type with its characteristic border are usually woven beginning at the bottom of the design, as in this example, illustrated right side up both from the design and the technical perspective. The inclusion of paired extra wefts of a different color on either side can be observed in other examples of this subgroup.

Entering the Saint Louis Art Museum in 1972, this last of Ballard's four splendid Ladik carpets in St. Louis to be catalogued here exhibits the distinctive border that the Turkish scholar Belkis Balpinar determined to denote an origin in the village of Innice near Ladik. Otherwise in its single-arch layout it is quite similar to CAT.42, except for the somewhat eccentric choice by the weaver to fill the spandrels of the arch with small octagons rather than trying to echo the complex vegetal forms passed down over centuries. It appears that Ballard's daughter, who may have had her preferred choice of carpets to keep for herself, favoured the Innice border over the more conventional one found in Ballard's other three Ladiks in the Saint Louis Art Museum.

Length: Approximately 198 cm

Width: Approximately 116 cm

Warp: Undyed white wool, two Z-spun yarns plied S, alternate warps moderately depressed

Weft: Mostly brown (probably undyed) wool, all one Z-spun yarn; shot twice (one straight + one sinuous); on both sides there are occasional extra parallel pairs of wefts, both straight and sinuous, of one-ply Z-spun blue-dyed wool that extend from the edge between 10 and 15 cm into the fabric

Pile: Wool dyed red, eggplant-purple, pale purple, dark blue, light blue, yellow, corrosive dark brown, undyed white; all consisting of two Z-spun yarns plied S

Knot: Symmetrical, sharply pulled to the left (raising the right warp of each knot pair); approximately 48V x 32H per decimeter

Edges: Mostly original selvedge, consisting (inside to outside) of one, then 2// + 2// + 2// warps, wrapped in purple wool

Ends: Bottom: remains of orange and red tapestry weave. Top: stripped, restored by reweaving on a white cotton warp

Detail

Reverse view

Transcaucasian Carpets

fig. 18
Dragon carpet, Transcaucasus,
17th century. Metropolitan
Museum of Art, New York, Gift of
James F. Ballard, 22.100.122

Transcaucasia lies between the Black and Caspian Seas, encompassing the Greater and Lesser Caucasus mountains. It includes the modern countries of Georgia, Armenia and Azerbaijan as well as regions such as Chechnya and Ossetia that are part of the Russian Federation. Situated between formerly Ottoman Anatolia to the west and Safavid Iran in the south, over the centuries this complex land of many peoples, religions, and languages was subject to a rich mixture of artistic influences and inspirations.

The most important early carpets woven in Transcaucasia, probably in or near urban areas on the Caspian coast, are known as Dragon carpets: their powerful, geometric designs incorporate, among other real and imaginary animal representations, those of dragons. Charles Grant Ellis conclusively showed that the origin of these designs of animals, huge palmette blossoms, and craggy leaves goes back to a group of seventeenth-century Persian carpets from Kerman, only a few small fragments of which have survived. The depictions of dragons in those early Kerman carpets were, as with almost all dragons seen in later Persian art, directly inspired by Chinese prototypes.

Unlike the Kerman rugs with dragons in their designs, Transcaucasian Dragon carpets were from the outset heavily stylized and the forms were highly geometric—so much so that they were even occasionally found in mosques, where figural representations were forbidden. Many early Dragon carpets were quite large, following the model of their Persian prototypes. This apart, their technique and coloration was very similar to that of Anatolian carpets.

Transcaucasian carpets invariably have a symmetrical knot, usually a warp on two levels. Apart from the frequent use of three-ply rather than two-ply wool for warp and pile— they are often technically indistinguishable from Anatolian carpets. Despite an attempt to attribute them to Tabriz in northwest Iran, the consensus is that the early Dragon carpets are from the Caspian littoral.

James Ballard gave the Metropolitan Museum two large Dragon carpets with the typical layout of ogival compartments filled with floral or animal forms (22.100.119 and 22.100.122; **FIG.18**). The carpet in St. Louis is very small for the genre, and only the halves of two misunderstood dragons can be seen at each side of the field. The border, with its rosettes and sprays of stylized hyacinths, is directly inspired by Ottoman court carpets. Despite an artistic lineage from China, central Persia, and Anatolia, the style of Dragon carpets is entirely distinctive. It was much admired and influenced the style of other groups of carpets outside Transcaucasia, in places such as western Anatolia [**CAT.23**].

A commercial weaving revival in east Transcaucasia in the nineteenth century led to the production of large, handsome carpets such as **CAT.46**, a long rug on a blue ground with a Persian-inspired floral design. Such carpets in turn served as the models for an explosive increase in the production of smaller Transcaucasian carpets in the late nineteenth and early twentieth centuries. Their many different types often borrowed designs from the Dragon carpets and the large floral carpets.

Further reading: Schürmann 1964, Dimand 1975, Ellis 1975, Wright and Wertime 1995

45

Small Dragon Carpet

Probably East Transcaucasia, late 18th century

Gift of James F. Ballard, 109:1929

Published: Dimand 1935, pl. LX

Typical of Dragon rugs from Transcaucasia in its materials, colors, three-ply wool, and stiff and inflexible handle, this carpet is unusual in its atypically very small size. The border, with its rosettes and sprays of stylized hyacinths, is borrowed from Anatolian neighbors, and the remains of two highly stylized dragons, simplified from earlier prototypes, are seen to each side of the center of the carpet.

The famous Dragon carpets woven commercially in the Caspian littoral of eastern Transcaucasia from the 17th century onward present us with a curious combination of Anatolian coloration and weaving structure on the one hand, and Iranian scale and size on the other. The extreme stylization of the original Kerman prototype designs may account for the fact that a number of carpets of this type have been found in Anatolian mosques, where recognizable animal forms would have been shunned.

This small carpet is distinguished among early Dragon carpets primarily by its unusually small size. The central field is in essence a small excerpt from a larger Dragon carpet that has been doubled by making it symmetrical end to end. The vestiges of the original dragon forms may be seen cut by the border to either side of the middle of the field. A full understanding of nature of this visual excerpt is best attained by looking at a Dragon carpet of more conventional size, such as Ballard's large Dragon carpet in the Metropolitan Museum [**FIG.18**].

Due to the abbreviated nature of the field, the yellow-ground border attains an unusual prominence in the overall design. The four-lobed forms are derived from the classical Ottoman rosette seen in the border of Ballard's famed coupled-column carpet in the Metropolitan Museum of Art [**FIG.14**], and closely resemble forms of similar derivation in the Ottoman-style borders of many Ladik carpets, including three in St. Louis [**CAT.41-43**]. The delicate sprays of red hyacinths are an entirely original approach to the Ottoman prototype, and lend this small carpet much of its charm.

Ballard also gave a small 19th-century Transcaucasian carpet with a dragon design in sumak-brocaded technique to the Metropolitan Museum (22.100.21).

Length: Approximately 182 cm

Width: Approximately 106 cm

Warp: Apparently undyed light brown, dark brown and white wool, three Z-spun yarns plied S, alternate warps strongly depressed

Weft: Dyed pink and apparently undyed brown wool; one Z-spun yarn, shot mostly four times (2// + 2//) between each row of knots

Pile: Wool dyed red, dark blue, medium blue, light blue, blue-green, eggplant-purple, yellow-tan; all two Z-spun yarns plied S; and undyed white wool, three Z-spun yarns plied S

Knot: Symmetrical, pulled strongly to left, approximately 40V x 36H per decimeter

Edges: Both restored

Ends: Both stripped

Detail

Reverse view

46

Blossom-pattern Long Carpet

Probably East Transcaucasia, Shirvan or Kuba district, early 19th century

Gift of James F. Ballard, 118:1929

Published: Dimand 1935, pl. LXIII

Typical of east Transcaucasian rugs conventionally ascribed to the Shirvan district are the multicolor undyed wool warps, and the tightly integrated edge finishes. Undyed brown wool is almost useless for carpet pile, as its color varies greatly and it cannot be dyed other hues, but it makes fine material for the foundations, where it is hidden.

Caucasian carpets from the nineteenth century exhibiting this overall pattern of blossoms are probably derived from Persian prototypes, and the design often referred to as the *harshang* pattern in the carpet literature. Conventionally dated to the early nineteenth century, carpets such as this are much larger than the great bulk of later Transcaucasian carpets produced in vast numbers in the mid and later nineteenth century, and tend to reflect in their shape and to an extent in their dimensions the older Kuba carpets in the so-called "sunburst" and Dragon designs. Although the field design is definitely of Persian origin, many Transcaucasian carpets of this type frequently exhibit a border clearly derived from the kufesque borders of early Anatolian carpets woven far to the west. The Ballard *harshang*-design carpet, by contrast, exhibits an unusual border of arrow-like forms alternately pointing toward and away from the central field, set in a lattice of delicate vines that have lost their original blue color except at the very top of the carpet. Ballard gave a somewhat larger *harshang*-pattern carpet to the Metropolitan Museum of Art (22.100.121), as well as an unusual narrow runner incorporating a fragment of the *harshang* pattern (22.100.120).

Length: Approximately 384 cm

Width: Approximately 191 cm

Warp: Undyed dark-brown and white wool, all warps two Z-spun yarns plied S, some all dark brown, some white, some one-ply of each; alternate warps slightly depressed

Weft: Apparently undyed light brown wool, one Z-spun yarn; shot twice (1+1) and three times (1+2//)

Pile: Dyed wool, dark blue, medium-blue-green faded to yellowish-tan, medium blue abrashed to light blue, medium red, purple, dark yellow, corrosive dark brown, and undyed white; all two Z-spun yarns plied S

Knot: Symmetrical; approximately 32V x 30H per decimeter

Edges: Both two bundles of two warps wrapped in tan (faded blue-green?) wool; wrapping intrudes four warps into the body of the rug between each row of knots

Ends: both ends stripped

Detail

Reverse view

Turkmen Carpets

I n the early twentieth century, few serious collectors paid any attention to the red rugs of Central Asia that today we call Turkmen carpets. Unrepresented in European painting, without lineage or documentation, and with many examples woven for specific functions within the nomadic environment, these rugs were erroneously called "Bukhara" in the marketplace. They were of little interest to North America, except to James Ballard in St. Louis and George Walter Vincent Smith in Springfield, Massachusetts. Around the time that Ballard was collecting his few Turkmen examples, a retired Russian officer named Bogolyubov published the first scholarly work on Turkmen carpets in St. Petersburg, but the artistic and historical importance of this group of carpets was not fully to emerge until the second half of the twentieth century.

The bulk of Turkmen carpets can easily be assigned to one of six major nomadic tribal groups, whose history can be documented for the past thousand years in the writings of their settled neighbors. Ballard's two Turkmen carpets both exhibit the predominately red or red-brown coloration typical of the entire range of Turkmen weaving. It is derived from the dried root of the ubiquitous madder plant that forms the basis of the red on most of the rugs in the Ballard collection woven from Spain to Samarkand. Both Ballard carpets are what we term "main carpets," the largest weavings made by these nomadic peoples. They were used on the floors of their domical felt-covered portable dwellings, conventionally called yurts in English-language publications.

The basis of the design in both carpets is a small medallion called a gül that symbolizes the tribal group and subgroup as a sort of coat-of-arms or emblem. The rows of güls in the Tekke main carpet are connected by a single row of knots in dark blue, giving a grid-like pattern over the entire carpet that quarters the main güls and surrounds the smaller cruciform secondary motifs. On the Ersari main carpet the primary güls, the rectangular-stepped cruciform motifs, are in stacked rows, and the diamond-shaped secondary güls that alternate with them are almost the same size.

Despite the impression of overall red or red-brown coloration (Turkmen dyers produced an amazing range of reds from scarlet to mahogany from the madder plant) both of these carpets have a wide range of colors, usually about the same as Anatolian rugs woven by their Turkish cousins some 2,000 kilometers to the west. Knots in Turkmen pile weaving vary from symmetrical to asymmetrical open right to asymmetrical open left. Main carpets typically have a broad tapestry-woven *elem* panel at each end. As a touch of luxury a few main carpets may include silk in the design, which almost always is magenta in hue (often dyed with a red derived from scale insects), and occasionally light blue.

The visual relationship between the designs of nineteenth-century Turkmen carpets and those of fifteenth-century carpets of Anatolia, such as the small-pattern Holbeins [**CAT.18**], strongly supports the hypothesis that much of the traditional weaving design repertoire of Anatolia was brought westward into Anatolia by migrating Central Asian Turkmen tribal

weavers in the aftermath of the Battle of Manzikert in 1071. There, the Seljuk Turkish Sultan Alparslan defeated the Byzantine Emperor Romanus, setting in motion the gradual process of change from medieval Hellenism to Turkic Islam in Anatolia.

In the wake of Ballard's 1922 gift to the Metropolitan Museum, he apparently did not feel any urge to continue collecting in the Turkmen area. His Turkmen carpets in the Metropolitan [**FIG.12**] comprise a very handsome group, including three Yomut main carpets (22.100.44, 46, 47), a Tekke main carpet (22.100.46), a pair of Arabachi chuval tent bag faces (22.100.40a, b), a door surround (22.100.37), a Yomut tent band (22.100.38) and several other bag faces from various tribes. A number of contemporary Turkmen carpet aficionados feel that, of the two splendid Tekke main carpets from Ballard's collection, the Saint Louis Art Museum got the older and more attractive example. Following Ballard's example, Joseph V. McMullan also donated a number of splendid Turkmen examples to the Metropolitan.

Further reading: Thompson and Mackie 1980, Denny 1982

47

Tekke Turkmen Main Carpet

Turkmenistan, 19th century
Gift of James F. Ballard, 113:1930

Despite the stretched condition at the top end, brought about by the splaying of the warps on the loom, this is a handsome example of an early nineteenth-century Tekke carpet. It has fine color variation, generally good condition, is of typically supple and substantial handle, and typically superb weaving quality.

Before the eventual subjugation of the Turkmen tribes by imperial Russian forces in the nineteenth century, the Tekke had emerged as the most important of the six major tribal groups in what is today Turkmenistan. Perhaps the best known of all Turkmen carpet types, surviving in fairly large numbers, is the main carpet woven by the women of the Tekke tribe. The Ballard example in St. Louis is a particularly handsome example, with nine rows of four major güls each, in contrast to the ten rows of five güls each in the Metropolitan's example from Ballard.

The vibrant *abrash* or color variations of the red ground contribute a sense of artistic suppleness and resiliency, and heighten the visual interest of this carpet. Its relative simplicity and openness compared to many Tekke examples further enhances the visual impact of this carpet. The border consists of repeated octagons embellished with four motifs each, in most places the conventional four six-petaled flowers in a diamond arrangement, but in few cases a far more unusual arrangement of two rows of two eight-pointed stars. The "spacers" between each octagon on the two vertical borders show a variety of interesting traditional Tekke forms, including chevrons and eight-pointed stars. Typically for Tekke carpets, a grid consisting of single lines of dark-blue knots bisects each major güls vertically and horizontally. The colors, eight in number, are also typical of the best Tekke main carpets. The tapestry-woven skirts at either end, known as elem, are probably about half of their original length.

Further reading: Thompson and Mackie 1980, Denny 1982

Length: Approximately 254 cm

Width: Approximately 196 cm

Warp: White undyed hard wool, two Z-spun yarns plied S, uniform, alternate warps slightly depressed

Weft: Wool dyed dark brown, one Z-spun yarn, uniform, shot twice (1+1), packing very regular

Pile: Wool, uniform thickness, dark red, red-orange, dark blue, light blue, blue-green, yellow, undyed white and dark brown; all two Z-spun yarns plied S

Knot: Asymmetrical, open right, approximately 68V x 36–37H per decimeter

Edges: Original edges consist of two warps wrapped in a selvedge of blue wool; some over-wrapping and replacement of original edges

Ends: Top: Approximately 9 cm of red tapestry-woven elem with blue stripes at the top, with a rewoven top right corner. Bottom: Approximately 14.5 cm of red tapestry-woven elem at bottom

Detail

Reverse view

48

Small Ersari Turkmen Main Carpet

Probably southern Uzbekistan, 19th century
Gift of Nellie Ballard White, 319:1972

A very small main carpet, with unusual gül medallions and borders, in generally very good condition, with lustrous wool and silk pile.

The overriding impression of this small carpet is the incredible lushness of its thick wool pile, enhanced by the highly reflective magenta silk pile that is used very lavishly in this example. The Ersari Turkmen are a coalition of many sub-tribes. They are found in the southeast part of the broader Turkmen area of Central Asia, with many tribal groups settled in what is today northwest Afghanistan, and others occupying villages along the Amu Darya (Oxus) River. Not surprisingly, there is a huge variation in designs, coloration, and to a considerable extent weaving technique, among these far-flung and diverse groups.

When Ballard was collecting, carpets such as this one were essentially orphans—their exact tribal origins were often unknown unless they happened to correspond exactly to one of the chromolithographed illustrations in General Bobolyubov's massive tome published in St. Petersburg in 1906.

Length: Approximately 191 cm

Width: Approximately 127 cm

Warp: White undyed soft wool, two Z-spun yarns plied S, all warps on one level

Weft: Light undyed brown wool, pattern of shots highly variable: two (1+1), three (1+1+1), three (1+2//), and four (1+1+1+1).

Pile: Wool, dyed dark red, light red, medium blue abrashed to dark blue, light blue blue-green, yellow, dark brown, and undyed white; all two Z-spun yarns plied S, highly variable in thickness. Silk, magenta, apparently two Z-spun yarns plied S

Knot: Asymmetrical, open right, pulled strongly to right, approximately 48V x 43H per decimeter

Edges: Original selvedge was probably flat and wide; now replaced by a bundle of two warps wrapped in blue yarn

Ends: Top: Approximately 10.5 cm of tapestry-woven red elem with blue stripes. Bottom: Original missing; approximately 10 cm of tapestry-woven red elem with blue and green stripes, taken from a Tekke main carpet, has been sewn on

Detail

Reverse view

Mughal Carpets

The art of Mughal India, the empire established in the early 16th century by the Central Asian Turkic conqueror Babur that ruled first over northern Indian and then over much of the subcontinent down until the 19th century, represents a complex blend of Islamic, Turkic, and indigenous Indian cultures. Much of India, like Egypt, lacks the traditional pre-requisites for carpet manufacture; a temperate climate with cold winters, an abundance of marginal land, and a nomadic tradition. But the Turkic rulers of India, like the Turkic rulers of Egypt, although outsiders to the local culture, imported many of their own traditions and customs, and the pile carpet appears to have been one of the most important.

It is often said of Mughal art of India that it loves hyperbole: the largest gems, the most lavishly illustrated manuscripts, the smallest illustrated manuscripts, and of course the greatest mausoleums. In the case of carpets, the Mughal tradition has given us the largest carpets and by far the most finely-woven carpets, as well as carpets incrusted with thousands of pearls, and carpets woven to fit specific non-rectangular architectural spaces. These carpets were woven in a wide variety of techniques in a wide variety of weaving sites, from northern Kashmir and Lahore to the Deccan principalities of central India.

The Mughal presence in the Ballard collection of carpets in St. Louis is small but exquisite: it consists of two very small carpet fragments, that utilize a density of knotting far higher than anything seen in the rest of the Ballard Collection. The pile is made of pashm—which in the West we call cashmere, named after the region of Kashmir in the northern subcontinent – and the designs reflect a curious combination of naturalistic flowers peculiar to Mughal art, and a kind of framing or compartment border that may have originated in Baroque Europe.

Other fragments, many of them much larger, from the same carpets represented in St. Louis by **CAT.49** and **CAT.50**, are known in other museum collections; larger fragments from the Metropolitan Museum [**FIG.19**] and the Gulbenkian Foundation in Lisbon [**FIG.20**] help us to contextualize James Ballard's two small but astounding bits of a greater artistic whole.

In looking at the Spanish carpet in the Ballard Collection in the St. Louis Art Museum [**CAT.6**], we saw a tradition in which artistic elements from many different places, some at a great distance from the others, blended together to form a unique synthesis. The same is true of Mughal carpets in India. The Mughal courts hosted visitors from Europe, and the Mughal emperors collected European prints and other works of art sent to them as gifts by the East India Companies of Holland, Portugal, and England. The cultural ties to the Turkish homeland of the Mughals in Central Asia persisted long after the dynasty had settled into urban centers in India. The Mughal court was in many respects dominated by the cultural influence of Iran to the west. And the vast subcontinent of India, over which the Mughals ruled, maintained and continued to assert its own age-old and powerful cultures based on strands of Hindu and Buddhist belief, custom, and mythology. The two small Mughal carpet fragments in the Ballard collection therefore represent a great tradition, which despite their small size they express with artistic eloquence and visual impact.

Further reading: Walker 1997

49

Fragment of a Mughal Court Carpet

Northern Indian subcontinent, possibly Lahore, probably mid-17th century

Gift of James F. Ballard, 73:1929

Published: *Dimand 1935, plate IX*

Despite the small size of this fragment, it gives a good idea of the overall pattern: an ornamental ogival lattice composed of white leaf-like forms superimposed on a blue and green lattice of floral vines: the white lattice frames the elaborate palmette-like blossoms springing from the blue and green vines. This was a favored design layout for the finest of all Mughal carpets: those, like the present example, evidently woven in northern India, possibly Lahore, with an exceptionally fine weave, brilliant colors, and a luxurious pile of pashm. Other fragments from the same carpet [**FIG.19**], and examples of carpets with similar lattice and blossom layouts woven in both pashm and silk, are seen in the landmark Metropolitan Museum catalogue of 1997 by Daniel Walker (figs. 111-114).

There was a definite hierarchy of Mughal weaving; the expensive Lahore carpets were difficult to obtain, as attested by documents from the British and Dutch East India Companies. While certain commissions were successfully completed, such as the famous "Girdler's Carpet" in London that was woven in Lahore with specific inscriptions in English, finding a workshop willing to execute a commission for the foreign companies was often a frustrating enterprise. Certainly in the first half of the seventeenth century, the great age of Mughal arts under the emperors Jahangir (r. 1605-27) and Shah Jahan (r. 1628-58), when carpets such as this example were certainly woven, commissions from the imperial Mughal court had precedence in the market for these expensive, rare, and difficult-to-produce carpets.

Further Reading: Walker 1977

fig. 19

Mughal lattice carpet fragments, Northern India, circa 1650. 150 x 417 cm. Metropolitan Museum of Art, New York, Bequest of Benjamin Altman, 1913, No,14.40.172

fig. 19

Length: Approximately 58.5 cm

Width: Approximtely 28 cm

Warp: Dyed dark red silk, also white and green, evidently 2 z-spun yarns plied s; alternate warps moderately depressed

Weft: Dyed red silk, one unspun or z-spun yarn, uniform and regular, shot three times (1+1+1)

Pile: Pashm (cashmere) dyed dark red, light pink, dark green, dark blue-green, light green, tan-yellow, and undyed white; all consisting of 4 z-spun yarns plied s

Knot: Asymmetrical open to the left; approximately 68-69V x 95H per decimeter

Edges: None

Ends: None

Detail

Reverse view

50

Fragment of a Mughal Court Carpet

Northern Indian subcontinent, possibly Lahore, probably mid-17th century

Gift of James F. Ballard, 74:1929

Publication: Dimand 1935, plate X; Walker 1997, catalogue number 31, Figure 113

Somewhat darker in coloration than the other St. Louis Mughal fragment, this small excerpt from a large Mughal carpet contains a white-ground guard border as well as elements of a central field again composed of two lattices, one constituting a frame for major elements and the other a sort of trellis on which large flowers, mostly chrysanthemums, are displayed along with buds, smaller five-petaled blossoms, and leaves. As in **CAT.49**, the artistic conception relies in part on a coloristic practice known as *ton-sur-ton* (in French, literally, "color value on color value"), the juxtaposition of two different values of the exact same hue, in this case green and light green, purple-red and pink. These different values are accomplished by using exactly the same dyestuffs, but leaving the wool (or, in this case, pashm) yarns for a longer or shorter time in the dye-pot. While *ton-sur-ton* coloration is practiced in a number of different textile traditions, it seems to have been a particularly characteristic feature of Mughal carpet-weaving, and displays the legendary talents of Indian dyers to a high degree.

fig. 20
Mughal carpet fragment,
Northern India, circa 1650.
140 x 320 cm. Calouste
Gulbenkian Foundation,
Lisbon, inv. T60

fig. 20

Length: Approximately 76 cm

Width: Approximately 33 cm

Warp: Dyed dark red silk, also white and green, evidently 2 z-spun yarns plied s; alternate warps moderately depressed

Weft: Dyed red silk, one unspun or z-spun yarn, uniform and regular, shot three times (1+1+1)

Pile: Pashm (cashmere) dyed dark red, pink, dark blue, medium blue-green, light green, tan-yellow, and undyed white; all consisting of 4 (and more rarely 5) z-spun yarns plied s

Knot: Asymmetrical open to the left; approximately 85V x 96H per decimeter

Edges: None original

Ends: None original

Detail

Reverse view

Two Persian Tents

The two Persian tents given by James Franklin Ballard to the Saint Louis Art Museum are not particularly old. Nor do they find close parallels in the Ballard carpets in St. Louis, especially as only two significant Ballard carpets from Iran found their way into the Saint Louis Art Museum, one in 1929 and another in 1972. Without any definitive documentation, we might well imagine that these colorful examples of fabric architecture may have been bought by Ballard on a whim; and further that, given their good condition and relative modernity, they may have been used by Ballard for entertaining family and friends outdoors.

From another perspective, however, these two small decorative tents may be seen as surviving artefacts of an enormously important tradition within Islamic art, which unfortunately is drastically under-represented in North American museums. Fabric architecture, even late fabric architecture such as this, casts light on two major elements of Islamic weaving cultures that are almost always given little consideration in the museum context. The first element is the importance of nomadic survivals in the art of later Middle Eastern urbanized and settled agricultural cultures: the artistic persistence of tribal memory. The second element is what we might call the "outdoor culture" of the Islamic world. Anyone who has ever traveled in the Middle East knows the phenomenon whereby on warm weekends urban families head en masse for the countryside, where they roll out carpets on the grass, put up fabric sunshades or awnings, and enjoy a cook-out in the midst of nature. Countless Persian paintings in particular chronicle the outdoor pleasures of kings and courtiers, and Persian literature abounds in descriptions of outdoor feasts, ceremonies, and romantic dalliances. In the late fifteenth century the Venetian traveler Josafa Barbaro describes a visit to an outdoor celebration near Tabriz, where the White Sheep Turkmen sultan and his court enjoyed a banquet among beautiful tents, with countless exquisite carpets spread on the green grass of a meadow.

For many centuries Persian masonry architecture both sacred and secular has been dominated by the iwan, a vaulted hall with one side completely open, a form that characterized some of the most important royal structures of the Sasanian dynasty that predated the Islamic conquest of Iran. The iwan form and the fabric architecture of tents provide an ideal mediation between indoors and outdoors. The fabric tent, especially in forms where the side walls open up, is a logical product of societies where textiles are a major artistic form and nomadic lifestyles coexist with village and urban life. Furthermore fabric structures, in addition to being portable and easy to store, have one signal advantage over masonry ones: they are not susceptible to the earthquakes that have devastated much of the legacy of masonry building in Iran and Central Asia.

Middle Eastern tents come in a variety of shapes destined for a variety of uses. Although few older examples have survived,

old Islamic tents are well documented in Islamic paintings, and have been thoughtfully and thoroughly discussed in a masterly two-volume study by the British scholar Peter Andrews, published in 1999. The Imperial tents of the Ottoman Turkish sultans, their courts and their armies, have likewise been studied by Professor Nurhan Atasoy. This knowledge has been shared through another lavishly illustrated publication (2000) in which most of the important surviving examples from museum collections are illustrated. Because the Ottoman armies traveled with a huge number of richly decorated tents of many different types, quite a few entered European collections as the fruits of the plunder of the Ottoman camp before Vienna by Polish troops in 1683. A few highly decorated Mughal tents from India have likewise survived. By contrast, a smaller number of old Persian tents have come down to us, most of these largely as textile fragments. For this reason the two small Ballard tents help to illuminate an older Persian tradition, in much the same way as many of the later Ballard carpets reflect light back on the earlier history of carpet weaving. The intimate association of carpet and tents, made clear in numerous Persian paintings [**FIG.21**], serves as the rationale for the inclusion of these two examples in this catalogue of the Islamic carpets from the Ballard Collection in St. Louis.

Further Reading: Andrews 1999; Atasoy 2000

51

Small Rectangular Pavilion Tent

Resht (Rasht), Iran, 19th century
Gift of James F. Ballard, 131:1929

This small pleasure-pavilion tent was designed so that one or more sides could be opened to provide air and a view, but it could also be completely closed, with a small door panel under an arch in the left rear as illustrated then giving access to the interior. Two large poles at each end supported the roof, and smaller poles served as rigid stays for the wall panels.

The simple if colorful exterior of this tent contrasts with the dramatic and elaborate embroidered decoration of the interior, probably accomplished in the Iranian town of Resht, a locale famous for its rich embroidery in chain-stitch technique.

Overall dimensions: composed of four walls, two approximately 10½ feet wide, two approximately 8½ feet deep, all 6½ feet high, with a door panel at the end of one long side; a gabled top composed of two large rectangular panels and two triangular pediments, one at each end.

Interior: appliquéd red, blue, green and yellow pieced wool plain-weave fabrics embellished with *tambour* chain-stitch embroidery (so-called *reshti* technique); leather added to reinforce points of potential stress, wear, and friction. Exterior: red cotton plain weave. At some point in its history the tent fabric was reinforced by additional fabric that was attached by adhesive. During treatment at the St. Louis Museum of Art the tent was reinforced, cleaned, and some later additions removed.

Cat. 51
Persian Small Rectangular Pavilion Tent (details and overleaf), 19th century; wool, cotton, silk, and leather; 290 x 305 x 213 cm; Saint Louis Art Museum, Gift of James F. Ballard 131:1929

Cat. 51
Persian Small Rectangular Pavilion Tent

Cat. 51
Persian Small Rectangular
Pavilion Tent (details)

52

Small Octagonal Pavilion Tent

Resht (Rasht), Iran, 19th century
Gift of James F. Ballard, 132:1929a, b

Doubtless designed for pleasurable use in a garden setting, this small tent was designed to be erected with eight poles in the corners held by ropes staked to the ground, and a central pole to hold up the conical roof canopy. An octagonal floor cloth purchased by Ballard along with the tent appears to have been an afterthought, perhaps added by a dealer when the tent was sold. The exterior of the tent is plain-weave cotton, which is resistant to sunlight and less likely to be damaged by rain, while the interior is lined with more fragile and luxurious silk fabric.

The form of this small pavilion tent inevitably recalls the shape of medieval Iranian octagonal tomb structures or *gunbad*, whose decorative brickwork frequently includes corner columns or "tent poles." One of the eight wall panels is designed to open as an entrance, and the central part of each wall panel is embellished by a fabric "grille" that clearly imitates Persian wooden or metal grille-work. The design provides plenty of shade

and privacy coupled with maximum air circulation, and the door panel could be closed for additional privacy.

The tent comprises eight contiguous panels each measuring 211 x 135 cm, and an octagonal canopy of eight triangular pieces. The plain-weave cotton exterior is embroidered with silk and metallic yarns, and the interior is lined with woven silk panels.

The tent appears to have been altered in the late nineteenth or early twentieth century, possibly by the dealer who sold it to Ballard. The separate silk floor cover (see p. 217) is probably unrelated to the original tent.

A stylistically similar tent on a much more splendid scale, made for Muhammad Shah Qajar (r. 1834-1848) in the first half of the 19th century, was recently acquired by the Cleveland Museum of Art (Purchase from the J.H. Wade Fund, 2014.388) and was recently published in *HALI* ("The Shah's Tent", Issue 185, Autumn 2015, pp. 94-95).

Cat. 52

Cat. 52
Persian Small Octagonal Pavilion Tent (and details overleaf), 19th century; silk, cotton, and metallic yarns; 345 x 406 x 406 cm; Saint Louis Art Museum, Gift of James F. Ballard 132:1929a,b

Cat. 52
Persian Small Octagonal
Pavilion Tent (details)

Appendix:
The Ballard Collection

Persia

**Corner fragment of a carpet
with vegetal lattice design**

Persian, Kerman region
Safavid period, c. 1650-1750
wool and cotton
58 x 53 in. (147.3 x 134.6 cm)
Gift of James F. Ballard
No. 47:1930

**"Polonaise" carpet with split-
leaf arabesque and palmette
design on silver ground**

Persian
Safavid period, 17th century
silk pile and metallic thread brocading
58 x 42 in. (147.3 x 106.7 cm)
Gift of James F. Ballard
No. 120:1929

**Carpet with design of cloud
bands and floral palmettes on
red ground**

Persian
Safavid period, early 17th century
wool
76½ x 47½ in. (194.3 x 120.7 cm)
Gift of James F. Ballard
No. 72:1929

Carpet with field design of cloud bands and floral palmettes on a red ground

Persian
Safavid period, late 17th century
wool and cotton
13 ft. 6 in. x 70¼in. (411.5 x 178.4 cm)
Gift of James F. Ballard
No. 71:1929

***Jufti*-knotted Khurasan carpet with palmette lattice design**

Persian
Qajar period, 19th century
wool and cotton
139½ x 66½ in.(354.3 x 168.9 cm)
Gift of Nellie Ballard White
No. 294:1972

Carpet with design of leaves and flowers on red ground

Persian
Qajar period, late 19th century
wool
12 ft. 10½ in. x 76¾ in. (392.4 x 194.9 cm)
Gift of James F. Ballard
No. 69:1929

Persia

Horse caparison

Persian
Qajar period, late 19th century
wool
74 x 62 in. (188 x 157.5 cm)
Gift of James F. Ballard
No. 68:1929

Saddle cover with *herati* pattern in spandrels

Persian
Qajar period, late 19th century
wool and cotton
66 x 34 in. (167.6 x 86.4 cm)
Gift of James F. Ballard
No. 70:1929

Carpet in a seventeenth-century style

Persian
Qajar period, late 19th or early 20th century
wool and cotton
71 x 51½ in. (180.3 x 130.8 cm)
Gift of Nellie Ballard White
No. 286:1972

Carpet in a seventeenth-century style

Persian
Qajar period, late 19th or early 20th century
wool and cotton
68 x 49½ in. (172.7 x 125.7 cm)
Gift of Nellie Ballard White
No. 287:1972

Carpet in a sixteenth-century style

Persian
Qajar period, late 19th or early 20th century
wool and cotton
83 x 54 in. (210.8 x 137.2 cm)
Gift of Nellie Ballard White
No. 288:1972

Carpet in a sixteenth-century style

Persian
Qajar period, late 19th or early 20th century
wool and cotton
51 x 71 in. (129.5 x 180.3 cm)
Gift of Nellie Ballard White
No. 289:1972

Persia

Persian
Qajar period, late 19th century
wool
134 x 34½ in. (340.4 x 87.6 cm)
Gift of Nellie Ballard White
No. 111:1973

Persian
Qajar period, late 19th century
wool
21 ft. 10 in. x 34½ in. (665.5 x 87.6 cm)
Gift of Nellie Ballard White
No. 112:1973

Baluch small carpet in prayer rug layout

Persian, Khurasan province
Qajar period, late 19th century
wool
70 x 34 in. (177.8 x 86.4 cm)
Gift of James F. Ballard
No. 110:1930

"Sehna" carpet with diamond-shaped central medallion

Persian, Sanandaj region
Qajar period, c. 1900
wool and cotton
14 ft. 7 in. x 78 in. (444.5 x 198.1 cm)
Gift of James F. Ballard
No. 114:1930

"Serabend" carpet with rows of *boteh* on pink ground

Persian
Qajar period, c. 1900
wool and cotton
76 x 54 in. (193 x 137.2 cm)
Gift of James F. Ballard
No. 112:1930

Persia

Tabriz medallion carpet

Persian
Qajar period, late 19th century
silk
55½ x 52½ in. (141 x 133.4 cm)
Gift of Nellie Ballard White
No. 290:1972

Tabriz white-ground two-column prayer carpet in Gördes style

Persian
Qajar period, late 19th century
silk
70 x 47 in. (177.8 x 119.4 cm)
Gift of Nellie Ballard White
No. 310:1972

"Sofreh" sumak-brocaded open-field carpet

Persian or Transcaucasian, Azerbaijan,
late 19th century
cotton, including the brocading
54½ x 39 in. (138.4 x 99.1 cm)
Gift of Nellie Ballard White
No. 293:1972

Tent floor covering composed of various textile materials

Persian
Qajar period, probably assembled late 19th/
early 20th century
silk and cotton
12 ft. 1 in. x 141 in. (368.3 x 358.1 cm)
Gift of James F. Ballard
No. 128:1929

Spain

Mudejar carpet with design derived from Anatolian "Lotto" carpets

Spanish, probably Cuenca, 17th century
wool
14 ft. 7 in. x 94¾ in. (444.5 x 240.7 cm)
Gift of James F. Ballard
No. 127:1929

Turkey

Ushak Carpet with *çintemani* pattern on white ground with cloud band border

Ottoman period, late 16th–early 17th century
wool
61 x 52½ in. (154.9 x 133.4 cm)
Gift of James F. Ballard
No. 112:1929

Turkey

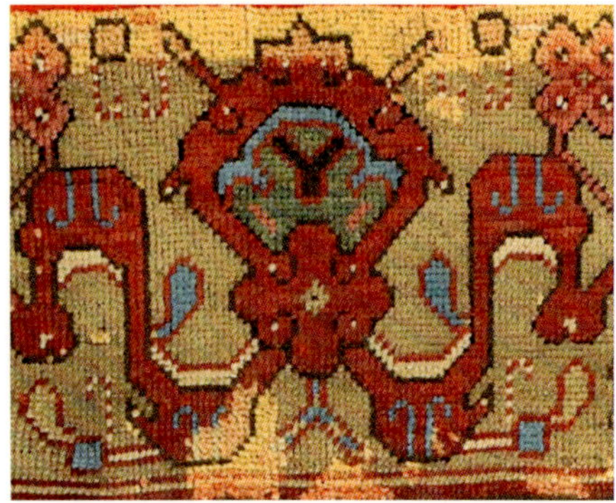

Small "double-ended" Ushak carpet with red ground

Ottoman period, mid-17th century
wool
69¼ x 36½ in. (175.9 x 92.7 cm)
Gift of James F. Ballard
No. 105:1929

"Transylvanian" prayer carpet with yellow ground

Ottoman period, late 17th–early 18th century
wool
56 x 46 in. (142.2 x 116.8 cm)
Gift of James F. Ballard
No. 93:1929

Fragmentary "Smyrna" carpet with *saz* arabesque design on red ground

Ottoman period, late 18th–early 19th century
wool
82 x 40 in. (208.3 x 101.6 cm)
Gift of James F. Ballard
No. 115:1929

Small Ushak carpet with oval quatrefoil medallion

Ottoman period, c. 1700–1800
wool
90 x 51 in. (228.6 x 129.5 cm)
Gift of Nellie Ballard White
No. 303:1972

Gördes prayer carpet with blue ground

Ottoman period, late 18th–early 19th century
wool
75 x 55 in. (190.5 x 139.7 cm)
Gift of James F. Ballard
No. 77:1929

Gördes prayer carpet with columns on blue ground

Ottoman period, late 18th–early 19th century
wool and cotton
68 x 50 in. (172.7 x 127 cm)
Gift of James F. Ballard
No. 78:1929

Turkey

Gördes prayer carpet with red ground

Turkish
Ottoman period, 18th century
wool
66½ x 47½ in. (168.9 x 120.7 cm)
Gift of James F. Ballard
No. 81:1929

Gördes prayer carpet with blue ground

Turkish
Ottoman period, 19th century
wool
77 x 53 in. (195.6 x 134.6 cm)
Gift of Nellie Ballard White
No. 48:1975

Two-column Gördes prayer carpet with red ground

Turkish
Ottoman period, 19th century
wool
55 x 49½ in. (139.7 x 125.7 cm)
Gift of Nellie Ballard White
No. 309:1972

**Two-column Gördes prayer
carpet with white ground**

Turkish
Ottoman period, early 19th century
wool
65 x 50 in. (165.1 x 127 cm)
Gift of Nellie Ballard White
No. 47:1975

**Two-column Gördes prayer
carpet with white ground**

Turkish
Ottoman period, 19th century
wool
67 x 51½ in. (170.2 x 130.8 cm)
Gift of Nellie Ballard White
No. 308:1972

**Gördes carpet with narrow
red ground**

Turkish
Ottoman period, 19th century
wool
74¼ x 43 in. (188.6 x 109.2 cm)
Gift of Nellie Ballard White
No. 306:1972

Turkey

Small West Anatolian medallion carpet

Turkish
Ottoman period, 19th century
wool
59¼ x 50½ in. (150.5 x 128.3 cm)
Gift of James F. Ballard
No. 111:1930

Ladik prayer carpet with triple arch and columns on red ground

Ottoman period, mid-19th century
wool
68¼ x 44 in. (173.4 x 111.8 cm)
Gift of James F. Ballard
No. 95:1929

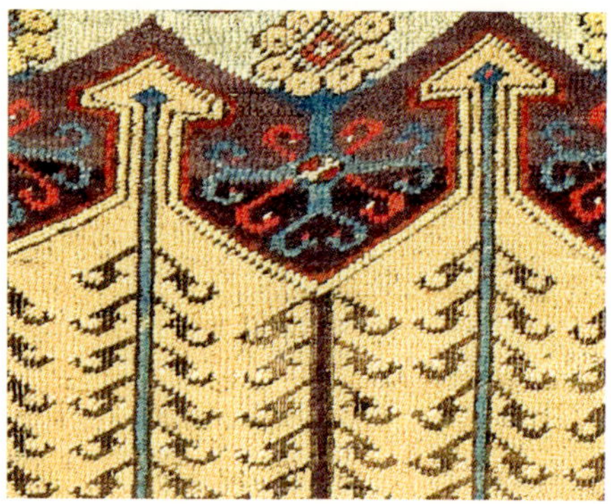

Ladik prayer carpet with vestigial triple arch on yellow ground

Turkish
Ottoman period, c. 1850
wool
68½ x 45½ in. (174 x 115.6 cm)
Gift of Nellie Ballard White
No. 312:1972

Two-column Kula prayer carpet with red ground

Turkish
Ottoman period, c. 1800
wool
65½ x 47½ in. (166.4 x 120.7 cm)
Gift of Nellie Ballard White
No. 305:1972

Yürûk carpet with ogival layout

Turkish
Ottoman period, late 18th–early 19th century
wool
88½ x 67½ in. (224.8 x 171.5 cm)
Gift of Nellie Ballard White
No. 110:1973

Two-column Kula prayer carpet with red ground

Turkish
Ottoman period, 19th century
wool
78¾ x 51½ in. (200 x 130.8 cm)
Gift of Nellie Ballard White
No. 314:1972

Turkey

**Two-column Kula prayer carpet
with blue ground and multiple
narrow borders**

Turkish
Ottoman period, 19th century
wool
74 x 47 in. (188 x 119.4 cm)
Gift of Nellie Ballard White
No. 315:1972

**Two-column Kula prayer carpet
with blue ground and multiple
narrow borders**

Turkish
Ottoman period, 19th century
wool
68½ x 44 in. (174 x 111.8 cm)
Gift of Nellie Ballard White
No. 316:1972

**Kula prayer carpet with blue
ground**

Turkish
Ottoman period, 19th century
wool
75 x 50 in (190.5 x 127 cm)
Gift of Nellie Ballard White
No. 317:1972

Kula prayer carpet with small bouquets on blue ground and multiple borders

Turkish
Ottoman period, late 18th–early 19th century
wool
71 x 47 in. (180.3 x 119.4 cm)
Gift of James F. Ballard
No. 87:1929

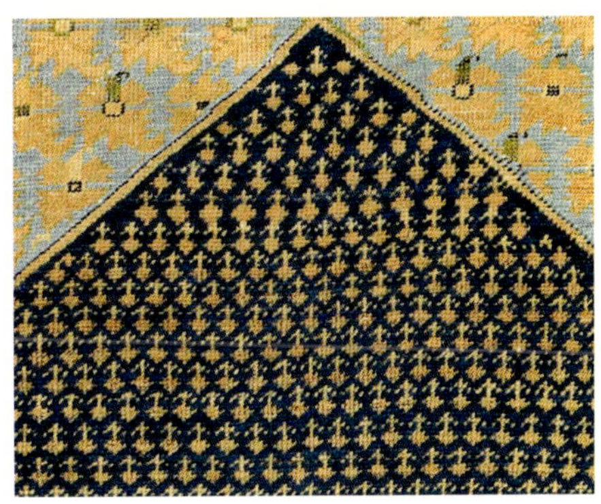

Kula prayer carpet with blue ground, light blue spandrels and multiple borders

Turkish
Ottoman period, late 18th–early 19th century
wool
69 x 46¼ in. (175.3 x 117.5 cm)
Gift of James F. Ballard
No. 86:1929

Two-column Kula prayer carpet with blue ground

Turkish
Ottoman period, 19th century
wool
64¼ x 41 in. (163.2 x 104.1 cm)
Gift of Nellie Ballard White
No. 313:1972

Turkey

Demirci prayer carpet with flowering tree design

Turkish
Ottoman period, 19th century
wool
52 x 44 in. (132.1 x 111.8 cm)
Gift of James F. Ballard
No. 84:1929

Small Demirci carpet with red ground

Turkish
Ottoman period, 19th century
wool
54¾ x 46½ in. (139.1 x 118.1 cm)
Gift of Nellie Ballard White
No. 318:1972

Southeast Anatolian carpet with two diamond-medallions

Turkish
Ottoman period, late 19th century
wool
59 x 46 in. (149.9 x 116.8 cm)
Gift of Nellie Ballard White
No. 307.1972

Transcaucasus

Shirvan long carpet with narrow field of palmettes

Transcaucasian, late 19th century
wool
141½ x 41 in. (359.4 x 104.1 cm)
Gift of Nellie Ballard White
No. 295:1972

Fragmentary South Caucasus carpet with blossom design

Transcaucasian, 19th century
wool
116¼ x 64½ in. (295.3 x 163.8 cm)
Gift of Nellie Ballard White
No. 324:1972

Transcaucasus

Shirvan prayer carpet with lattice pattern on white field

Transcaucasian, late 19th century
wool
59 x 39¾ in. (149.9 x 101 cm)
Gift of Nellie Ballard White
No. 297:1972

Shirvan prayer carpet with lattice pattern on white field

Transcaucasian, late 19th century
wool
67 x 39 in. (170.2 x 99.1 cm)
Gift of James F. Ballard
No. 117:1929

Small Shirvan carpet with kufesque border and "Perepedil" pattern

Transcaucasian, late 19th century
wool
78 x 51 in. (198.1 x 129.5 cm)
Gift of Nellie Ballard White
No. 296:1972

Shirvan carpet with field of staggered rows of small motifs

Transcaucasian, late 19th century
wool
50½ x 36½ in. (128.3 x 92.7 cm)
Gift of Nellie Ballard White
No. 298:1972

Shirvan carpet with rows of star-like blossoms

Transcaucasian, early 20th century
wool
61 x 42 in. (154.9 x 106.7 cm)
Gift of Nellie Ballard White
No. 322:1972

Small East Caucasus carpet with two cruciform medallions

Transcaucasian, early 20th century
wool
57 x 33½ in. (144.8 x 85.1 cm)
Gift of Nellie Ballard White
No. 323:1972

India

China

North Indian carpet with rows of flowering plants

Indian
Mughal period, second half 17th century
wool and cotton
208½ in. x 99 in. (529.6 x 251.5 cm)
Gift of James F. Ballard
No. 125:1929

Daybed cover with design of five medallions

Chinese
Qing dynasty, Yongzheng period, early 18th century
wool and cotton
101 x 67 in. (256.5 x 170.2 cm)
Gift of James F. Ballard
No. 119:1929

Daybed cover with design of the "Hundred Antiques"

Chinese
Qing dynasty, Kangxi period, early 18th century
wool
113 x 66 in. (287 x 167.6 cm)
Gift of James F. Ballard
No. 126:1929

Central Asia

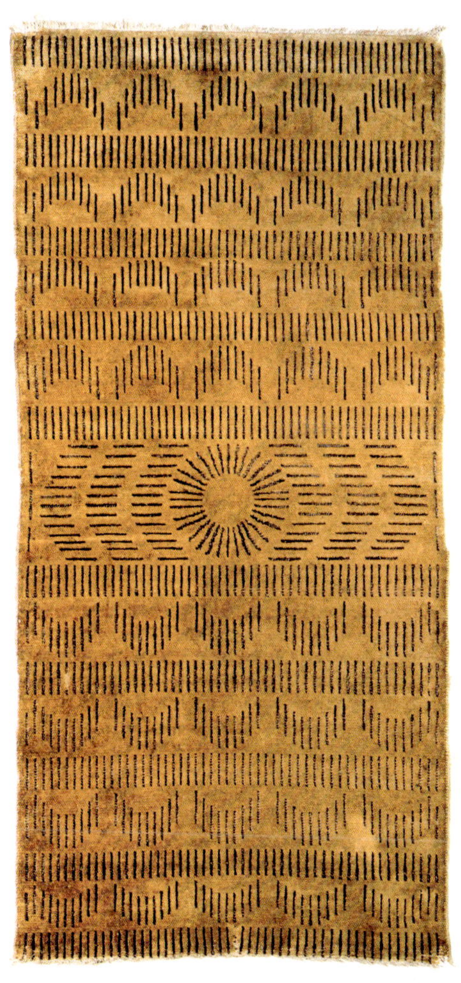

Small carpet on ivory ground

Chinese
Qing dynasty, 19th century
wool and cotton
66 x 31 in. (167.6 x 78.7 cm)
Gift of Nellie Ballard White
No. 321:1972

"Khotan" carpet with pattern of small circles on blue ground

Central Asian, 19th century
wool and cotton
132 x 75¾ in. (335.3 x 192.4 cm)
Gift of James F. Ballard
No. 124:1929

Yomut Turkmen sumak-brocaded cover

Central Asian, 19th century
wool
119 x 78¼ in. (302.3 x 198.8 cm)
Gift of Nellie Ballard White
No. 320:1972

Endnotes

Chronology

1. Virginia Gardner, "Ballard Rug Collection Shows Brilliant Colors and Wealth of History", *The St. Louis Times*, October 28, 1927.

2. Board of Control meeting minutes, April 1929, City Art Museum, Saint Louis Art Museum Archives.

Thomas J. Farnham

3. Ballard, during the early stages of his collecting, kept lists of what he spent on rugs. These lists are undated but appear to be complete through 1916, by which time he had expended approximately $80,000 for 303 rugs. John D. Rockefeller, Jr. paid $110,000 for a single Polonaise rug and Charles T. Yerkes, nearly $180,000 for an early Tabriz carpet. Both are now in the Metropolitan Museum of Art, acc. nos. 45.106 and 10.61.3. (Objects from the Metropolitan will hereinafter be cited as MMA, with appropriate accession numbers.) Ballard's lists are in The James F. Ballard Rug Collection Papers, Archives, Saint Louis Museum of Art (hereinafter cited as Ballard Papers, SLAM).

4. After the passage of the Pure Food and Drug Act, Ballard was on several occasions charged by the United States Attorney for the Eastern District of Missouri with "false and fraudulent" advertising, charges to which Ballard in each instance pled guilty and paid a nominal fine of $10.

5. James F. Ballard, *Illustrated Catalogue and Descriptions of Ghiordes Rugs of the Seventeenth and Eighteenth Centuries from the Collection of James F. Ballard* (St. Louis, 1916), xi.

6. Ibid.

7. This carpet is now in the Philadelphia Museum of Art, acc. no. 43-28-1. (Hereinafter objects in the Philadelphia Museum of Art will be cited as PMA, with appropriate accession numbers.)

8. Levon Babayon, *The Romance of the Oriental Rug* (Toronto, various dates), 11.

9. Ballard, *Ghiordes Rugs*, xi–xii.

10. *The Furnishing Trader Advisor,* London, October 1923, pp. 220ff. See also Ballard's foreword in Arthur MacLean and Dorothy Blair, *Catalogue of Oriental Rugs in the Collection of James F. Ballard* (Indianapolis: Herron Art Institute, 1924), and the *Louisville Courier-Journal*, January 6, 1929.

11. Typically rugs are identified by the names of the locations where they were supposedly made. Thus a "Ghiordes" rug would be a rug woven in that western Anatolian town or an Isfahan carpet would be one created in that Iranian city. But some rugs are identified on the basis of the objects their motifs appear to represent, as is the case with "Dragon" or "Bird" rugs. Several early Turkish rugs derive their names—"Holbein", "Lotto", "Tintoretto", "Ghirlandaio"—from the names of artists who used rugs of certain types as props in their paintings. Other rugs carry the names of the ethnic groups that produced them, such as Turkmen or Mamluk, and some bear names that have nothing whatsoever to do with any of these criteria, "Polonaise" and "Transylvanian" rugs being examples. Prayer rugs are those bearing *mihrabs* or prayer niches, whether or not actually used by adherents of Islam for prayer.

12. Ballard, *Ghiordes Rugs*, xii.

13. Evidence of Dilley's enthusiasm for Gördes prayer rugs can be found in his book, *Oriental Rugs* (Boston, 1909), 56.

14. These figures are taken from Ballard's lists of what he paid for rugs, Ballard Papers, SLAM.

15. James F. Ballard, "Antique Ghiordes Rugs, Six Illustrations," *International Studio* 53, No. 212, pp. lxxxvi–xc.

16. Ballard maintained an exhausting work schedule even after he began collecting. It was described in *The Practical Druggist and Spatula* 38 (November 1920): 49.

17. Dilley subsequently wrote catalogues for Ballard's other exhibitions, and he regularly traveled to the cities where Ballard's rugs were displayed in order to lecture about them. See *An Exhibition of Oriental Rugs Lent by James F Ballard*, November 17–January 31 [1923–24], Department of Fine Arts, Carnegie Institute. When they were exhibited in San Francisco, for example, Dilley spent three weeks there offering daily explanations of why they should be admired.

18. Saint Louis Museum of Art, acc. nos. 111.1973 and 112.1973. (Hereinafter objects in the Saint Louis Museum of Art will be cited as SLAM with appropriate accession numbers.)

19. Parke-Bernet Galleries, *Rare Oriental Rugs, Chinese Art, Paintings from the Estate of the Late Berenice C. Ballard*, New York, 1950, Lot 187. (Hereinafter cited as Berenice Ballard, with the appropriate lot number.)

20. MMA, 22.100.94.

21. MMA, 22.100.85.

22. Among the Ballard Papers, SLAM, is a list of the rug books Ballard owned. Although the document is not dated, it can be assumed the list was made before 1916.

23. David Sylvester, "On Western Attitudes to Eastern Carpets," in *Islamic Carpets from the Joseph V. McMullan Collection* (London, 1972), 17.

24. The whereabouts of the rugs mentioned in this paragraph are as follows: Gördes, MMA, 22.100.94; Isfahan, whereabouts unknown; Isfahan, MMA, 22.100.72; Cairene, MMA, 22.100.53 and 22.100.54; Mamluk, whereabouts unknown; Spanish, MMA, 22.1000.126; Polonaise, SLAM, 120:1929; Lotto, SLAM,104:1929; Star Ushak, SLAM, 103:1929; Medallion Ushak, SLAM, 301:1972; Karapinar, Private Collection, St. Louis.

25. Both Sharpless rugs are in the PMA, 48-83-1 and 48-83-2.

26. *Special Loan Exhibition of Carpets and Other Textiles from Asia Minor*, Philadelphia, Pennsylvania Museum and School of Industrial Art, 1919.

27. Los Angeles County Museum of Art, acc. no. 53.502.

28. PMA, 43-40-68 and 43-40-63.

29. The whereabouts of the rugs mentioned thus far in this paragraph are: Mughal fragments, SLAM, 73:129 and 74:1929; Persian fragment, MMA, 22.100.67; Kuba, MMA, 22.100.74; Dragon, MMA, 22.100.119; Polonaises, SLAM, 120:1929 and whereabouts unknown; Isfahan, MMA, 22.100.76; and Floral, MMA, 22.100.77.

30. Oriental Rug Exhibition, December 15, 1919–February 15, 1920, supplement to the *Bulletin of the Cleveland Museum of Art*, January 1920.

31. *New York Herald*, February 18, 1925.

32. A receipt for the rugs sold to Merner on August 14, 1923, can be found in the Ballard Papers, SLAM. Because he did sell and gave away many pieces, certain of his rugs are now with family members (see Hali 124 [September–October 2002]: 104–06), and others have even found their way into the hands of dealers and collectors. Maurizio Battilossi illustrated a Ballard rug in his 1985 exhibition catalogue, *Selezione di Tappeti d'Antiquariato*, Turin, Italy.

33. *New York Times*, October 7, 1921.

34. The whereabouts of the rugs mentioned in this paragraph are: Tabriz, MMA, 22.100.75; Spanish, MMA, 22.100.126; Isfahan Tree, MMA, 22.100.76; Vase fragment, MMA, 22.100.68; Dragon, MMA.100.49; and the Ottomans, MMA, 22.100. 51, 52, 53, 54, 55, 56, and 57.

35. *Loan Exhibition of Oriental Rugs from the Collection of James F. Ballard of St. Louis, Missouri*, New York, The Metropolitan Museum of Art, 1921.

36. James F. Ballard to Edward Robinson, May 4, 1922. The Metropolitan Museum of Art Archives. Ballard, James Franklin. Gift. Rug Collection, November 11–May 17, 1922. Office of the Secretary, Correspondence Files, 1870–1950.

37. "The James F. Ballard Gift," *The Bulletin of The Metropolitan Museum of Art* 17, No. 6 (June 1922). In his exchange of letters with Robinson, Ballard urged the director to acquire the Charles F. Williams collection for the Metropolitan; if both his and the Williams rugs were there, he argued, the Met collection would be without parallel. James F. Ballard to Edward Robinson, March 7 and 17, 1923. Ballard, James Franklin. Gift Addition to the Rug Collection, 1923. Office of the Secretary, Correspondence Files, 1870–1950, The Metropolitan Museum of Art Archives. Instead the Williams collection went to the Philadelphia Museum of Art.

38. *New York Times*, May 23, 1922.

39. Ibid.

40. The whereabouts of the rugs mentioned in this paragraph are: Ottoman, MMA, 22.100.51; Bird, MMA, 22.100.127; Garden, MMA, 22.100.128; Ghiordes, MMA, 22.100.129.

41. Joseph Breck and Frances Morris, *The James F. Ballard Collection of Oriental Rugs* (New York: Metropolitan Museum of Art, 1923).

42. All the rugs in the photograph are now in the Saint Louis Museum of Art—SLAM, 106:1929, 101:1929, 102:1929, 72:1929—with the exception of the one that went to the Metropolitan Museum of Art—MMA, 22.100.113—and the Ushak medallion rug; it was purchased by Henry Francis duPont in 1950 (Berenice Ballard, Lot 186) and is currently in the Winterthur Museum, Garden and Library, Winterthur, Delaware, acc. no. 1969.1393. (Hereinafter objects from the Winterthur will be cited as Winterthur with appropriate accession numbers.)

43. The rugs mentioned in this paragraph are: Çintemani, SLAM, 112:1929; Indo-Persian, SLAM, 72:1929.

44. Edith Rockefeller McCormick brought the carpet from Cardinal and Harford. It was later purchased by the Metropolitan, MMA. 43.121.1. A companion piece is in the Austrian Museum of Applied Art, Vienna, acc. no. T 8334/ 1922 KB.

45. London, *The Times*, August 19, 1926.

46. The rugs mentioned in this paragraph are all in the Saint Louis Museum of Art: Vase, 285: 1972; Tekke, 113:1930; and Mudejar, 122: 1929.

47. The five rugs mentioned in this paragraph are in the Saint Louis Museum of Art: Variant Star, 98:1929; Ghiordes, 79:1929; Kula, 186:1929; Ladik, 94:1929; Karapinar, 116:1929.

48. A report to Ballard from French's Press Cutting Agency can be found in the Ballard Papers, SLAM.

49. Berenice Ballard, Lot 185.

50. MMA, 22.100.127.

51. This was a story Ballard repeated over and over. See examples in the *New York Evening Post*, October 12, 1923 and the *New York Tribune*, November 18, 1923.

52. See note 59 below for more about his Chinese carpet.

53. SLAM, 72:1929.

54. *New York Times*, October 26, 1922, June 1, 1924; *St. Louis Globe-Democrat*, March 17, 1925; Albany Knickerbocker Press, April 15, 1926.

55. *St. Louis Globe-Democrat*, March 17, 1925; *New York Herald Tribune*, March 20, 1927. The whereabouts of the two rugs mentioned in these articles cannot be determined; Ballard did not specifically identify them.

56. *New York Herald,* February 18, 1925.

57. T*he Furnishing Trader Advisor,* London, October, 1923, pp. 220 ff.

58. *St. Louis Globe-Democrat*, April 24, 1931.

59. As Ballard became more and more preoccupied with his travels and adventures he seems also to have become less and less discerning toward the rugs he bought, especially in instances involving those rugs that supposedly required his greatest efforts to find and about which he elaborated most

expansively. The Indo-Persian rug, the one he claimed to have traveled 40,000 miles to locate, is an undistinguished piece, and his so-called imperial Chinese carpet, for which he allegedly journeyed 30,000 miles, clearly never decorated the interior of The Hall of Supreme Harmony or any other palace. That carpet became the property of Berenice Ballard and was sold at auction in 1950, Lot 185.

60. *St. Louis Post Dispatch*, October 26, 1927; *St. Louis Daily Globe-Democrat*, October 26, 1927; *St. Louis Post Dispatch Sunday Magazine*, August 31, 1930.

61. Administrative Board of Control of the City Art Museum to James F. Ballard, June 5, 1929, Ballard Papers, SLAM.

62. *Inaugural Exhibition of a Collection of Oriental Rugs Presented to the Museum by James F. Ballard*, St. Louis, City Art Museum, 1929.

63. The rugs mentioned in this paragraph are all in the Saint Louis Museum of Art: Spanish, 122:1929; Chinese, 126:1929; Indian fragments, 73 and 74:1929; tents, 131 and 132: 1929; Holbein, 106:1929; Lotto, 100 and 101:1929; Tintoretto, 102:1929; Ghirlandaio, 130:1929; Yuruk, 89:1929, Mudéjar, 108:1929; Ushak, 102:1929; Transylvanian, 92 and 93:1929, Karapinar, 116: 1929; and Tekke, 113:1930.

64. SLAM, 48:1975.

65. Vase, SLAM, 285:1972; Animal rugs, SLAM, 286-289:1972.

66. Before donating her rugs to the Saint Louis Art Museum, Nellie exhibited her collection in St. Louis in 1932, in Chicago in 1933, and again in St. Louis in 1934.

67. The whereabouts of the rugs mentioned in this paragraph are: Berenice Ballard, Lots 144 and 170, Ushak and Spanish, The Textile Museum, Washington, D.C, accession Nos. R34.1.5 and R44.004; Lots 156 and 159, Transylvanians, MMA, 1974.149. 13 and 15; Lots, 180, 181, 186, Winterthur, Kula, 1952.0047; Feraghan, 1969.1405, Ushak, 1969.1393; Lot 171, Kula prayer rug, to Karekin Beshir and eventually to Maurizio Battilossi of Turin, Italy, from whom it was stolen in February 2005.

68. MMA, 67.22.

Walter B. Denny

69. See W. Denny, "Saff and Sejjadeh: Origins and Meaning of the Prayer Rug," *Oriental Carpet & Textile Studies 2* (1990): 92–104, and S. Blair and J. Bloom, eds., *Images of Paradise in Islamic Art* (Hanover, NH: Hood Museum of Art, 1991).

70. Fakery, no matter how skillful, relies on a set of visual suppositions and methods that reflect the time of creation of the fake, rather than of the originals on which the fake is always in some way based. In the same way, the "unmasking" of fakes relies on similarly restricted suppositions and methods peculiar to the time in which such judgments are made. This means that the process of evaluating genuineness in a carpet must be extremely circumspect and thoughtful, and that allegations of fakery should be carefully considered not only in light of what we do know about carpets, but what we inevitably don't know about carpets. We now recognize that the overwhelming majority of carpets originally made in earlier eras, probably including entire classes and groups of carpets, have disappeared over time. False accusations of fakery usually stem from three categories of misunderstanding. The first is when an old carpet survives in very good condition (we now know that beyond any doubt a certain number of old carpets certainly did). The second is when the design or coloration exhibits variation with the bulk of surviving examples. (We should not fall into the so-called "Orientalist" trap of assuming that traditional carpet weavers from the Islamic world were somehow completely bound by tradition, but should recognize that artistic originality and innovation are essential parts of the artistic process in all cultures.) Third, we need to pay more attention to reconstructing original artistic process. (Today, for example, we realize that "errors" or "imprecision" in design of classical Persian carpets are common to almost all surviving early examples; and that they did not utilize the knot-by-knot instructions for weaving common to high-end Persian weavings of the past century, but rather allowed for a certain degree of latitude and flexibility in the hands of highly trained weavers.)

71. See W. Denny, "Classical Roots of Anatolian Kilim Designs" *HALI* 2/1 (Summer 1979): 105–09. While art historians widely proclaim their respect for the visual power and beauty of art, practically speaking it is indeed difficult for many traditionally trained individuals to write about works that lack written documentation. It is a fact of life that we often do not respect, purchase, write about, or exhibit that work of art for which we cannot easily give a named artist, a title, a precise date, and a precise area of manufacture, together with precise iconographical information. Since all of these are lacking in the bulk of surviving early kilims, they have been largely ignored by "traditional" art historians, and on the other hand have been subject to a huge volume of (often mostly) dubious mixes of conjecture, hyperbole, and wishful thinking, too often published by collectors, dealers, and other enthusiasts with scant command of method or historical resources, and great resources of imagination and salesmanship.

72. The reference is to a paper by Dr. Thomas Farnham given in New York City in April of 2008 on the history of the New York Hajji Baba Club: see "The Pioneers", *HALI* 158 (Winter 2008): 60–69.

73. Among the many catalogues of the Ballard collection published over the years, the most important early publications, likely to be encountered in most major research libraries, are *Metropolitan Museum of Art, Loan Exhibition of Oriental Rugs from the Collection of James F. Ballard of St. Louis* (New York: The Metropolitan Museum of Art, 1921); Joseph Breck and Frances

Morris, *The James F. Ballard Collection of Oriental Rugs* (New York, 1923); *James F. Ballard, Catalogue of Oriental Rugs in the Collection of James F. Ballard* (Indianapolis, 1924); City Art Museum of St. Louis, *Inaugural Exhibition of a Collection of Oriental Rugs Presented to the Museum by James F. Ballard, opening November 21st* (St. Louis, 1929); Maurice S. Dimand, *The Ballard Collection of Oriental Rugs in the City Art Museum of St. Louis* (St Louis, 1935).

74. Saint Louis Art Museum 98.1929, cat. 12 in this catalogue.

75. Metropolitan Museum of Art 22.100.51; most recently published in Walter Denny, *The Classical Tradition in Anatolian Carpets* (Washington D.C. and London, 2002).

76. The revolution in perception of carpets that has taken place in the last two or three decades, in combination with new standards for conservation practice in museums, has resulted in a re-examination of the ethics of restoration, and a new tolerance for exhibition of fragmentary works of art without extensive restoration. In selecting Ballard Collection carpets for inclusion in this catalogue and for a related exhibition, some carpets that had previously been highly regarded, and illustrated in color in earlier catalogues (for example, plate XXV in Dimand 1935) have been omitted due to their large amount of restoration, and the fact that the early restoration has now badly faded, making an aesthetic appreciation of the work difficult if not impossible. Good examples of the growing acceptability of exhibiting and publishing fragmentary works can be seen in Nazan Ölçer and Walter B. Denny, *Anatolian Carpets: Masterpieces from the Museum of Turkish and Islamic Arts, Istanbul* (Bern, 1999), and Heinrich Kirchheim et al., *Orient Stars: A Carpet Collection* (London, 1993).

77. Maurice S. Dimand and Jean Mailey, *Oriental Rugs in the Metropolitan Museum of Art* (New York: The Metropolitan Museum of Art, 1972), 110.

78. Metropolitan Museum of Art, 22.100.115 (see Dimand and Mailey 1972, catalogue entry 75 and figure 166).

79. Metropolitan Museum of Art 22.100.92, 22.100.86, 22.100.90, and 22.100.91 (see Dimand and Mailey 1972, catalogue entries 89–92, pp. 226–27.)

80. See note 75 above.

81. Metropolitan Museum of Art 22.100.113 (Dimand and Mailey 1972, catalogue entry 84, figure 170).

82. In a private collection in Europe. See *HALI* 73 (February–March 1994): 131–32; see also Eberhart Herrmann, *Asiatische Teppich und Textilkunst* Bd. 5 (Munich, 1997), pl. 23.

83. See Friedrich Spuhler, *Oriental Carpets in the Museum of Islamic Art, Berlin* (Washington, D.C., 1987).

84. See Ölçer and Denny 1999, entries 1 and 2; Spuhler 1987, entry 73; and Belkis Balpinar, *Carpets of the Vakıflar Museum, Istanbul*; Wesel, 1986, pl.s 58 and 59.

85. See Dimand and Mailey 1972, catalogue entry 96 and figure 117; also Joseph V. McMullan, *Islamic Carpets* (New York, 1965), catalogue entry 3.

86. Daniel Walker, "Turkish Rugs," *Bulletin of the St. Louis Art Museum* 17, No. 4 (Summer 1988); see also George O'Bannon, "The Ballard Collection: The St. Louis Art Museum," *Oriental Rug Review* 11, No. 3, also on the Internet at http://www.rugreview.com/orr/113ball.htm.

87. See Mills 1983 and London 1983.

88. Wilhelm von Bode, director of the Prussian State Museums and an important scholar of Renaissance painting, was responsible for much of this nomenclature; see Bode 1955.

89. See Geijer 1963, where the author published her important discovery that because one carpet from the group was demonstrably a copy of a fourteenth-century Chinese Yuan silk damask, the so-called "Seljuk" carpets of Konya and Beyşehir must have been produced in the fourteenth century rather than in the thirteenth, as previously supposed.

90. See Mackie 1977, where the author discusses a Spanish carpet copy of a Turkish carpet copy of a Yuan Chinese silk damask design.

91. Metropolitan Museum of Art 22.100.124, gift of James Franklin Ballard.

92. Philadelphia Museum of Art 55-65-21, The Joseph Lees Williams Memorial Collection; see Ellis 1988, 240–47.

93. See Felton 2012, where the author posits a Jewish connection with a famous Spanish carpet.

Bibliography

Andrews 1999
Andrews, Peter Alford. *Felt Tents and Pavilions: The Nomadic Tradition and Its Interaction with Princely Tentage.* 2 vols. London: Melisende, 1999.

Atasoy 2000
Atasoy, Nurhan. *Otağ-ı Hümayun: The Ottoman Imperial Tent Complex.* Istanbul: MEPA, 2000.

Bailey 1985
Bailey, Julia. "Ladik Prayer Rugs," *HALI* 28 (1985): 19–25.

Balpinar 1988
Balpinar, Belkis, and Hirsch, Udo. *Carpets of the Vakıflar Museum Istanbul.* Wesel: Uta Hülsey, 1988.

Bátari 1994
Bátari, Ferenc. *Ottoman Turkish Carpets: The Collections of the Museum of Applied Arts, Budapest.* Budapest: Museum of Applied Arts, 1994.

Beattie 1976
Beattie, May Hamilton. *Carpets of Central Persia: With Special Reference to Rugs of Kirman.* London, 1976.

Bode 1955
Bode, Wilhelm von, and Kühnel, Ernst. *Vorderasiatische Knüpfteppiche aus alter Zeit.* Berlin, 1955.

Boralevi 1987
Boralevi, Alberto. *L'Ushak Castellani-Stroganoff.* Florence, 1987.

Bruschettini 2014
Bruschettini Foundation. *Arte Ottomana, 1450-1600, Natura e Astrazione: uno Sguardo sulla Sublime Porta* (Genoa, Palazzo Lomellino, October-December 2014).

Chicago 1922
Descriptive Catalogue of an Exhibition of Oriental Rugs from the Collection of James Franklin Ballard Exhibited in Gallery Fifty and on the Main Staircase from November 28, 1922 to February, 1923. Chicago: The Art Institute of Chicago, 1922.

Denny 1979
Denny, Walter B. "Origin of the Designs of Ottoman Court Carpets," *HALI* 2, No. 1 (Spring 1979): 6–11.

Denny 1986
"The Origins and Development of Ottoman Court Carpets," in R. Pinner and W. Denny, eds. *Oriental Carpet & Textile Studies II: Carpets of the Mediterranean Countries 1400–1600.* London 1986: 243–59.

Denny 1988
"Tradition and Change: Islamic Carpets and Artistic Heritage," pp. 39–53, and "A Note on Technical and Structural Analysis," pp. 63–69. In Walter Denny and D. Walker, *The Markarian Album.* Cincinnati, 1988.

Denny 1990
"Saff and Sejjadeh: Origins and Meaning of the Prayer Rug," in R. Pinner and W. B. Denny, eds. *Oriental Carpet & Textile Studies III, part 2* London 1990: 92–104.

Denny 1991
"Reflections of Paradise in Islamic Art," 33–43. In S. Blair and J. Bloom, eds. *Images of Paradise in Islamic Art.* Hanover, NH: Hood Museum of Art, Hanover, 1991.

Denny and Ölçer, 1999
Denny, Walter B., and Ölçer, Nazan. Anatolian Carpets: *Masterpieces from the Museum of Turkish and Islamic Arts, Istanbul.* With photographs by Ahmet Ertug. Bern, 1999.

Denny 2002
Denny, Walter B. *The Classical Tradition in Anatolian Carpets.* Washington, D.C.: The Textile Museum, 2002.

Denny 2003
Denny, Walter B. "Beyond the Carpet Design Revolution: Perspectives in 15th Century Carpet History," In T. Farnham and D. Shaffer, eds. *Oriental Carpet & Textile Studies VII.* London, 2011: 21–33.

Denny 2007
Denny, Walter B. "Oriental Carpets and Textiles in Venice." In Stefano Carboni, ed., *Moments of Vision: Venice and the Islamic World 828–1797.* New York: The Metropolitan Museum of Art, 2007.

Denny 2012
Denny, Walter B. and Krody, Sumru Belger, *The Sultan's Garden: The Blossoming of Ottoman Art.* Washington, D.C.: The Textile Museum, 2012.

Denny 2014
Denny, Walter B., *How to Read Oriental Carpets.* New York and New Haven, 2014.

Dimand 1935
Dimand, Maurice, *The Ballard Collection of Oriental Rugs in the City Art Museum of St. Louis.* St. Louis: City Art Museum, 1935.

Dimand 1973
Dimand, Maurice S., and Mailey, Jean, *Oriental Rugs in the Metropolitan Museum of Art. New York*: The Metropolitan Museum of Art, 1973.

Ellis 1969
Ellis, Charles Grant, "The Ottoman Prayer Carpets" in *Textile Museum Journal* II, No. 4 (1969), 5–23.

Ellis 1975
Ellis, Charles Grant, "The Lotto Pattern as a Fashion in Carpets," *Festschrift fur Peter Wilhelm Meister.* Hamburg, 1975, 19–31.

Ellis 1986
Ellis, Charles Grant, "On 'Holbein' and 'Lotto' Rugs," in R. Pinner and W. Denny, eds. *Oriental Carpet & Textile Studies II: Carpets of the Mediterranean Countries 1400–1600.* London 1986: 163–76.

Ellis 1988
Ellis, Charles Grant, *Oriental Carpets in the Philadelphia Museum of Art.* Philadelphia, 1988.

Ellis 1990
Ellis, Charles Grant, *Early Caucasian Rugs.* Washington, D.C.: The Textile Museum, 1990.

Erdmann 1970
Erdmann, Kurt, *Seven Hundred Years of Oriental Carpets,* trans. May H. Beattie and Hildegard Herzog. Berkeley, 1970.

Erdmann 1976
Erdmann, Kurt, *Oriental Carpets: An Account of their History,* trans. Charles Grant Ellis. London, 1976.

Felton 2012
Felton, Anton, *Jewish Symbols and Secrets: A Fifteenth-Century Spanish Carpet.* London, 2012.

Franses 2007
Ölçer, Nazan, and Franses, Michael, *In Praise of God: Anatolian Rugs in Transylvanian Churches 1500–1700.* Istanbul, 2007.

Geijer 1963
Geijer, Agnes, "Some Thoughts on the Problems of Early Oriental Carpets" in *Ars Orientalis* V, 79–87.

Ionesco 2005
Ionesco, Stefano, *Antique Ottoman Rugs in Transylvania*. Rome, 2005.

Indianapolis 1924
Catalogue of Oriental Rugs in the Collection of James F. Ballard. Indianapolis, 1924.

Istanbul 1996
Ölçer, Nazan, Volkmar Enderlein, Ferenc Batári and John Mills, *Turkish Carpets from the 13th–18th centuries*. Exhibition in the Museum of Turkish and Islamic Arts, Istanbul 1996.

Kirchheim 1993
Kirchheim, E. Heinrich, Michael Franses, Friedrich Spuhler, Jürg Rageth and Eberhart Herrmann, *Orient Stars: A Carpet Collection*. Stuttgart and London, 1993.

Kühnel 1957
Kühnel, Ernst and Bellinger, Louise, *Cairene Rugs and others Technically Related*. Washington, D.C.: The Textile Museum, Washington, 1957.

Kühnel 1953
Kühnel, Ernst and Bellinger, Louise, *Catalogue of Spanish Rugs XI–XIX Century*. Washington, D.C.: The Textile Museum, Washington, 1953.

London 1983
King, Donald, and David Sylvester, *The Eastern Carpet in the Western World from the 15th to the 17th Century,* selected and arranged by Donald King and David Sylvester. London: Hayward Gallery, London, 1983.

Mack 2001
Mack, Rosamond, *Bazaar to Piazza: Islamic Trade and Italian Art 1300–1600*. Berkeley and Los Angeles: University of California Press, 2001.

Mackie 1977
"Two remarkable fifteenth-century Carpets from Spain", in *Textile Museum Journal*, 1977, 15–32.

May 1977
May, Florence Lewis, *The Hispanic Society of America: Rugs of Spain and Morocco*. Chicago & London, 1997.

McMullan 1965
McMullan, Joseph V., *Islamic Carpets*. New York, 1965.

Metropolitan 1923
Breck, Joseph and Morris, Frances, *The James F. Ballard Collection*. Metropolitan Museum of Art, New York, 1923.

Metropolitan 2011
Ekhtiar, Maryam D., et. al., eds., *Masterpieces from the Department of Islamic Art in the Metropolitan Museum of Art*. New York, 2011.

Mills 1983
Mills, John, *Carpets in Paintings*. London: The National Gallery, 1983.

Mills 1986
Mills, John, "Near Eastern Carpets in European Paintings" R. Pinner and W. Denny, eds. *Oriental Carpet & Textile Studies II: Carpets of the Mediterranean Countries 1400–1600*. London 1986:109–22.

Oakley 2010
Oakley, Penny, 'Fact or Fiction?', *HALI* 166 (2010):40-51.

Okumura 2007
Okumura, Sumiyo, *The Influence of Turkic Culture on Mamluk Carpets*. Istanbul, 2007.

Paquin 1992
Paquin, Gerard, "Çintamani" in *HALI* 64. (1992), 104–19, 143–44.

Paquin 1996
Paquin, Gerard, "Silk and Wool: Ottoman Textile Designs in Turkish Rugs," www.galaxy.com/rvw46643-678513/Gerard-Paquin-Silk-and-Wool-Ottoman-Textile-Designs-in-Turkish-Rugs.htm; alternatively: www.tcoletribalrugs.com/article59Silk&Wool.html.

Raby 1986a
Raby, Julian, "Court and Export: Part 1. Market Demands in Ottoman Carpets 1450–1550" in R. Pinner & W. B. Denny, eds. *Oriental Carpet & Textile Studies II: Carpets of the Mediterranean Countries 1400–1600*. London 1986: 29–38.

Raby 1986b
Raby, Julian, "Court and Export: Part 2: The Ushak Carpets" R. Pinner & W. B. Denny, eds. *Oriental Carpet & Textile Studies II: Carpets of the Mediterranean Countries 1400–1600*. London 1986: 177–88.

Sherrill 1996
Sherrill, Sarah B., *Carpets and Rugs of Europe and America*. New York, London and Paris, 1996.

Spuhler 1986
Spuhler, Friedrich, "Chessboard Rugs" in R. Pinner & W. B. Denny, eds. *Oriental Carpet & Textile Studies II: Carpets of the Mediterranean Countries 1400–1600*. London 1986: 261–69.

Spuhler 1987
Spuhler, Friedrich, *Die Orientteppiche im Museum für islamische kunst Berlin*. Munich, 1987.

Spuhler 2012
Spuhler, Friedrich, *Carpets from Islamic Lands*. London and New York, 2012.

Thompson 2006
Thompson, Jon, *Milestones in the History of Carpets*. Milan, 2006.

Walker 1997
Walker, Daniel, *Flowers Underfoot*. New York: The Metropolitan Museum of Art, 1997.

Index

Acknowledgments

It has been a great pleasure to collaborate with an array of talented people in order to realize this exploration of the extraordinary James F. Ballard Collection of Oriental Rugs. I am also grateful to the numerous individuals who shared their knowledge, experience, and enthusiasm for this subject, especially Dr. Sidney M. Goldstein, former Curator of Ancient and Islamic Art, who spearheaded the catalogue and exhibition projects from their inception through his retirement in 2009, and Zoe Perkins, Textile Conservator, who has worked with me closely for well over a decade on the Ballard project, and with whom I have had the privilege of being Co-Curator for the 2016 exhibition. I also thank my long-time colleague and distinguished historian Thomas Farnham, whose contributions to the catalogue broadened our understanding of Ballard as a collector.

At the Saint Louis Art Museum, I am indebted to Brent R. Benjamin, Director, and Jason T. Busch, Deputy Director for Curatorial Affairs and Museum Programs, for their enthusiastic support throughout this process. Philip Hu, Associate Curator of Asian Art, has been instrumental in bringing the exhibition and catalogue to completion.

I am also grateful to Kristen S. Watts, Director of Exhibitions and Design; Mariah R. Keller, Head of Publications and Digital Media; and Elisabeth P. Ellis, Exhibitions Assistant; Jon Cournoyer, Senior Graphic Designer; Lauri Kramer, Graphic Design and Production Specialist and Fontella Bradford, Publications Associate, expertly handled the exhibition graphics. I also thank Jessica Slawski, Manager of Digital Assets; Rachel Aubuchon, Photography and Image Rights Manager; Cathryn Gowan, Digital Imaging Specialist; Brian Van Camerick, Collections Care Technician and Jean Paul Torno, Contract Photographer, for their assistance in procuring images and rights for the catalogue and exhibition. Philip Atkinson, former Head of Exhibition Design, developed an elegant and engaging presentation for the exhibition. In registration, I thank Jeanette Fausz, Director of Collections and Head Registrar, and Ella Rothgangel, Associate Registrar and TMS Administrator, for their skillful management of exhibition loans. Amanda Thompson Rundahl, Director of Learning and Engagement, and her staff, especially Ann M. Burroughs, former Research Assistant, Department of Ancient and Islamic Art, and currently Head of Engagement and Interpretation, contributed greatly to the catalogue and exhibition, and Lindsey Schifko, Kress Interpretive Fellow, guided me through the development of the exhibition's interpretive materials and programs. The librarians and archivists at the Richardson Memorial Library, SLAM, and the Metropolitan Museum of Art Archives were most helpful. The late Melanie Michailidis, former Mellon Postdoctoral Fellow in Islamic Art, and Linda Thomas, former Director of Exhibitions, helped carry the project forward.

Bill Ballard has been extraordinarily generous with his great grandfather's papers over the years, making them available to the many individuals involved in this project as well as previous scholars and interested collectors. Thanks to former Ancient and Islamic Art research assistants Theresa Huntsman, Stephanie Lovett, and Elizabeth Donnelly, for their persistence in sorting through and making chronological sense of this fascinating yet challenging material.

Norma Sindelar, the Museum's archivist, is ever a source of amazement given her ability to retrieve references that seem hopelessly vague or seemingly lost. Barbara File in the Archives of the Metropolitan was extremely helpful in making Ballard's letters available. I also want to thank Daniel Walker, former Chair of the Department of Islamic Art at the Metropolitan, for his support of the Ballard exhibition and publication project. The support continued with Stefano Carboni, former Managing Curator, Qamar Adamjee and Aysin Yoltar, research assistants in the Department and Britt Eilhardt.

Finally, my grateful thanks for the editing and publishing of this catalogue go to my colleagues at Hali Publications in London; to my long-time friend Daniel Shaffer for his patient and adept editing and helpful suggestions, to Ben Evans, Malin Lonnberg, and Rachel Meek who carefully read the manuscript, to Steven Cohen for his help with the Mughal entries, and to Kanittha Mairaing and Liz Dixon who created the beautiful design.

Walter B. Denny,
Amherst, Massachusetts, 2015